War and Children

War and Children

A Reference Handbook

Kendra E. Dupuy and Krijn Peters

Foreword by Ishmael Beah

Contemporary Military, Strategic, and Security Issues

PRAEGER SECURITY INTERNATIONAL
An Imprint of ABC-CLIO, LLC

A B C CLIO

Santa Barbara, California • Denver, Colorado • Oxford, England

Library of Congress Cataloging-in-Publication Data

War and children : a reference handbook / Kendra E. Dupuy and Krijn Peters ; foreword by Ishmael Beah.
    p. cm. — (Contemporary military, strategic, and security issues)
    Includes bibliographical references and index.
    ISBN 978–0–313–36208–8 (hard copy : alk. paper) — ISBN 978–0–313–36209–5 (ebook)

1. Children and war. 2. Child soldiers. 3. War and society. I. Peters, Krijn. II. Title.
HQ784.W3D87   2010
305.23—dc22   2009026681

14 13 12 11 10   1 2 3 4 5

This book is also available on the World Wide Web as an eBook.
Visit www.abc-clio.com for details.

ABC-CLIO, LLC
130 Cremona Drive, P.O. Box 1911
Santa Barbara, California 93116-1911

This book is printed on acid-free paper (∞)

Manufactured in the United States of America

Contents

Foreword

The nature of warfare and the tactics used by various armed groups have changed tremendously since the end of the Cold War. In particular, intrastate or civil conflicts seem to be much more intensive and their high levels of violence cause incredible damage. The availability of small arms or the plundering of natural resources in certain conflicts prolong and intensify the violence which is often deliberately directed to the most vulnerable members of societies: young people and women.

One of the relatively new dimensions of such conflicts has been the unprecedented use of large groups of children and young people as combatants. This appalling phenomenon changes the nature of societies, communities, and cultures during and after a conflict—probably for decades to come. There are myriad facets to look at in order to understand the impact of the use of children and youth in war.

When war breaks out it brings about chaos, physical destruction of places, separation of families, and psychological exposure to horrors that will scar the memory of people, communities, and societies forever. Armed violence often undermines societal and community norms. Ethical and moral standards and traditions are shattered and all that is left is the uncertainty of whether things will ever change for the better. Added to this already dramatic situation is the loss of belief in the very innocence of children and youth, as they are forced to bring horrors to their own communities.

As a young boy affected by the civil war in my country, Sierra Leone, fighting in the conflict and undergoing rehabilitation and reintegration, I experienced the above scenario myself. The attitudes and perceptions of the population toward children and young people—particularly those who participated in the war—have changed forever. A place where once your innocence as a child was celebrated quickly became a place where children were treated with suspicion and sometimes even fear. Rehabilitation was a difficult and long-term process. I and other ex-child soldiers in the rehabilitation program had to learn how to reconnect with our childhood and humanity again by facing our traumas. We all had to find ways to change the behaviors which we developed to survive the terrible years of violence. When this first step in the rehabilitation process was finished and we left the rehabilitation center, we then had to reintegrate into the community. At this stage, successful reintegration depended as much on ourselves as on the communities which received us. Our acceptance into civilian society and the opportunities provided after we left the rehabilitation center were incumbent on our successful recovery. And beyond the community level, the wider post-conflict political and social environment needed to be favorable for us as well if we were ever to live as ordinary young people again.

I am deeply grateful that Krijn Peters, whom I met for the first time in 1996 in Sierra Leone after I had completed my rehabilitation, and Kendra Dupuy have produced this necessary work. The book goes beyond looking at only the trauma and the horrors which are associated with war. Rather, it looks at how armed conflict impacts young people—child soldiers and war-affected young people in general—and what the social, political, and economic effects are on them. The text looks at the far-reaching implications in the way societies function when such wars have ended. It is my hope that this text will not only deepen our understanding on how war affects children and young people, but will also help to better understand the challenges they face in the post conflict rehabilitation process.

—Ishmael Beah (Author of: *A Long Way Gone: Memoirs of a Boy Soldier*), 20 April 2009, New York

Preface

"The Secretary-General has the honor to transmit herewith to the General Assembly the study on the impact of armed conflict on children, prepared by Ms. Graça Machel, the expert appointed by him on 8 June 1994, pursuant to General Assembly Resolution 48/157 of 20 December 1993." It was with these words that the former United Nations Secretary General, Boutros Boutros-Ghali, presented a milestone document to the UN General Assembly's fifty-first session on 26 August 1996. The document proved to be agenda-setting for the next decade, for two reasons: (1) it was the first major and multi-country study on the impact of war on children, and (2) it covered a wide range of topics, ranging from child soldiers, sexual exploitation, and gender-based violence to promoting psychological recovery and social reintegration.[1]

In 1993, when at the time the General Assembly requested for the appointment of an expert to undertake a comprehensive study of the impact of conflict on children, the world was in turmoil. Three years before, the Soviet Union had collapsed, bringing to an end nearly five decades of tensions between the USA and the USSR and their respective allies. The end of this so-called Cold War period raised hopes that the world would be moving toward global peace. Yet, the opposite happened. The number of conflicts increased and around 1995, there were 30 major armed conflicts raging in different places in the world. These conflicts, mainly taking place within states themselves, had devastating effects on the well-being of entire populations, including children.

The expert Graça Machel[2] was asked to make recommendations in her report about five areas: (1) the participation of children in armed conflict; (2) the reinforcement of preventive measures; (3) the relevance and adequacy of existing standards; (4) the measures required to improve the protection of children affected by armed conflict; and (5) the actions needed to promote the physical and psychological recovery and social reintegration of children affected by armed conflict.[3]

The authors of this book have chosen to dedicate the preface to a discussion of the 1996 Machel report. By doing so, they pay their respects to this landmark document. But more importantly, by highlighting the various sections in the report, the reader will get a basic idea of the most important issues regarding children and armed conflict which have set the agenda for the last 15 years. Obviously, the report reflects the knowledge and situation of more than a decade and a half ago. Much has changed, much has been achieved, and much has been learned ... but not enough! Millions of children and young people today still become victims of war, despite the increase in our knowledge about best practices in minimizing the impact of war on young people, despite the treaties and conventions aimed at helping during wartime, and despite the fact that the world has become a more peaceful place since the early 1990s. Many, if not all the issues brought up in the Machel report are (sadly) still relevant today. This textbook will discuss these issues in more detail in the following chapters, although the authors had to be selective in what could be discussed within the space of six chapters. It will become clear from this preface that the impact of war on children and young people remains major and diverse, with issues ranging from child soldiers and peace education to international human rights law and post-traumatic stress disorder.

The 1996 Machel report on the Impact of Armed Conflict on Children starts with the observation that the character of warfare is changing; increasingly, wars are waged within countries and often involve, in addition to regular standing national armies, one or more rebel organizations and / or armed militias. Atrocities and acts of terror have become weapons of war, and are increasingly aimed at civilians. Reports indicate that between 1985 and 1995, an estimated 2 million children were killed during armed conflict and 6 million were seriously injured or disabled for the rest of their lives—often as a result of land mines.[4] Many more have been uprooted by armed conflict and have been forced to seek sanctuary either within or outside their country. Of the total number of internally displaced people (IDP) and refugees, an estimated 80 percent are women and children.[5] However, IDP and refugee camps do not necessarily provide people with sufficient protection and even the most basic human needs in these camps are not guaranteed to be met.

It is worth noting here that the Machel report does not automatically use a discourse of "victimization" when it describes the impact of war on children, nor does not consider children—understood as those below the age of 18—as a homogenous group. With regards to the main section of the report, it "emphasizes the importance of considerations of age—in particular, that adolescents have special needs and special strengths. Young people should be seen in that light; as survivors and active participants in creating solutions, not just as victims or problems."[6] While legislation (including international child-related treaties and conventions) in many cases used and still use a singular definition of a child—everyone below the age of 18—policy makers, development practitioners, humanitarian workers and academics use more stratified definitions, recognizing several categories within the below-18 years age-group." Avoiding the all too easy pitfalls of describing children in situations of armed conflicts solely as victims, the Machel report pays respect to the agency children and young people have and express in some of the most difficult circumstances one can imagine. The acknowledgement of (at least some level of) agency, which can be defined as the capacity of individuals to act independently and to make their own free choices, forces policy makers, practitioners and researchers to take children seriously. To better understand the impact of war on children, it is no longer sufficient to talk only to parents, teachers, practitioners, specialists, etc.; instead, the children in difficult circumstances themselves are the experts and are often surprisingly capable of reflecting on their situation and suggesting solutions. Listening to children and taking them more seriously has also proven to be essential for postwar programs aimed to help war-affected children.

The Machel report then continues by documenting some of the gravest impacts of armed conflict on children. Firstly, it discusses the phenomenon of child soldiers—those under the age of 18 actively involved in combat or serving the army or a rebel movement in supportive roles, such as cooks, porters, or spies. It is recognized that there has been an increase in the number of child soldiers and that they are often specifically targeted by commanders looking to increase their number of fighters. The report acknowledges that not all child soldiers claim to be forcibly recruited, although it states that is misleading to understand this as voluntary conscription, since the choice is not exercised freely.[7] Both scholars and practitioners have challenged this view and claim that in many armed conflicts children do choose to take part in armed groups during conflict under circumstances which we would label "voluntary" if it would concern adults, as will be discussed later in this book. Drawing attention to the participation—whether voluntary or forced—of children in armed conflicts is important also because only then can their specific needs can be reflected in peace-accords, which include details of the disarmament, demobilization, and reintegration process.[8]

In times of war relatively few children take up arms. But the numbers of refugee and internally displaced children can be enormous and is rising, from 5.7 million at the beginning of the 1980s to 14.8 million at the end of the decade.[9] The number of internally displaced people was estimated to be 30 million during the early 1990s.[10] At least half of these numbers are children.[11] As was already pointed out, IDP and refugee camps can be deprived of even the most basic levels of safety, protection, and assistance. Unaccompanied children—those who arrive without their parents or another adult caregiver—are in a particularly vulnerable position.[12] The Machel report advocates that extended family or the community should try to take care of these unaccompanied minors, and that both institutionalization in centers as well as adoption should be prevented as much as possible.[13]

Armed conflict increases the chance of sexual exploitation and gender-based violence. The Machel report observes that gender-based violence, such as rape, sexual humiliation, and mutilation and trafficking is used as a weapon of war and therefore it argues that these should be denounced as war crimes.[14] One shocking finding is that in many cases the arrival of peacekeeping troops has been associated with a rapid rise in child prostitution, making clear that an end to the fighting does not mean an end to the suffering of children.[15]

Another peril which does not stop with the end of a war is the danger posted by land mines and unexploded ordnance. This a major threat to the safety of millions in the world.[16] The chance to become a victim of mines or unexploded ordnance is largest among the poorest in the world, those who have no other choice than to go out in the fields or on the roads to cultivate crops, herd cattle, or fetch water and firewood. Many of these tasks are normally assigned to children. When children become victims and lose one or more limbs, they will need new prostheses on a regular basis since they are still growing.[17] This is a financial burden that can often be too much for a family.

As is the case with land mines, economic sanctions on a country often hit the poorest and most vulnerable sections of society the hardest. Sanctions—used to put a regime under pressure and enforce change—can be preferred by the international community, which might feel that a military intervention cannot (yet) be justified or because it is unwilling to risk its soldiers in an intervention. Although in theory critical humanitarian aid is exempted from a sanction, in practice the provision of necessary items to a country under an embargo is often seriously disrupted, to say the least. Various studies have showed a clear link between economic sanctions and increasing levels of malnourishment among children.[18]

Malnourishment among children only increases during times of war. Malnutrition and diseases—the latter going untreated because of the destruction of health facilities during times of war, or because people simply cannot reach health centers—claim more victims during wars than bombs and bullets do. Large-scale food relief can be used to address urgent needs, but it is not guaranteed that this will actually reach the most needy, including children. Food convoys are vulnerable to ambushes by the fighting parties and much can be lost through corruption and bribery. According to a study by the World Health Organization on average only 50 percent of malnourished children attend the special feeding centers created.[19] Poor attendance was explained by the fact that these centers may be too far away, or that mothers cannot afford to spend too much time with their malnourished child waiting at these centers at the cost of their other children's needs.[20]

As much as the physical health of children is at risk during war, so too is their mental health. Many children have lost family members and sometimes have even witnessed their killings. In the case of child soldiers, the young recruits may have been forced to kill one or more of their family members themselves, as a kind of initiation process and to lower the chance of defection. The destruction of homes and communities and the increased levels of distrust caused by war affect the developmental process of children. The report states that the long-term psychosocial effects of protracted armed conflict on children and young people is not well understood[21], and warns against the uncritical application of western psychotherapeutic approaches in non-Western settings.[22]

To protect the developmental process of children against the impact of war, schools play a vital role. As long as schools remain open, there is some sense of normality and children have the opportunity to be among peers, away from the adult and outside world. For those who have been forced to flee because of the war, schools can be created in IDP or refugee camps for the same reasons.[23] But schools are often targeted by armed forces, looted, their teachers killed, and in some cases, the pupils abducted in order to be turned into child soldiers. And as we will see in the following chapters, once schools stop functioning, there is an increased chance that young people will affiliate themselves with fighting forces.

It is clear that armed conflict has a major and wide-ranging impact on the lives of children and young people, and it is difficult to meet even the most basic needs of children in times of war. Increasingly, the basic needs of children are formulated as rights. The 1989 United Nations Convention on the Rights of the Child (UNCRC) stipulates the rights of children, and States which have signed and ratified the convention become responsible for all children in their territory, a responsibility shared with the International Community.[24] International Humanitarian law and Human Rights Law (including the UNCRC) together provide nearly all the protection for children that would be needed during times of war, but the problem is the limited implementation (of standards) and monitoring[25] of violations in practice.[26]

Once a conflict draws to an end, the immense task of rebuilding society will have to start.[27] Children's needs should be prioritized and young people must be "key contributors in the planning and implementation of long-term solutions."[28] The reconstruction of roads and bridges, the rebuilding of houses and schools, and the clearing of overgrown fields are only one part of the postwar rehabilitation process. Of equal importance to a successful rehabilitation and enduring peace are processes of reconciliation. Local mechanisms of reconciliation, nationwide Truth and Reconciliation Commissions and the establishment of International Tribunals to prosecute those who bear responsibility for atrocities and human rights violations—and hence facilitate reconciliation by providing justice—are some of the most important means to achieving reconciliation. However, the Machel report expresses its concern where ex-child soldiers are put on trial. For instance, after the 1994 genocide in Rwanda, nearly 2000 children were held in detention, of whom more than 500 were under the age of 15—which is beneath the age of criminal responsibility under Rwandan law.[29]

One of the last sections of the report deals with conflict prevention. Conflict resolution techniques should be part of the postwar school curriculum so that young people learn how to settle disputes in nonviolent ways. Many conflict countries—or countries at risk—already have these programs.[30] Equally important for conflict prevention is a process of demilitarization, where States "shift the allocation of resources from arms and military expenditures to human and social development."[31] Such a shift would benefit children even more than adults since the educational sector is often the first to be sacrificed when a government wants to increase its military budget, and thus may be the first to benefit when demilitarization takes place. Finally, to reduce the dangers of armed conflict for children, early warning systems and stand-by capacity should be improved.[32]

In conclusion, the report recommended the establishment of a special representative of the Secretary General on Children and Armed Conflict.[33] This and the other recommendations in the report were welcomed by the General Assembly. The findings and recommendations have found their way in legislation, policy, practice, and further research. This will be illustrated by the following chapters, which will discuss some of the most important implications of war on children and young people and present the current state of affairs in these matters.

Notes

1. Graça Machel, "The Impact of Armed Conflict on Children", 1996, accessed at http://www.unicef.org/graca/.

2. Graça Machel was the former Minister for Education and Culture in Mozambique, widow to the late President Samora Machel, and remarried to former President Nelson Mandela of South Africa. See her biography in the key documents section of this book.

3. Machel 1996, 6.

4. Ibid, 5.

5. Ibid, 10.

6. Ibid, 11.

7. Ibid, 12.

8. Ibid, 14.

9. Machel 1996, 22.

10. Ibid, 23.

11. Ibid, 17.

12. Ibid.

13. Ibid, 18.

14. Ibid, 22.

15. Ibid, 24.

16. On 1 March 1999, the 1997 Convention on the Prohibition of the Use, Stockpiling, Production and Transfer or Anti-Personnel Mines and on Their Destruction entered into force after the 40 required ratifications were deposited to the UN Secretary General. For more information, see the International Campaign to Ban Landmines at http://www.icbl.org.

17. Machel 1996, 27.

18. Ibid, 30.

19. Ibid, 48.

20. Ibid, 38.

21. Ibid, 40. It is here where the 1996 Machel report is (fortunately) slightly outdated. Over the last 10 to 15 years, much has been learned about the psychosocial impact of

war on children and young people. Issues such as post-traumatic stress disorder in war-affected children and factors influencing the resilience of children in difficult circumstances have been fairly well researched. Equally, the report is outdated in its observations that "adolescents, during or after wars, seldom receive any special attention or assistance" (Machel 1996, 40). These days, adolescents have moved to the center stage, with numerous programs helping them during and after armed conflicts.

22. Machel 1996, 41.

23. Ibid, 45.

24. Ibid, 48.

25. Security Council Resolution 1612 (2005) established a monitoring and reporting mechanism of grave violations of child rights.

26. Machel 1996, 52.

27. If an armed conflict is contained in a specific part of the country, the reconstruction is likely to start in those places free of conflict well before the final peace-accord is signed.

28. Machel 1996, 55.

29. Ibid, 55.

30. Ibid, 58.

31. Ibid, 59.

32. Ibid.

33. Ibid, 60.

Acknowledgments

Krijn Peters would like to express his thanks to the Centre for Development Studies, Swansea University, for allowing time to write this textbook, and to his family for their encouragement.

Kendra E. Dupuy wishes to thank the International Peace Research Institute, Oslo (PRIO), for support in writing this textbook, as well as her family.

Abbreviations

ALP	accelerated learning program
CBO	community-based organization
CZOP	Children as Zones of Peace
ECOMOG	Economic Community of West African States Monitoring Group
FTR	family tracing and reunification
GDP	gross domestic product
GNP	gross national product
ICC	interim care center
ICC	International Criminal Court
IDP	internally displaced person
ILO	International Labour Organization
IMF	International Monetary Fund
INEE	Inter-Agency Network on Education in Emergencies
IO	international organization
LRA	Lord's Resistance Army
MDG	Millennium Development Goal
NGO	nongovernmental organization
PTSD	post-traumatic stress syndrome
RUF	Revolutionary United Front
SALW	small arms and light weapons
SZOP	Schools as Zones of Peace
UN	United Nations
UNCRC	United Nations Convention on the Rights of the Child
UNDP	United Nations Development Program
UNESCO	United Nations Education, Scientific, and Cultural Organization
UNHCR	United Nations High Commissioner for Refugees
UNICEF	United Nations Children's Fund
USSR	Union of Soviet Socialist Republics
WWII	World War Two

CHAPTER 1

Children, Youth, and Armed Conflict

Human history is largely written in blood. For thousands of years, tribes, popula-tions, kingdoms, and whole empires have fought and waged war on each other. Many of the ancient civilizations are known to us today because they were so suc-cessful in their military endeavors, expanding their territories from obscurity into history through violence. More recently, the twentieth century was witness to two World Wars in its first half, and the second half was by no means more peaceful. Post-WWII, each and every region in the world has been involved in war. To give just a few examples: in Latin America conflict has affected Peru and Colombia, among other countries. The Central American region has witnessed a series of armed conflicts, including those in Guatemala, El Salvador, and Nicaragua. Sub-Saharan Africa has been literally plagued by it in entire regions: the Horn of Africa (in Ethiopia, Somalia, Sudan, and Eritrea); West Africa (for example in Sierra Leone, Liberia, and the Ivory Coast); and the Great Lakes district (in the Democratic Republic of Congo, Rwanda, and Burundi). The Middle East and North Africa are experiencing prolonged conflicts in Israel, and the Middle East has been the theatre of two Gulf Wars. The Central and South Asian regions are experiencing conflict in some of the former Soviet republics and in countries such as Afghanistan, Pakistan, India, and Nepal. East and South East Asia were the the-atre of some of the deadliest post-WWII conflicts in Vietnam, Korea, China, and Cambodia and more recently in the Philippines and Timor Leste.

North America, Oceania, and Europe seem to have done reasonably well, although Europe experienced a significant armed conflict during the 1990s in for-mer Yugoslavia. It may therefore come as a surprise that post-WWII, the United States, Australia, the United Kingdom, and France are among the countries that have most often gone to war (as discussed later in this chapter), although these conflicts were seldom if ever fought on their home soil. Economically well-off countries generally do not experience many armed conflicts on their home soil. It is the poor and lower middle income countries in the world, which often have undemocratic or transitional governments, which are most likely to experience armed conflict. The consequences for these countries are devastating. Living standards and social provisions—already low before the start of a conflict—are likely to further deteriorate. Infrastructure is damaged, state resources reallocated in favor of the military sector, and human capital lost, because people are killed or flee the country.

Some conflicts in the world have been going on for many years, experiencing some level of stability after a cease-fire agreement or peace agreement, only to fall back again into full-scale war after a number of years. For example, in Sudan, armed conflict started in 1955 and is—despite several peace-accords—still ongoing this day, with heavy fighting now occurring in the Darfur region. Another example of a protracted conflict is Colombia, where an armed struggle started in the mid-1960s, and again does not have an end in sight. Whole generations have grown up in these countries knowing only violent conflict. War is one of the most destructive activities of mankind. Its effects are both direct and indirect: hundreds or thousands of people can be killed in the course of an armed struggle and many more are wounded and disabled, some for the rest of their lives. The considerable physical damage to civilian infrastructure, such as homes, schools, roads, and health clinics—all too often deliberately inflicted—not only brings the need for a long and costly postwar reconstruction process, but also has significant and long-term implications for children and young people as individuals and therefore for societies as a whole. Experiencing armed conflict and its traumas during a phase when one is still developing both physically and psychologically will likely have long-term detrimental psychosocial consequences, in particular if those institutions which can mitigate these effects (schools, health facilities, community centers, etc.) have been destroyed too.

This book illustrates and discusses the different ways armed conflict affects children and young people. In many war-affected countries, children and young people make up the largest section of the population. Young people are often referred to as the "future of a country." But what kind of future does a country have if the majority of its population has known only war? What happens to these young people and their future when they are deprived of the conditions and institutions which are central for their physical, psychological, and mental development? What will happen if they cannot grow up in a safe environment, and do not have access to educational and health facilities?

Most children and youth in countries experiencing armed conflict are affected by it, but to varying degrees. And the specific ways children and young people respond to situations caused by armed conflict also vary, depending as much on the nature of the person as on external circumstances. The majority of children and young people in regions experiencing armed conflict just try to survive, in their communities, as internally displaced people in camps, or abroad as refugees. But there is a significant group of young people who either resist or participate more actively in armed conflict. To pay full justice to the agency of children and young people, it is important to acknowledge both these responses; children and young people use a wide range of tactics to survive during times of war, even in situations where there seems to be little choice left. Young people in conflict zones around the world actively survive, resist, and participate in conflicts by, for instance, taking up arms as combatants to fight in government armies or opposition groups, by helping their families to survive the difficulties of conflict situations, or by leading positive and peaceful initiatives during and after times of war.

War is not a recent phenomenon in the world, nor is its impact on children and young people or their involvement as active participants. However, the nature of war has changed considerably during the last 60 years or so. The number of wars between two or more states (interstate conflicts) has gradually declined since the end of WWII, with nearly all armed conflicts taking place today being civil (or intrastate) conflicts. Most of the conflicts that took place during the Cold War had some geopolitical element to it, due to the involvement of either the United States or the former USSR (or both), although often by proxy. But the end of the Cold War did not bring global peace. It did, however, change some of the characteristics of war, removing in many cases the geopolitical element and replacing it with other characteristics. The changing character of war also had an impact on children and young people. Young people have been victims of and participants in wars throughout history, but never to the extent that they are today. So what has changed about warfare in recent years?

Understanding "New Wars"

It is November 9, 1989. Crowds are gathering in the center of Berlin and marching to the wall which divides the eastern and communist part of the German city from the western, capitalist half. The Berlin Wall has for decades now been the symbol of a divided world in which the USSR and the United States compete for global domination. Some of the people in the crowd carry sledgehammers and climb on top of the concrete wall. The demolition starts. Others join in and not long afterward the first cracks appear. Cracks become gaps and for the first time since 1961, the people of a divided city, of a divided nation, of a divided world, can meet each other as one people.

Definitions of War and Armed Conflict

What exactly is a "war"? War is an armed conflict with at least a thousand battle-deaths per year during the course of a conflict. Battle-deaths are deaths of civilians caught in the crossfire and the deaths of combatants. If there are less than a thousand battle-deaths per year, it is called an armed conflict. Armed conflict is political violence between two or more parties involving armed force. If there are less than 25 battle-deaths it no longer is counted as a conflict.

The two main types of armed conflict are non-state conflicts—fought between ethnic groups, or militias, without the involvement of the state—and state-based conflicts, which can further be divided into:

— **Interstate conflict** is armed conflict between two or more states.
— **Intrastate conflict (civil war)** is armed conflict inside a state.
— **Extra-state conflict (e.g., colonial wars)** is armed conflict involving a state which takes place outside its geographical borders.
— **Internationalized intrastate conflict** is a conflict inside a state in which one or more outside states have sent their own armed forces to support one side or another.[1]

For many, on that historic day in November in Berlin, the Cold War—the period of tension, competition, and conflict between the Soviet Union and the United States and their respective allies—came to an end and expectations ran high of a "global peace" with each country soon uniting under the banner of democracy and capitalism. It was, as one author referred to it; "The End of History" with liberal democracy as human government's final form.[2] Of course, there were still many "walls" in the world that had to be broken down; there were still political struggles going on and in the far corners of the world, armed conflicts still needed a peace-accord. But these conflicts would soon come to an end—or so was the globally shared expectation. These wars were the "remnants" of the Cold War period, where the Superpowers fought their geopolitical battle through proxy wars in Third World Countries. Other conflicts were considered to be the "leftovers" of unfinished anticolonial struggles, of which the majority took place between the 1950s and 1980s. The expectation was that these too would soon come to a peaceful end in the new era of peace.

But moving into the 1990s, it became clear that we were too optimistic. Rather than countries cashing in on the "peace dividend"—using funds for development which were before committed to the defense budget—the number of armed conflicts actually increased in the world. In Central and South America, South East Asia, and the Middle East, conflicts did not necessarily come to an end, and in Africa, organized violence and armed conflicts actually increased, often posing a region-wide problem. Halfway during the 1990s much of West Africa, the Horn of Africa, and the Great Lakes area were experiencing armed conflict. Moreover, these conflicts did not fit the standard explanations; they were neither Cold War remnants, nor "leftovers" of the anticolonial struggles. They appeared to be a new type of conflict with distinctive features. Hence international observers and scholars started to refer to these conflicts as the "New Wars."

60 Years of Conflict

Straight after the end of World War II, the number of intrastate conflicts in the world was below 10. Since then this number has steadily increased—fluctuations aside—and peaked in the year 1995 with nearly 50 intrastate conflicts. Since 1995, there has been a sharp decline in the number, and 10 years later it had already dropped to half the number. Inter-state, extra-state and internationalized intrastate conflicts have never exceeded more than 10 conflicts at a time in the world, with extra-state conflicts having been null since 1975.

Interestingly, countries involved in the most international conflicts between 1946 and 2005 are the United Kingdom (22 conflicts), France (19), and the United States (17), followed by Australia, the Netherlands, and Portugal, which all have been involved in 8 conflicts. However, if we look at the list of countries which experienced the highest number of conflicts on their home soil between 1946 and 2005, we do not find any of the above countries at the top of the list. Instead, we see India, which has fought 14 conflicts on its home soil, followed by Myanmar (9), China (8), Ethiopia (8), Indonesia (7), and Israel, the West Bank, and Gaza (7). All these countries, with the exception of Israel, are poor or lower-income countries.[3]

You can find more statistics on war and armed conflict, human rights abuse and peacekeeping operations on the Web site of the Human Security Report Project at http://www.hsrgroup.org/.

In the 1990s the number of intrastate conflicts peaked, while the already few interstate and internationalized conflicts further decreased. In an intrastate conflict, the state (often of an oppressive or dictatorial nature) is challenged for its authority by one or more opposition groups, within the national boundaries. In other words, these "new" conflicts are civil wars, although often they have had regional destabilizing influences. Related to that was another characteristic of the "New Wars," the high level of civilian casualties. Increasingly it seemed that the civilian population was explicitly targeted by the armed factions, whether government troops or rebels; civilian casualties were no longer "collateral damage." For example, in World War I, the percentage of civilian casualties was around 5 percent of the total number. Clearly the majority of casualties were soldiers. In World War II, the percentage of civilian casualties had risen to half of the total number of casualties. In the so-called New Wars, the civilian casualty percentage reaches as high as 90 to 95 percent of the total casualty number.[4]

For many observers the high number of civilian casualties was also related to what was considered as probably the most shocking feature of the New Wars, namely the extreme brutality of the armed factions waging war and the apparently "senseless" violence. It looked like violence was no longer the last resort if all other diplomatic means had failed, but that using violence and excessive violence had become the norm in political and social behavior. In the West, people were now exposed to footage and images of civilians—including women and children—who had their limbs cut off by rebels; of alleged collaborators of the enemy who were burnt alive with car-tires set on fire around their necks; and children—sometimes as young as eight—executing civilians while probably under the influence of drugs. Both the level of violence and targets of the atrocities seemed to refute any claim that this was politically or ideologically-motivated violence.

State-Based Conflicts on Home Soil

WAR AT HOME

Number of armed conflicts involving government forces fought within a country or its territorial waters
1946–2005

13
7 – 9
4 – 6
1 – 3
0
no data

Three-quarters of countries have had one or more state-based armed conflicts within their own borders since 1946.

All but one of Myanmar's nine home-soil conflicts, that with China in 1969, pitted the government against a rebel group.

India's 13 home-soil conflicts include war with Pakistan, and insurgencies in Punjab, in Kashmir, and in five states in the north-east.

Apart from Israel, these are all developing countries with large, multi-ethnic populations. Most of these conflicts have involved insurgents seeking secession or greater autonomy.

MOST HOME-SOIL CONFLICTS

Countries that have fought the highest number of conflicts at home *1946–2005*

India	13
Myanmar	9
China	8
Ethiopia	8
Indonesia	7
Israel and West Bank & Gaza	7
Nigeria	6

The previous map counted all international wars. For colonial states and for the "great powers," many of these were fought abroad. This map only counts conflicts involving government forces fought wholly or partially on a state's home soil or in its territorial waters. It excludes non-state conflicts – those between rival warlords and militias – and genocide and other acts of one-sided violence. Of the nine most conflict-prone states identified in the previous map, three (Australia, Netherlands and Portugal) have had no home-soil conflicts at all; France had one and the UK had two.

Figure 1.1. State-Based Conflicts on Home Soil, 1946–2005. © World Bank, 2008. Used by permission. Reprinted with the permission of the World Bank.

6

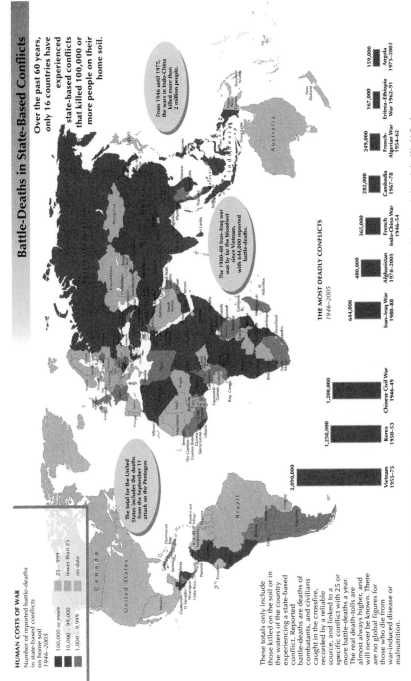

Battle-Deaths in State-Based Conflicts

Over the past 60 years, only 16 countries have experienced state-based conflicts that killed 100,000 or more people on their home soil.

From 1946 until 1975, the wars in Indo-China killed more than 2 million people.

The 1980–88 Iran–Iraq war was by far the bloodiest since Vietnam, with 644,000 reported battle-deaths.

The total for the United States includes the deaths from the September 11 attack on the Pentagon.

HUMAN COSTS OF WAR

Number of reported battle-deaths in state-based conflicts on home soil
1946–2005

- 100,000 or more
- 10,000 – 99,000
- 1,000 – 9,999
- 25 – 999
- fewer than 25
- no data

These totals only include those killed on the soil or in the waters of the country experiencing a state-based conflict. Reported battle-deaths are deaths of combatants, and civilians caught in the crossfire, recorded by a reliable source, and linked to a specific conflict with 25 or more battle-deaths a year. The real death-tolls are almost always higher, and will never be known. There are no global figures for those who die from war-induced disease or malnutrition.

THE MOST DEADLY CONFLICTS
1946–2005

Conflict	Battle-deaths
Vietnam 1955–75	2,090,000
Korea 1950–53	1,250,000
Chinese Civil War 1946–49	1,200,000
Iran–Iraq War 1980–88	644,000
Afghanistan 1978–2005	480,000
French Indo-China War 1946–54	365,000
Cambodia 1967–78	282,000
French-Algerian War 1954–62	249,000
Eritrea-Ethiopia War 1962–91	167,000
Angola 1975–2002	159,000

Figure 1.2. Battle-Deaths in State-Based Conflicts, 1946–2005. © World Bank, 2008. Reprinted with the permission of the World Bank.

7

Such a claim also became problematic when one looked at the way the armed factions supported themselves. Before, governments and armed factions could often count on financial support—overt, but more often covert—from one of the Superpowers. This reduced the need of the armed factions to generate revenues themselves. But after the end of the Cold War, in the New War era, this support was no longer available. Armed groups had to look for other ways to fund their struggle and increasingly involved themselves in a range of illicit activities, such as looting, drug-trafficking, kidnapping, and the exploitation of mineral resources, such as diamonds, gold, or timber. It was unclear if the revenues raised were used to pursue the struggle or if it ended up in the private bank accounts of the leaders of the often multiple armed groups. Armed factions were sometimes run as private armies by these leaders or "warlords," who executed control through personal authority rather than through the hierarchical military structures of command and control associated with formal armies. Rebel leaders appeared to be economic entrepreneurs as much as they were freedom fighters. The line between a politically-motivated versus a criminal organization became increasingly blurred with fighting factions tapping into regional and sometimes global criminal networks, to strengthen their financial situation. Clearly, international observers and scholars were up against a major challenge. What to make of these New Wars? Over the following years, different explanations were put forward to explain these new conflicts with their distinctive features.

The first explanation—sometimes referred to as "New-Barbarism"—partly reflects the widespread confusion among observers when the number of conflicts increased in the early 1990s. The New Barbarism thesis argues that conflict-affected countries would have experienced conflict and a breakdown of law and order anyway, if it was not for the policing of the Superpowers which had a clear stake in not provoking each other. In other words, it was argued that many of these countries were and—this is the tricky part—always will be prone to conflict, because of unresolved and irresolvable hatreds between their civilians dating back to ancient times. Irresolvable since these countries harbored populations which were deeply divided among ethnic or religious lines. It was therefore no surprise that these hatreds erupted when the wider geopolitical balance of nuclear terror was removed.

Other scholars turned their attention to some of the characteristics of the countries in which the conflicts of the 1990s emerged. Most of these countries were characterized by a combination of a high population growth and increasing difficulties around environmental resources, which were often depleting or eroding. Thomas Malthus, a nineteenth-century British political economist, had already pointed out that if population growth is faster than the increase of environmental resources—in particular food—there is a problem. The balance between these two, Malthus argued, is reinstated by disease, famine, or violent conflict. Perhaps the conflicts of the New War era were the result of a "natural" process of balancing the population with its resource base?

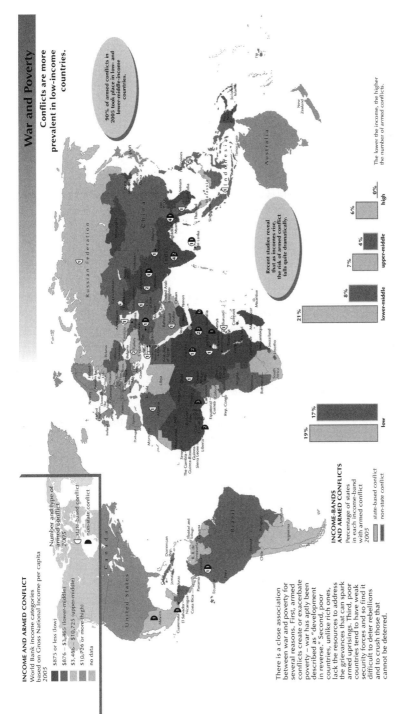

War and Poverty

Conflicts are more prevalent in low-income countries.

90% of armed conflicts in 2005 took place in low- and lower-middle-income countries.

Recent studies reveal that as incomes rise, the risk of armed conflict falls quite dramatically.

The lower the income, the higher the number of armed conflicts.

INCOME AND ARMED CONFLICT

World Bank income categories based on Gross National Income per capita 2005

- $875 or less (low)
- $876 – $3,465 (lower-middle)
- $3,466 – $10,725 (upper-middle)
- $10,726 or more (high)
- no data

Number and type of armed conflict 2005

- state-based conflict
- non-state conflict

There is a close association between war and poverty for several reasons. First, armed conflicts create or exacerbate poverty — war has aptly been described as "development in reverse." Second, poor countries, unlike rich ones, lack the resources to address the grievances that can spark armed uprisings. Third, poor countries tend to have weak security forces and so find it difficult to deter rebellions and to crush those that cannot be deterred.

INCOME-BANDS AND ARMED CONFLICTS

Percentage of states in each income-band with armed conflict 2005

- state-based conflict
- non-state conflict

19% 17% low

21% 8% lower-middle

7% 4% upper-middle

6% 0% high

Figure 1.3. War and Poverty. © World Bank, 2008. Reprinted with the permission of the World Bank.

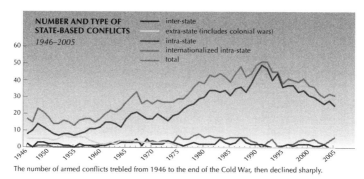

The number of armed conflicts trebled from 1946 to the end of the Cold War, then declined sharply.

Figure 1.4. Number and Type of State-Based Conflicts, 1946–2005. © World Bank, 2008. Used by permission. Reprinted with the permission of the World Bank.

Another group of academics and policy advisors looked for a less evolutionarily-inspired explanation, and took one of mankind's main interests as a starting point: wealth accumulation. Clearly, armed conflict brought major human and economic loss to a country, with infrastructure, schools, and hospitals destroyed and international investments significantly reduced. But not everybody was losing out during conflicts. These scholars realized that there were people who were financially getting better off from a conflict. Arms dealers, rebel leaders, officers of the national army, even the rank-and-file fighters, could all profit from war and thus had no interest in stopping it. To back up this insight, statistical data showed that countries which were "blessed" with an abundance of easily exploitable natural resources were more likely to have armed conflicts (this paradox was referred to as the "resource curse").[5] Perhaps it was "greed, not grievance" which explained the new kind of wars?

But not everybody was convinced by this economic explanation. Obviously, some people benefited from war and often access to resources could prolong a conflict (it is difficult to fight a war without resources anyway), but was it the cause for conflict? Taking a closer look at those countries which had high levels of natural resources and which were experiencing war, it was found that in many cases the income of these resources was divided in a highly unequal way. These scholars found that there was a particular kind of political system—the so-called patrimonial system—common in many (especially African) countries, which was particularly vulnerable to violent collapse. In these patrimonially organized states, state resources were handed out as marks of personal favor by government officials. In this way, people were made loyal to the ruling clique, who could buy off the opposition. However, when government resources declined, for example as the result of a decline in world market prices for raw materials in the 1980s or because of the end of support by one of the Superpowers at the end of the 1990s, less resources remained for the patrons to buy the loyalty of their clients. An increasingly large group of people—in particular at the very low end of the patrimonial ladder—had to do without the handouts, and these individuals can be easy recruits for any opposition leader willing to take his or her struggle to the next—and more violent—level.

A last explanation discussed here is the destructive impact of the globalization process, taking off after the end of the Cold War. It was observed that neoliberal economic reforms, propagated by international financial institutions, such as the World Bank and the International Monetary Fund, did not produce the economic growth and prosperity which they had promised. In many cases these reforms brought increased unemployment, disparities in income, and an erosion in the provisions of social sectors—such as education and health—and in effect undermined the legitimacy of the state. This grim environment proved to offer fertile grounds for increasing corruption, the development of black markets and for the trafficking of drugs, weapons, or humans. In the face of eroding state authority, opposition groups started to claim power, often on the basis of a particular identity, be it a national, religious, or clan identity. Hence, the causes of these new wars are "identity politics" turned violent, against the background of an increasingly weaker state.

Above, the most important features of many contemporary conflicts have been described. In addition, the dominant explanations which try to shed light on these conflicts and provide us with an analytical framework for how to interpret these have been provided. For the content of this book, which addresses children and youth in the context of war, it is important to remember that never before in history have children and youth become so central in conflicts, as victims and as participants. As we have seen above, New Wars have an unprecedented number of civilian casualties, many of which are children and young people. But equally, children and young people actively participate in armed conflicts on a scale never witnessed before. Children have become "stakeholders" in conflict, and thus also "stakeholders" in peace. This urges us to reconsider the effects that armed conflicts have on children and young people, the roles they have during conflict, and what they can offer in the postwar peace-building process. But we first need a better understanding of who falls into the category of children and young people.

Who Are Children and Young People?

Up to this point, the terms children and young people have been used without clearly defining what we specifically mean by these. Few of us would label an 8-year-old boy or girl as not being a child, while equally few of us will consider a 40 year-old man or woman as not being an adult. However, when and at what age does a child become an adult? And what kind of criteria do we use to determine this: do we use an age-based definition—in most countries children legally become adults with their 18th birthday—or do we use physical appearance? Another method is to use social indicators—for instance, once a child is able to sustain himself or herself independently of his or her parents, he or she can be considered to be an adult. Clearly, this varies from place to place; in Western countries many young people obtain independent livelihoods as late as their mid-twenties, while in many developing countries young people of the age of 15 or 16 are (often forced to be) economically independent (or in the case of child-headed households, the breadwinner for their brothers and sisters as well). Many cultures have special initiation rituals—rites of passage—to mark the transition from childhood to adulthood. The timing of these rites seldom coincidences with a person's 18th birthday. And there is a gender dimension to the whole issue as well: in many cultures girls are considered to be women once they have given birth and thus, a 15-year-old mother is considered to be an adult. Equally, boys become men when they are married and their wife has given birth, but to be able to marry, young men often need a regular income first in order to provide for their new family. In many developing countries, young men are not able to generate sufficient resources to marry and hence are not considered as full adults, even if they are 30 or 40 years of age.

The division of the categories of child and adult, with 18 years of age as the moment of (instant) transition, is not very helpful or accurate in many circumstances. Even where it concerns legal issues, a more stratified model is used, enabling the law to give a different kind of punishment for the same violation to a 16- or 17-year-old person than it would give to a 12- or 13 year-old one. The similarities between a boy or girl of 7 and one of 17 years are much fewer than those between a 17-year-old and a 19 year-old person, although in the latter case, the first one is a child and the second one an adult. The need for more subtle categories is clear. The United Nations, for instance, uses the following terms:

- Child: 0–17 years
- Adolescent: 10–19 years
- Teenager: 13–19 years
- Young adult: 20–24 years
- Youth: 15–24 years

Ironically, a 15- or 16 year-old person is thus, according to the United Nations, a child, an adolescent, a teenager, and a youth, all at the same time. Nevertheless, these divisions do more justice to the reality than the child-adult one. Recently, the category of youth (ages 15–24)—and in particular the "problem of the youth," referring among other things to the inability of many youths to find employment and thus to become adults (see above)—has moved center stage on many development-related agendas and policies.[6] Now that the concept of youth is clearly established as a category, a "child" is often to be understood as someone below the age of 15, so anyone younger than a youth.

Childhood and Youth

Different factors determine whether one is considered to be a "child," a "youth," or an "adult," and chronological age is just one of these. Other factors include

Table 1.1 Views of Childhood

Dionysian	Apollonian
Children should be seen and not heard	Childhood is a time for play, and not for
Children need protection from themselves	work
Childhood is a time to learn discipline	Children need protection from the world
	Children are innocent
	Children are passive
	Childhood should be happy
Both	
Childhood is a time set apart from the adult world	
Children belong in families	
Children are closer to nature than adults	
Children are incomplete—less than adult	

Source: Nicola Ansel, *Children, Youth and Development* (London: Routledge, 2005): 11

cultural and social norms and beliefs, economic status, gender, religion, and different aspects of national and international law. Ideas about what is (and should be) "childhood" and "adulthood" diverge widely between different societies and groups. They not only differ from group to group, but also over time. The understanding of childhood as a time of innocence and play is only a fairly recent construction. During medieval times in Europe, there was no childhood, only a phase of infancy when there was physical dependency, after which those who are today considered to be children, entered the (expanded) phase of adulthood.[7]

A useful, although rather simplified model, is provided by Chris Jenks in his 1996 book *Childhood: Critical Concepts in Sociology*.[8] It distinguishes two contradictory concepts of childhood; the "Dionysian" and the "Apollonian."

In the Western world, before the twentieth century, people held a more "Dionysian" perspective on childhood, but this changed into a more "Apollonian" one during the previous century. The concept of childhood in many non-Western countries is probably closer to the Dionysian perspective than it is to the Apollonian, although one should be careful to use these Western concepts in non-Western settings. However, one can observe a certain level of "apollonianization" taking place in many developing countries, partly as a result of the activities of Western child-focused nongovernmental organizations and international organizations such as the UN.

Lately, the "apollonian" perspective—in particular where it is "imported" by Western NGOs—has come under scrutiny; it is argued that because it perceives children as passive, it denies their agency and turns a blind eye to all the situations where children actively contribute—or are forced to contribute—to society, economically, socially, and politically. The recent focus in development studies on a discourse of rights, including so-called "rights-based approaches" come some way in changing the view of children as passive, powerless, and excluded. Children have "rights" (the right to health, clean drinking water, education, etc.), rather than "needs," which would make them passive recipients of charity. And with children as rights bearers, there are also duty bearers (most notably the state[9]) which can be held accountable if they do not realize these rights.

The 1989 United Nations Convention on the Rights of the Child—the most widely signed and ratified treaty of the United Nations ever—forms (with other treaties) the basis of these rights. Its near universal support implies that there is now a globally shared perspective on the rights of children and, by default, some level of shared perspective about what childhood should entail. But some differences in perspectives remain. For instance, the 1990 African Charter on the Rights and Welfare of the Child, formulated by what is now the African Union, states in Article 31 a series of responsibilities and duties for children, including 31a:*to work for the cohesion of the family, to respect his parents, superiors and elders at all times and to assist them in case of need*; and 31d: *to preserve and strengthen African cultural values in his relations with other members of the society, in the spirit of tolerance, dialogue and consultation and to contribute to the moral well-being of society*. Such an article on duties or responsibilities is not present in the UNCRC. One of the critiques on the UNCRC is that it represents a recent and Western, urban middle-class perspective on childhood, while the majority of children are non-Western, poor, and from working-class backgrounds.[10]

Whether or not this critique is correct, by virtue of signing and ratifying the UNCRC, State Parties—whether they represent countries in Latin America, sub-Sahara Africa, or Asia—legally bind themselves to uphold its content, in peace and in times of conflict (whether or not they are capable or genuinely willing to do so is another story). Hence, it is important to look at some provisions of international law which concern children and young people in situations of armed conflict or war.

International Law and Its Provisions

International law is increasingly becoming an effective tool to protect the rights of young people affected by conflict. It is used by practitioners, policy makers, politicians, and aid donors when formulating policies; in the design of interventions and programs; for advocating purposes; and to decide on the allocation of donor money. For instance, those states which have signed and ratified the UNCRC but which still have underage combatants in their armies are likely to be publicly "named and shamed" and can face political and economic reprimands from the international community. In the twentieth century, a significant number of international laws have been formulated, signed, and ratified by state bodies, which are of relevance for children and young people in war and post-conflict situations. Some of these laws apply to both adults and children. For example, the 1949 Geneva Conventions stipulate the rules of war and provide protection for civilians and those who can no longer fight. Other laws are specifically designed for underage persons, covering peace—and/or wartime, like the UN Convention on the Rights of the Child. Hereafter, some of the most important international laws protecting children and young people in conflict situations will be briefly discussed.[11]

The International Save the Children Union, founded in 1920—after Eglantyne Jebb and her sister Dorothy Buxton founded the first Save the Children organization in 1919 in the United Kingdom—formulated the "Declaration of Geneva" in 1923. One year later, in 1924, the League of Nations (the predecessor to the United Nations) adopted the **Declaration on the Rights of the Child (CRC)**, which was based on the Geneva declaration. It contained five articles, of which Article 3 is of relevance to conflict situations, stating that "The child must be the first to receive relief in times of distress."

The 1948 **Universal Declaration of Human Rights (UDHR)** provides basic human rights varying from "the right to life, liberty and security of person" (Article 3) to the right for everyone "to freedom of thought, conscience and religion" (Article 18). No article deals specifically with times of war, although all rights should be upheld during war and armed conflict. Article 14.1, however, has significance for refugees where it states that: "everyone has the right to seek and to enjoy in other countries asylum from persecution." The UDHR is translated and disseminated into more than 300 languages and dialects, making it the most translated document in the world.

The 1949 **Geneva Conventions** came into existence to try to limit the barbarity of war. Its predecessor—the 1864 Geneva Convention for the Amelioration of the Condition of the Wounded in Armies in the Field—was based on a draft convention prepared by the International Committee of the Red Cross/Red Crescent. The Geneva Conventions protect people who do not take part in the fighting and those who can no longer fight. There are four conventions, namely: the 1st Convention, which addresses wounded soldiers on the battlefield; the 2nd Convention, which addresses the wounded and shipwrecked at sea; the 3rd Convention, which addresses prisoners of war; and the 4th Convention, which addresses civilians under enemy control. These conventions refer to children only in limited ways. The Geneva Conventions and their Additional Protocols (see hereafter) form the core of *international humanitarian law.*

The UN's **1951 Convention** and 1967 **Protocol Relating to the Status of refugees** stipulate the rights of refugees. A central issue of these documents is the "Principle of unity of the family"; it is recommended that "Governments . . . take the necessary measures for the protection" especially with a view to "the protection of refugees who are minors, in particular unaccompanied children and girls, with special reference to guardianship and adoption."

In 1959, the United Nations—which was established in 1945—formulated the **UN Declaration on the Rights of the Child**, building on and expanding the 1924 Declaration. Principle 8 reaffirmed that "The child shall in all circumstances be among the first to receive protection and relief."

The 1977 **Additional Protocols I & II to the 1949 Geneva Conventions** relates to the Protection of Victims of International and Non-International Armed Conflict, and includes specific articles referring to children. For example,

Additional Protocol I, Article 77: Protection of Children, states that "parties to the conflict shall take all feasible measures in order that children who have not attained the age of 15 years do not take a direct part in hostilities and, in particular, they shall refrain from recruiting them into their armed forces." Additional Protocol II, covering the majority of conflicts and wars, formulates the above more firmly in *Article 4: Fundamental guarantees*, in stating that "children who have not attained the age of 15 years shall neither be recruited in the armed forces or groups nor allowed to take part in hostilities." More generally it states that "Children shall be provided with the care and aid they require."

The 1989 **UN Convention on the Rights of the Child**—the result of 10 years of negotiations and drafting—is the most widely signed and ratified convention ever,[12] and it lays out the civil, political, economic, social, and cultural human rights of children. Three articles are of particular relevance to situations of armed conflict: *Article 38: Armed conflicts; Article 39: Rehabilitative care*; and *Article 40: Administration of juvenile justice*. Article 38 refers to the obligations State Parties have under international humanitarian law with respect to children in situations of armed conflict. It again marks 15 years as the cutoff point for lawful armed recruitment and participation in hostilities. Article 39 states that "State Parties shall take all appropriate measures to promote physical and psychological recovery and social reintegration of a child victim of . . . armed conflict." Article 40 is of particular relevance where children have been involved in, for instance, acts of atrocities. It asks "State Parties to recognize the right of every child alleged as, accused of or recognized as having infringed the penal law . . . to take into account the child's age and the desirability of promoting the child's reintegration and the child's assuming a constructive role in society."

The UNCRC states in Article 1 that "For the purposes of the present Convention, a child means every human being below the age of eighteen years unless under the law applicable to the child, majority is attained earlier." The 1990 **African Charter on the Rights and Welfare of the Child** does not offer this exception: for the purpose of the Charter "a child means every human being below the age of 18 years" (Article 2). Hence, there is, according to the African charter no (legal) way for those under the age of 18 but above the age of 15 to be recruited or to take part in hostilities. Most African countries have signed and ratified the Charter.

The International Labour Organization (ILO) is a specialized agency of the United Nations that deals with labor issues. It was founded in 1919 and has its headquarters in Geneva, Switzerland. In 1999 it adopted **ILO Convention 182: Convention Concerning the Prohibition and Immediate Action for the Elimination of the Worst Forms of Child Labor**. Article 3 of this convention is of relevance to children directly involved in conflict as combatants but also more widely to children in the context of war, since it covers certain scenarios which are more likely to happen during wartime (as a time of reduced authority and increased lawlessness). Article 3a outlines what *the worst forms of child labor* are: "all forms of slavery or practices similar to slavery, such as the sale and trafficking of children, debt bondage and serfdom and forced or compulsory labor, including forced or compulsory recruitment of children for use in armed conflict."

Many felt that the UNCRC failed to fully protect the rights of the child (under 18 years) with regards to armed recruitment. Hence the 2000 **Optional Protocol to the Convention on the Rights of the Child on the Involvement of Children in Armed Conflict** was adopted, which prohibited compulsory recruitment of anyone below 18 years and made (legal) voluntary recruitment of those between 15 and 18 years nearly impossible (Articles 2 & 3). In addition, in Article 4 it states that "armed groups that are distinct from the armed forces of a State should not, under any circumstances, recruit or use in hostilities persons under the age of 18 years."

It is clear from the above that the rights of children in general—and in situations of armed conflict in particular—are well provided for. States have signed and ratified these documents and thus made firm commitments to uphold these rights. Nevertheless, the rights of children are violated worldwide, during times of peace and particularly during times of war. Sometimes states are not willing to live up to their obligations, but more often they are just not capable of providing and protecting the rights of children. Lacking the resources and capacity is an important reason for this failure—particularly so in the case of poor countries. And even in situations of armed conflict where the state—as a signature to these conventions and protocols—genuinely tries to honor its obligations, it is likely not able to put any pressure on the armed opposition to do the same. While rebel organizations have not signed these conventions, they too are bound by it. In short, the conventions and protocols aimed to protect the rights of children in situations of armed conflict are an important precondition to realizing these rights. But the signing and ratification of these conventions do not guarantee that these rights are truly realized.

For more about Human Rights declarations, see the following sources:

— The United Nations: http://www.un.org/.
— The International Labour Organization: http://www.ilo.org/.

Conclusion

There can be no doubt that the impact of war and armed conflict on children and young people is massive. To better understand the impact—and hence develop better ways to undo the negative consequences—it is important to have a good understanding of the changing character of wars. This introductory chapter provided on overview of the so-called "New Wars." It also discussed different theories which try to explain these wars. Peace initiatives and humanitarian interventions—aimed to help children, women and men—can become much more effective if there is a proper understanding of the root causes of an armed conflict.

This book focuses on armed conflicts and how they impact on children and youth. Hence, this introduction chapter continued with a discussion of the concepts of "children," "youth," and "childhood." Our understanding of these concepts has changed—and still is changing—over time and it varies widely among cultures. The "Western" view on "children" and "childhood" (if there is a uniform view in the first place) is just one perception among many, although an increasingly dominant one.

Finally, this chapter briefly discussed some of the most important international laws regarding children and young people in conflict situations. Some of these conventions concerning children and young people are among the most widely signed and ratified in the world. The rights of children and young people—and the obligations of states and the international community—in conflict situations are reasonably well stipulated, but the implementation and protection of these rights is still too often too limited.

Notes

1. The World Bank and the Human Security Report Project, *Mini Atlas of Human Security* (Brighton: Myriad Editions, 2008).

2. Francis Fukuyama, *The End of History and the Last Man* (New York: Free Press, 1992).

3. The World Bank and the Human Security Report Project, 2008.

4. Guy Goodwin-Gill and Ilene Cohn, *Child Soldiers: The Role of Children in Armed Conflict* (Oxford: Oxford University Press, 1994).

5. Paul Collier and Anke Hoeffler, "Greed and grievance in civil war." Washington, D.C.: The World Bank, Development Research Group, 2002.

6. See for instance, "World Development Report, 2007: Development and the Next Generation," Washington, D.C.: The World Bank, 2006.

7. Philippe Aries, *Centuries of Childhood* (New York: Vintage Press, 1962).

8. Chris Jenks, *Childhood* (London: Routledge, 1996) cited in: Nicola Ansell, *Children, Youth and Development* (London: Routledge, 2005).

9. State Parties have four types of obligations regarding the rights of children: to respect children's rights; to protect children's rights; to facilitate children's rights and; to provide children's rights. *Child Rights Programming: How to Apply Rights-Based Approaches in Programming.* International Save the Children Alliance 2002.

10. Ben White, "A World Fit for Children? Children and Youth in Development Studies and Policy," Institute of Social Studies, The Netherlands, 2003.

11. See Appendix II (Key Documents) for the text of many of these documents.

12. All countries have signed the UNCRC, but only the United States and Somalia have not yet ratified it. http://www.unicef.org/crc/index_30197.html (accessed 7 July 2009).

CHAPTER 2

Growing Up in the Context of War: The Impact of Armed Conflict on Children and Young People

The Lost Boys of Sudan

It is an afternoon in October 1995 in the Kakuma refugee camp in northwestern Kenya. 100 young people of varying ages sit packed together tightly on wooden benches in a classroom in one of the camp's primary schools. They listen carefully as the teacher reads aloud to them from a textbook on English language grammar. Peter sits among the students, toward the front, eagerly copying down the lesson written on the blackboard into the copy book that the students were given by the United Nations High Commissioner for Refugees (UNHCR), the UN entity mandated to assist refugees. Peter is 15 years of age and is older than many of the other children in the classroom, but he is extremely eager to learn.

Peter arrived at the refugee camp in 1992, along with many other boys and young men. He was one of many young refugees from southern Sudan who were separated from their parents and families during attacks on their home villages by the Sudanese government army during Sudan's second civil war (1983–2005). In the autumn of 1987, Peter was away from his village for a few days, herding cattle with his cousins and brothers. He returned to his village one morning to find the houses looted and burned down and the village nearly deserted. The inhabitants were wounded, killed, or gone, having fled to safety. Peter's family was killed during the raid on the village by the government army, leaving him with few other options than to leave his village. He started walking east, joining thousands of other young people going in the same direction. Some of them were only eight or nine years old, just like Peter. The boys and girls banded together and formed small groups, relying on each other to survive the long walk to the border with Ethiopia. Many of the young people died along the way from starvation, disease,

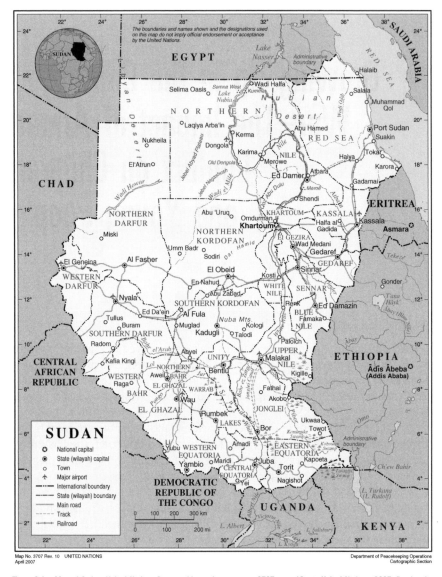

Figure 2.1. Map of Sudan, United Nations Cartographic section, map no. 3707, rev. 10. © United Nations, 2007. Reprinted
with the permission of the United Nations.

dehydration, exhaustion, and attacks by wild animals. The situation was so dangerous that the only humanitarian assistance provided for the young people was done from the air, with the Red Cross dropping food from its planes. In all, around 20,000 mostly boys and young men walked hundreds of kilometers from southern Sudan to Ethiopia, a journey that took many weeks.

The young refugees found sanctuary in refugee camps in Ethiopia, but not for long. In 1991, the Ethiopian government was overthrown by a coalition of opposition groups under the name Tigrayan People's Liberation Front (TPLF), which had been fighting a civil war against the Ethiopian government since the 1970s. The new government was hostile to the main resistance group in southern Sudan, the Sudanese Peoples Liberation Army/Movement (SPLA/M), which had been fighting a civil war against the Sudanese government since the 1950s. The new Ethiopian government suspected that the young Sudanese refugees who were living in the Ethiopian refugee camps were receiving military training to become SPLA/M combatants. As a result, the government forced the young refugees to leave Ethiopia, sometimes at gunpoint. The young people again made the dangerous crossing over the Gilo River on the border between Ethiopia and Sudan. Many of them were eaten by crocodiles, drowned, or shot dead by the Ethiopians as they tried to turn back. The survivors headed for Kenya, walking through Sudan. Finally, around 10,000 of them arrived at the Kakuma refugee camp in Kenya in 1992. They had walked for nearly a year and suffered greatly along the way. The young refugees were called the "Lost Boys"—a reference to the band of orphaned boys in the modern fairy tale of Peter Pan—by aid organizations working in the Kakuma camp, because they arrived at the camp without their parents. But, even though the refugees had finally found a more secure place to live in Kenya, life would be far from easy in the Kakuma camp, let alone like a fairy tale. As will be outlined in this chapter, the young refugees would face a number of challenges, such as accessing education and adequate health care, food, and clean water.[1]

Young People and the Wars in Sudan

The Sudanese civil war between the north and the south of the country was one of the longest ongoing civil wars in the world, and it has affected the lives of young people immensely—both during the long years of the conflict and during the more peaceful intervals. The first civil war broke out in 1955 and ended in 1972. The second phase of the civil war was fought between 1983 and 2005. The Sudanese government, based in the mostly Islamic and Arabic-speaking north, fought against the Sudan People's Liberation Army/Movement (SPLA/M), based in the largely Christian and animist, English-speaking south. But contrary to what these clear divisions might suggest, the conflict cannot be simplified to one over territory or religion. Political and social inequalities were also at stake, as the southern Sudanese were disenfranchised, excluded from the central Islamist government in Khartoum. In addition, natural resources were also an important factor in the start and continuation of the war, as the southern region of Sudan is endowed with vast tracks of fertile land and oil deposits, while the North is largely desert land.

Different components of a comprehensive peace agreement were signed between the Government of Sudan and the SPLA/M in 2004 and 2005. Despite this positive development, low-level conflict has been ongoing in the eastern region of Sudan, and civil conflict started in the western region of Darfur in 2003. The Darfur conflict has been largely fought between nomadic herders from the Arabic north and non-Arab ethnic groups living in Darfur, primarily over land and resources. The Sudanese government has been accused of sponsoring attacks by Arab "Janjaweed" militias against the black African population. Millions of children have fled the Darfur region and now live either as internally displaced people, or as refugees in the neighboring country of Chad—a country that faces its own political problems and has tense relations with Sudan over the Sudanese government's support for Chadian rebel groups fighting against the Chadian government (some of whom have military bases in Darfur). Many of the displaced children have physical health problems caused by malnourishment and poor health facilities. In addition, they often suffer from mental health problems, due to the forced displacement and atrocities they have witnessed. Young people have been orphaned and large numbers of young people have lost the opportunity to attend school. Many have served as combatants in the various fighting forces in the country (such as the SPLA/M).

In general, young people have been greatly and negatively affected by the long period of warfare in Sudan, a country 10 times as large as Great Britain. Southern Sudan in particular has very limited infrastructure such as schools, hospitals, or roads as a result of protracted fighting and deliberate disinvestment by the northern government, isolating communities and making service delivery and income generation difficult.

Sudan is an example of a protracted conflict, a war that has been ongoing for many years. There are a number of other armed conflicts in the world that have also been ongoing at varying levels of intensity for many years, such as in Sri Lanka, Israel, Afghanistan, Uganda, and India. Entire generations of young people in these countries have grown up knowing only war. These long-term conflicts—some of which have no solution in sight—have negatively affected young people in many ways and denied them the chance to grow up in their home communities without the threat of violence.

You can learn more about the story of the Lost Boys and about the wars in Sudan through the following sources:

On the Lost Boys:

- Nonfiction book: Joan Hecht, *The Journey of the Lost Boys*, 2005.
- Newspaper article: Sara Corbette, "The Lost Boys of Sudan: The Long, Long, Long Road to Fargo," *The New York Times*, April 1, 2001.
- Films: *The Lost Boys of Sudan* (2004) and *God Grew Tired of Us* (2006).
- Autobiographical and biographical works: Benson Deng, Alephonsion Deng, and Benjamin Ajak, *They Poured Fire on Us From the Sky*, 2006. Dave Eggers, *What is the What*, 2006.

On the North-South war in Sudan:

- Book: Douglas Hamilton Johnson, *The Root Causes of Sudan's Civil Wars*, 2003.

> • Internet Resource: http://www.crisisgroup.org has background information and many reports on both the North-South and the Darfur conflict in Sudan.

The Social and Economic Impact of War on Children and Young People

While Peter is a fictional character, the story is based on true events, and thus highlights some of the many ways in which war affects the lives of children and young people, both socially and economically. Children and young people are highly vulnerable to the effects of war, for multiple reasons. For instance, children are in many ways dependent on adults for their survival needs, such as food and water, and child-parent separation is a real danger during situations of armed conflict. Children and young people are still developing physically and psychologically. The consequences of war, such as mental trauma and physical injury, can thus have a very long-term impact on their development and growth into adulthood.

Armed conflict currently occurs most often in those regions that include very poor and low-income countries, such as in Africa, Asia, and Latin America. In most poor countries where war is not present, children and young people already experience difficulty in accessing schooling and health care and in receiving adequate nutrition. They may be required to work to earn income to help support their families and may be charged with carrying out domestic tasks to keep their households running, such as fetching water and caring for younger siblings. When a war breaks out, the situation for young people generally becomes much worse, as the overwhelming majority of victims of current conflicts are civilians, and the targets of various armed groups—whether government or opposition forces—are all too often civilian infrastructure, such as schools, hospitals, and houses. Thus, young people may be forced from their homes and deprived of access to the services and resources that help them to develop, while at the same time they are exposed to extreme levels of violence and intimidation.

Armed conflict has a significant effect on the foundations and structure of society, the economy, and the state. It is generally a period of great social, economic, and cultural disruption. The social order can be heavily disturbed as family members are killed, injured, or separated, and can even be turned upside down when friends become enemies or armed children command their former teachers or village authorities. The norms of society are broken and the rule of law is often absent, with people of all ages and walks of life committing acts of violence for which they may never be punished.

Yet, war can also offer opportunities for young people that did not exist prior to the outbreak of a conflict, and can be an opportunity for positive changes to occur. This happens when, for instance, young people have the opportunity to access education for the first time in their lives while living in refugee camps, or when local and international nongovernmental organizations advocate for and facilitate the implementation of children's rights.

It is important to realize that war does not have the same impact on all children and young people, as young people are not a homogenous category. War affects different groups of young people in different ways, depending on a wide variety of characteristics, such as the dynamics of the conflict (that is, the way in which the war is fought and where the fighting takes place) and the social and economic position of different groups of young people in society. Often, armed conflict affects girls differently from boys; this is the gendered impact of conflict. War can also affect younger children differently than those who are older, as well as those from urban areas versus rural areas. To fully understand the effects of armed conflict on children and young people, this chapter will explore the social and economic impacts of war on different groups of young people and in different armed conflicts around the world.

War-Induced Forced Displacement: Consequences for Young People

Profile of Forced Migration

Peter was forced to leave his home community in Sudan when his family was killed during the civil war and to live as a refugee first in Ethiopia, and then in Kenya. Forced displacement is the forced movement of people away from the communities and/or states in which they live due to either man-made or natural calamities. Forced migrants include both refugees and internally displaced persons (IDPs).

A refugee is someone who has been forcibly displaced from his or her home country and is living in another country—in other words, they are externally displaced. The internationally accepted legal definition of a (political) refugee is outlined in the 1951 United Nations Convention Relating to the Status of Refugees as being a person who,

> owing to a well-founded fear of being persecuted for reasons of race, religion, nationality, membership of a particular social group or political opinion, is outside the country of his nationality and is unable or, owing to such fear, is unwilling to avail himself of the protection of that country; or who, not having a nationality and being outside the country of his former habitual residence as a result of such events, is unable or, owing to such fear, unwilling to return to it.

The 1951 Convention stipulates a number of rights for refugees, such as the right to *non-refoulement*—that is, the right not to be forcibly returned to the country of origin.

Nearly every country in the world has been confronted with people seeking refuge, whether in receiving them for resettlement or hosting them temporarily. Most refugees seek asylum in a neighboring country. Refugees originate from and reside primarily in the Third World; it is "the world's poorest countries [who] continue to support the largest numbers of refugees."[2] There are currently around 10 million refugees in the world; some of the largest populations of refugees originate from war-affected countries such as Sudan, Iraq, and Afghanistan.[3]

As opposed to a refugee, an internally displaced person (IDP) is someone who has fled away from his or her place of living, but remains within the borders of his or her country of origin. Currently, there are around 26 million IDPs in the world.[4] Whereas the 1951 United Nations Convention Relating to the Status of Refugees provides protection for refugees, there is no similar international treaty or legal framework for the protection of IDPs[5], only a set of non-binding *Guiding Principles on Internal Displacement*, formulated in 1992 by the United Nations. According to international law, IDPs are under the protection of their national laws, but the state may itself be the reason for their displacement.

In general, women, children, and other vulnerable groups such as the elderly and the disabled constitute the bulk of any concentrated forced migrant population. Children under the age of 18 make up as much as half of all those forcibly displaced worldwide.[6] The table below shows the scale of some of the current major refugee and IDP crises in the world today. What becomes clear from the figures is that some conflict-affected countries have many more refugees than IDPs (e.g., Palestine, Afghanistan, Burundi) but that the opposite is much more common: of the total number of people who have fled their homes, the majority will look for refuge in their own country.

Many current refugees and IDPs belong to the most excluded and marginalized peoples in their society, often originating from rural and/or underdeveloped areas. Those who seek refuge outside their country are likely to end up in a refugee camp in a neighboring, host country. All too often, though, these host countries are

Table 2.1 Current Major Refugee and IDP Situations Worldwide (2008)

Country of origin	Estimated total number of refugees	Estimated total number of IDPs
Iraq	2.2 million	2.7 million
Turkey	227,232	954,000 to 1.2 million
Palestine (Occupied Palestinian Territory)	4.4 million	Between 24,500 and 115,000
Afghanistan	2,107,519	132,000
Colombia	72,796	Between 2 and 4 million
Uganda	21,752	1.1 million
Burundi	396,541	100,000
Sudan	686,311	Between 4.5 and 6 million
Chad	36,300	178,918
Somalia	464,253	1 million
Democratic Republic of Congo	401,914	1.4 million

Source: http://www.internal-displacement.org, and UNCHR (http://www.unhcr.org).

Figure 2.2. Refugee camp in Chad. © Mark Knobil, 2008. Used by permission.

equally poor and thus ill-equipped to deal with large refugee inflows. Poor host countries may find it hard to provide sufficient assistance to refugees when they cannot meet the needs of their own citizens, thus necessitating the intervention of nongovernmental and international organizations to deliver aid to forced migrants living in camps. Alternatively, forced migrants may be living in local communities or isolated areas such as forests where they receive no or only very little official assistance. While in some cases refugee camp populations have a higher quality of life than the host community outside the camp, aid agencies may be restricted by their budgets and low levels of security from delivering adequate amounts of food and other necessities. The physical location of a refugee camp may restrict farming, outside employment, and other income-earning activities, or the host government or community may limit these activities.

Forced displacement is not a new phenomenon, but it has taken on new dimensions in the twentieth and twenty-first centuries with the huge numbers of forced migrants that have been produced by many of the large-scale conflicts in poorer countries. Since the end of World War II, forced displacement has become longer in duration, with some forced migrants living in exile for weeks, months, and even years on end. It leaves people to live in a state of limbo, being unable to return to their communities of origin, settle as permanent residents in the host state, or be resettled abroad.[7]

Further Research: Organizations Providing Information About Forced Displacement and/or Working with Displaced People

- The Office of the United Nations High Commissioner for Refugees (UNHCR): http://www.unhcr.org
- Global International Displacement Monitoring Center: http://www.internal-displacement.org
- The Global Database on the Guiding Principles on Internal Displacement: http://www.idpguidingprinciples.org
- Norwegian Refugee Council: http://www.nrc.no
- Refugees International: http://www.refugeesinternational.org
- University of Oxford Refugee Studies Center: http://www.rsc.ox.ac.uk
- Forced Migration Review: http://www.fmreview.org
- Forced Migration Online: http://www.forcedmigration.org
- Human Rights Watch web page on child refugees and IDPs: http://www.hrw.org/en/category/topic/children%E2%80%99s-rights/migrants (accessed 8 July 2009).
- The Sphere Project Humanitarian Charter and Minimum Standards in Disaster Response: http://www.sphereproject.org/

Challenges Faced by Young Forced Migrants

Youthful forced migrants, both IDPs and refugees, face significant challenges while living in exile and growing up in abnormal conditions.[8] Among these challenges are difficulties in securing their basic needs, such as adequate levels of food, clean drinking water, and shelter and clothing. Young forced migrants also face problems in accessing education and health care due to the fact that schools and health clinics are likely to have closed down in war-affected areas, or simply be unavailable in camp settings. We will discuss the challenges that young forced migrants face in accessing education and health services and their basic needs as separate issues later in this chapter, and focus in this section on the security challenges faced by youthful forced migrants.

The lack of security is a considerable problem, one that can complicate the ability of young displaced people to secure their basic needs and to access social services. Forced migrants—whether living outside of or inside displacement camps—experience this insecurity. Displacement camps are regularly subject to attacks by armed groups, and unaccompanied and separated displaced children are particularly vulnerable to such attacks because they are deprived of the physical protection and developmental care that parents can provide.[9]

Unaccompanied children are those who are separated from both parents and are not being cared for by an adult who, by law or custom, is responsible to do so. A child is an **orphan** only if both parents are dead. **Separated children**, by contrast, are those who are separated from both parents, but not necessarily from other relatives. There are many reasons for children becoming orphaned, unaccompanied, or separated from their parents. Such reasons include abduction or recruitment, accidental separation, the death or imprisonment of a parent, or because children are sent to, or left in, a country of asylum for their safety by their parents, who may have returned or stayed in the home country. These children can find it hard to have their physical and developmental needs met, such as acquiring sufficient food and accessing education.[10]

An example of the security threats that refugee camps can pose for young displaced persons comes from the Kakuma refugee camp in Kenya where Peter, the young Sudanese boy we met at the beginning of this chapter, lived. This refugee camp faced the threat of raids on the camp by local Turkana herders. These attacks have stemmed primarily from fierce competition between the Turkanas and the refugee camp population over access to firewood, fuel, water, and other resources. The presence of a large number of refugees in the Kakuma area has strained the availability of these resources in an already harsh, desert-like environment. The Turkana raids have killed and wounded many young people. Other forms of violence which have impacted young people living in the camp are violent clashes between the different groups of refugees living in the camp, armed robberies, and domestic and sexual abuse.[11]

Displaced young women and girls face a constant risk of gender-based violence, such as rape and sexual abuse. Such threats come from both within the camp, and from outside, due to the poor security conditions of a refugee or IDP camp. Armed groups may attack and carry out acts of targeted sexual violence against displaced women and girls as a weapon of war, in order to humiliate or ethnically cleanse groups of people. For instance, hundreds of women and girls living in displacement camps in the Darfur region of Sudan and in Chad have been raped by armed groups when they were collecting firewood, fuel, and water in areas beyond the direct proximity of the camps, because of the increasing scarcity of these resources in the vicinity of the camps. These activities are traditionally considered to be the duty of girls and women.[12] But sexual violence can come from within a displacement camp as well. Displaced husbands and fathers may become more aggressive toward their wives or displaced female relatives due to the psychological stress of displacement and conflict, including feelings of idleness and frustration with living conditions.[13] Aid workers in displacement camps have also perpetuated the problem of sexual exploitation during war; a 2002 report stated that employees of national and international agencies, including the UNCHR, were sometimes sexually abusing young people in refugee camps in West Africa in exchange for food, money, and other favors.[14] The consequences of rape and sexual violence are multiple and can result in painful physical complications (including sexually transmitted diseases), mental trauma, and social ostracism.

The Night Commuters of Uganda

When night falls in northern Uganda, thousands of children and young people walk from their rural villages into the towns to spend the night. These young people try to escape the attacks of and abductions by the Lord's Resistance Army (LRA), a rebel group that has waged a civil war against the Ugandan government since 1987. Among its reasons to take up arms, the LRA lists discrimination against certain ethnic groups based in the north of the country and more generally the existence of inequalities between the northern and southern parts of the country. Children and young people have been targeted by the LRA on a large scale, evidenced by the fact that the majority of the LRA's fighters are children and young people., Many of them have been kidnapped and forced to fight or serve as sex slaves, cooks, porters, and spies.

The so-called "night commuter" phenomenon started in 2003, after the Ugandan army launched a military offensive against the LRA, leading to an increase in the level of violence in northern Uganda. Since then, around 50,000 young people have been walking several kilometers each evening to reach the safety of shelters and public spaces in urban areas. These children and young people often travel alone or in small groups but without adult protection, and sometimes experience sexual harassment along the way.

Many of the displaced persons in northern Uganda are living in crowded IDP camps, which are vulnerable to attacks by the LRA. Women and girls living in these camps are vulnerable to domestic and sexual abuse, and youths between the ages of 15 and 25 have few opportunities to go to school or to earn a living.

You can learn more about the night commuter phenomenon in Uganda through the following sources:

- Women's Commission for Refugee Women and Children, "No Safe Place to Call Home: Child and Adolescent Night Commuters in Northern Uganda" (2004), accessed at http://www.womenscommission.org/pdf/ug_nightcom.pdf.
- Lehnart Falk, Jessica Lenz, and Patric Okuma, "Sleepless in Gulu: A Study of the Dynamics Behind the Child Night Commuting Phenomena in Gulu, Uganda" (2004), Save the Children Denmark.

As Peter's story also shows, in some cases young displaced persons are recruited by armed groups who directly attack or infiltrate refugee or IDP camps. Refugee and IDP camps are characterized by a large and highly concentrated group of young people against a background of poor security, making it relatively easy for members of armed groups to slip into the camps and actively recruit young people into their ranks. Recruitment of young people in displacement camps has also occurred in the Democratic Republic of Congo, Sri Lanka, and Chad, amongst other countries.[15] In other cases, such as in the West African refugee camps in Guinea and Ivory Coast (where thousands of refugees from Liberia and Sierra Leone lived during the civil wars in these countries), armed groups directly attacked these camps and abducted children to serve as combatants in these groups.[16] Thus, while humanitarian aid is necessary for the survival of millions of war-affected people, particularly forced migrants, aid can also have negative consequences where it facilitates refugee and IDP militarization.[17] Lately, there has been an increasing understanding of the unintentional and negative consequences of aid. Humanitarian aid, however equally and neutrally provided, always brings political (real or perceived) implications with it.[18]

Young Forced Migrants in Colombia

Colombia has one of the highest rates of internal displacement in the world—between 2 and 4 million people in total. This high number is the result of a low-intensity conflict that has been ongoing in the country since the mid-1960s, fought between and among rebel groups, including the Revolutionary Armed Forces of Colombia (FARC) and the National Liberation Army (ELN)on the one hand, and the government and pro-government paramilitaries on the other. All parties to the conflict have committed and continue to commit atrocities and to violate human rights, and the rebel groups are heavily involved in the production and trafficking of illegal drugs, particularly cocaine, to fund their opposition activities. The conflict continues to claim thousands of lives and to displace people every year.

Half of Colombia's IDPs are children under the age of 18. Family disintegration is common for displaced Colombian families, with children and parents becoming separated when they try to reach safer urban areas. But even for displaced children who remain with their families, living conditions are difficult. Around 60 percent of Colombia's IDPs live in cities, where they often end up living in slums and shanty towns, characterized by high levels of (often gang-related) violence and very poor living conditions.[19] Displaced parents are more likely to be unemployed, thus making it less likely that their children will be able to attend school due to a lack of money. It is estimated that as many as 85 percent of the displaced Colombian children do not have access to education, partly the result of the fact that displaced Colombian children may have lost their records of previous schooling when they fled their home communities, barring them in some cases from restarting their schooling.[20]

Providing Sanctuary or Fuelling Conflict? Examining the Relationships Between Education, War, and Young People

Education is critical to the social and intellectual development of young people, and is a key determinant for their future socioeconomic opportunities. Yet, education is one of the first casualties of war, as young people are denied the opportunity to receive education or vocational training due to the violence and insecurity of a conflict. But in many conflict-affected countries, large numbers of young people may have been unable to fully benefit from education long before the outbreak of war. Frustration over poor educational opportunities can be one of the factors contributing to the outbreak of armed conflict, and is frequently stated by young combatants as a reason why they joined a fighting group or became vulnerable to armed conscription.[21]

The Impact of War on Education

Education refers to a broad social institution that includes formal schooling; vocational and apprenticeship training; and non-formal schooling. Below, each of these types of education is briefly defined[22]:

- **Formal education**: Mass schooling that transmits a mixture of academic knowledge and vocational training and is chronologically ordered from primary to tertiary (higher) education. Formal education is regulated, financed, and provided by the nation-state to its citizens; private organizations such as religious groups also provide formal schooling.
- **Vocational training**: training that is specifically intended to provide students with practical skills for employment within a profession.
- **Apprenticeship**: a type of vocational training carried out by craft-based organizations or individuals who train new practitioners, for example to become an electrician, carpenter, baker, or tailor.
- **Non-formal education**: any structured education or training that occurs outside of the formal education system, for instance adult literacy classes.

The formal education system of a conflict-affected country is usually negatively affected by fighting and violence.[23] As a result, enrollment and attendance levels can drop significantly during times of armed conflict. Over half of the approximately 72 million children who are out of primary school globally live in countries affected by armed conflict.[24] This has serious consequences for achieving the international *Education For All* target (an international advocacy campaign headed by UNESCO to improve access to basic education for people around the world) and for Millennium Development Goal number two of achieving universal primary education by the year 2015.[25]

War has a negative impact on the quality, the financing, and the physical and human capital of the education system. Students, teachers, and government officials can be killed, injured, displaced, and/or recruited or forced to join armed groups. Teachers are sometimes specifically targeted for recruitment, since their high-level literacy skills can be useful to an armed movement (for instance for intelligence or administrative purposes), or they can be singled out as a target for what armed groups interpret them to represent, such as modernists or agents of the state. The infamous Khmer Rouge in Cambodia prosecuted and killed thousands of teachers and intellectuals, accusing them of being the enemy of its Maoist-inspired rural revolution between 1975 and 1979. beside losses in human capital, the physical infrastructure of the education system is often also specifically targeted. School buildings and materials are damaged, destroyed, or used as barracks by fighting forces, making it impossible to provide lessons.

This loss of human capital and physical destruction take place against a background of diverted national spending for the educational sector, in favor of military spending. This lowers both the availability and the quality of educational provisions as teachers' salaries go unpaid and stationery supplies dwindle.[26] The example of Guatemala is illustrative in this respect: during Guatemala's long civil war (1960–1996), government spending for the education sector declined from 1.8 percent to 1.4 percent of the country's Gross Domestic Product (GDP) between 1978 and 1989, while the defense budget increased from 1.3 percent to 1.9 percent[27] During that time, only 50 percent of Guatemalan children were enrolled in primary school. This was a result of the reduced availability and poor quality of schooling, as well as of the climate of fear and insecurity that pervaded throughout the country.[28] Similarly, in Nicaragua and El Salvador, education spending was also dramatically reduced and defense spending increased during the civil wars in these countries in the 1980s. During the conflict in Nicaragua, government spending for the education sector was decreased from 3.8 to 2.5 percent of the country's GDP between 1978 and 1989, while defense spending was increased from 3.6 to 18.9 percent of the country's GDP. Government education spending in El Salvador decreased from 3.4 to 1.9 percent of the country's GDP during the same years, while defense spending increased from 1.5 to 2.9 percent of the country's GDP.[29] On top of the diversion of funds from the education sector, territories occupied by opposition forces are normally completely and purposively deprived of educational support by the state. The denial of education can thus be used as a weapon of war.[30] And while many rebel movements claim that they are fighting for better and fairer education for all, few groups actually provide these services in territories under their control. Even if these claims are genuine, rebel movements often need to divert their already limited resources to their military wings as much as governments do.

Children and young people thus lose out on the opportunity to go to school during war for several reasons. Schooling can be viewed as irrelevant when immediate survival needs are more pressing. With the prolongation of an armed conflict, it becomes increasingly likely that family incomes are either lowered or lost completely, forcing young people to engage in income-earning activities to help support their families. Older children, particularly girls, may be called back from school to start income-generating work or to carry out domestic duties such as caring for their siblings. Furthermore, fear for the safety of girls while walking to school during times of increased insecurity and lawlessness can make families to decide to withdraw them from school completely. The presence of land mines can also make it unsafe for both boys and girls to commute to school.

Altogether, an armed conflict environment is highly stressful for young people and often leads to higher wastage rates in the education system, that is, to higher rates of pupils repeating grades, higher dropout rates, and lower exam pass rates. This in turn, reduces the educational achievement on a national scale, which can have long-term effects, sometimes for decades after a conflict is over. Moreover, the concentration of education services to urban areas because of insecurity deprives rural people of access to education. This rural-to-urban "brain drain" can also sometimes be observed for personnel working in tertiary education, with professors and lecturers leaving their country to look for refuge and employment opportunities elsewhere.

Two recent examples illustrate the detrimental impact of war on education. The first example is that of Iraq, a country that used to have one of the best education systems in the Middle East before the outbreak of the Gulf War in 1991.[31] Its policy of free education resulted in high levels of school attendance, and as a result, the literacy level among the population was around 90 percent.[32] But cuts in the national education budget after the 1991 war and the poor economic conditions that resulted from UN and U.S. sanctions imposed on the country after the war had a negative impact on the education system. Primary and secondary school enrollment levels as well as literacy levels declined, teacher salaries were lowered, and educational facilities deteriorated. Then in 2003, the United States invaded Iraq to topple its president, Sadaam Hussein. Shortly after the invasion, large-scale violence engulfed the country when different armed militias (including religious-based groups) started to wage an intense campaign of violence against the American-dominated coalition forces, against the new Iraqi government, and against each other. The educational sector became one of the main targets of the post-2003 invasion violence. Schools were looted and/or burned down and those which still operate lack clean water supply, sanitation facilities, and basic materials such as books, desks, and chairs.[33] Teachers and academics have been killed and many young people became afraid to go school because of the constant threat of attacks.

The second example of the impact of war on education comes from Sierra Leone. During the country's civil war (1991–2002), approximately 70 percent of the school-aged population had limited or no access to schooling. Internally displaced children were particularly affected by this.[34] School enrollment rates remained low throughout the war, hovering around 45 percent for primary schools and at just 11 percent for secondary schools, with rates even lower for girls and children in rural areas.[35] In Sierra Leone, children and young people were denied access to schooling during the war for various reasons including the loss of family income, destroyed school infrastructure and materials (in particular in rural areas), a general climate of fear and violence (including the threat of recruitment into armed groups at school), and the absence of teachers. Most government spending during the war was channeled toward fighting the war rather than providing education; for instance, between 1998 and 2000, the Government of Sierra Leone spent on average only 1 percent of the national GDP on education.[36] By 1999, only 600 of the 2500 schools that had existed before the war were still functioning, and after the war ended in 2002, only 13 percent of schools in the country were in usable condition.[37] It looked like the targeting and destruction of the educational system was purposeful and a response to the highly unequal patterns of educational access that had prevailed before the outbreak of the war. In line with what has been suggested above, the education system played a critical role in the outbreak of war in Sierra Leone.

Providing Education During Times of War

During a humanitarian crisis such as armed conflict, so-called *emergency education* can be provided to crisis-affected groups of people. Emergency education is defined as the rapid provision of education for people affected by disasters, including war.[38] It is most often provided by non-government organizations (NGOs), though governments or even war-affected populations themselves may also be involved in providing emergency education. Such education includes formal schooling; peace education; HIV/AIDS awareness and health courses; literacy, numeracy, and basic life-skills and survival courses; and vocational and employment training.

The rapid reestablishment of teaching and learning is necessary in situations where the existing educational infrastructure has been damaged or destroyed. If no education is provided during emergency situations, it is likely that a whole generation will miss out on schooling. Providing education during a conflict can also protect young people from harm during a conflict by equipping them with the knowledge to survive during an emergency situation. For instance, sensitization campaigns within schools about the dangers of land mines in Afghanistan and Angola have saved many children's lives. Education can also provide young people with alternatives to engaging in armed combat, and can provide a sense of normalcy and thus help young people to recover from trauma and foster a sense of hope for the future. In addition, it can teach conflict resolution skills and values that emphasize peaceful coexistence and tolerance.

Education for All, Even in Times of War

According to international law, basic education is a considered to be a human right. The right to education is spelled out in the 1948 Universal Declaration on Human Rights (Article 26), the 1951 Refugee Convention (Article 22), and the 1989 Convention on the Rights of the Child. The United Nations Millennium Development Goal 2 aspires to all children having access to basic education by 2015. However, war is one of the major obstacles for achieving universal primary education.

International support for emergency educational provision culminated in the creation of the Inter-Agency Network for Education in Emergencies (INEE) which formulated the Minimum Standards for Education in Emergencies, Chronic Crises and Early Reconstruction in 2000. These are the minimum conditions that should be met in education during a crisis situation. These standards include ensuring access to educational opportunities in safe learning environments during a crisis, the training and employment of qualified teachers, the use of participatory teaching methods, and the teaching of a relevant curriculum which takes into account the learning needs of the affected population. The INEE network is composed of NGOs, UN agencies, donors, practitioners, researchers, and other individuals who help guide educational provision in emergency situations and work to ensure that the right to education is implemented in emergencies and post-crisis situations.

Two useful web sites to learn more about education during times of conflict and crisis are:

- The web site of the Inter-Agency Network on Education in Emergencies (INEE): http://www.ineesite.org.
- The web site of UNESCO's International Institute for Educational Planning (IIEP): http://www.unesco.org/iiep/eng/focus/emergency/emergency_1.htm.

One form of emergency education is the provision of education for refugee and IDP populations, which has increasingly become mainstreamed in humanitarian assistance programs. Refugee and IDP camps offer ample opportunities to provide emergency education programs since so many young people in need of schooling are concentrated in a small space, putting less demand on logistics. Recently, there has been a shift in the way the international community regards the provision of education in emergency contexts, such as in displacement camps. While in the past the provision of education was viewed as a central part of development—something to put effort into when a country is at peace—rather than a humanitarian activity, education is now widely advocated for as a fourth pillar of humanitarian assistance in addition to food, health, and shelter to crisis-affected people. This reflects an increasing awareness within the international community of the negative impact that conflict has on achieving universal primary education. But it also recognizes the fact that many forcibly displaced people consider education as a top priority. Some of the reasons for this are that conflict-affected populations such as refugees view education as a portable commodity, one that is an important asset in creating (future) livelihood opportunities through the attainment of knowledge and skills. In fact, displaced people often begin organizing some form of education well before the United Nations or NGOs do.

When we left Peter at the beginning of this chapter, he was attending primary school along with many other young refugees in the Kakuma refugee camp. But humanitarian agencies providing support to refugees and IDPs face a number of problems and dilemmas in trying to make education and skills training available, if their mandate allows it in the first place. Within a context of limited resources, there is a strong focus on satisfying immediate survival needs such as food, water, and shelter. The demands for these by large displaced populations can easily overwhelm the available resources, leaving no budget for other activities such as education. Where education programs have successfully been created, they can run the risk of becoming victims of their own success, as displaced persons may not want to return to their home communities where there is no good education. The educational facilities in a displacement camp may even become a pull factor, encouraging people to migrate away from their homes to the camps. And while camp-based refugees often have the opportunity to benefit from educational programs created by humanitarian agencies, IDPs and locally-integrated refugee populations face many more difficulties in accessing education, as they have no other choice than to attend local schools, which are often overcrowded, if they function at all. Finally, since primary education is the cheapest type of education to provide and is considered to be a fundamental human right, this often entails that displaced youths may be denied secondary schooling opportunities. Hence, they become increasingly vulnerable to military recruitment and/or sexual exploitation and violence.[39]

There are several issues that must be addressed before educational programs can be provided to forcibly displaced young people. These issues include whether or not the national curriculum of the host or home state should be followed, what the language of instruction should be, how qualified teaching personnel will be recruited, and how a good quality learning environment can be created. If refugee children attend school in a host community (where they often must pay school fees and purchase uniforms, books, and supplies—a significant financial burden for displaced families), they will learn the curriculum of the host country rather than of their own, and they are instructed in the language of the local community rather than in the language of the community or country they originate from. These young people will also take the exams of the host rather than home country. Once repatriation has taken place and children want to go back to the schools in their home communities, there is the chance that their certificates and diplomas are not recognized within their own educational system. Thus, the solution to a displacement situation (repatriation, resettlement, or local integration) can play a role in determining what type of education a displaced population receives.

Better than Silver and Gold: Education for Palestinian Refugees

The 1948 Arab-Israeli conflict and subsequent establishment of Israel as an independent state created a huge outflow of refugees from Palestine, many of whom settled in displacement camps in surrounding countries. As a result, the United Nations established the United Nations Relief and Works Agency (UNRWA) in 1949, the UN agency that provides aid and assistance to Palestinian refugees living in the Middle East. Since the 1950s, UNRWA has been helping to provide education to millions of Palestinian refugee children and youth living in Syria, Jordan, Lebanon, the West Bank, and Gaza. UNRWA currently runs one of the largest schooling systems in the Middle East, providing a restricted number of basic vocational training courses. In the UNRWA education system, there are currently around 700 schools providing free elementary and lower secondary education, eight vocational training centers, and nearly 500,000 students, of which 50 percent are female. Teacher training is also offered. Students in the UNRWA schools follow the curriculum and use the textbooks of the host country in which the various schools operate.

Some of the problems faced within the UNRWA schooling system are large class sizes and a lack of sufficient funding, as well as a lack of opportunities for refugee students to pursue higher academic education and more vocational training. Additional issues include the challenges of organizing an education system over the five localities where displaced Palestinians live, including coordination with the ministries of education in the host states. The outbreak of several armed conflicts in the region has also impacted schooling in UNRWA schools, prohibiting students and teachers from reaching schools and traumatizing students, while some UNRWA schools have even been destroyed in fighting or used for military purposes.

Nevertheless, Palestinian refugees place a high value on education and are one of the better educated groups of people in the Middle East. In some areas, refugee students at UNRWA schools perform better than those attending government schools in the host states. Education has helped Palestinian refugees to cope with life in exile and provides them with hope for the future, including the possibility of returning home. For many forcibly displaced people around the world, education is more important than "silver and gold," or material possessions.[40]

Relationships Between Education and War

While armed conflict often has a very negative impact on the provision of formal schooling and vocational education, grievances over poor education can be among the causes for the outbreak of an armed conflict, for instance when access to education is highly unequal or where education is used to suppress certain groups and identities while advocating the superiority of others.

So, education is not necessarily a benign institution. Sometimes, education creates, maintains, and legitimizes inequalities between groups in society. Since formal schooling is one of the means by which individuals can advance socially, economically, and politically, it can therefore be strictly controlled by the state. Access to schooling opportunities can be controlled by the government, and scholarships for tertiary education can be handed out only to the sons and daughters of the most loyal followers of a regime. In many countries in the developing world, formal, state-provided schooling was established during the period of European colonial rule (from the late nineteenth century through around the 1960s), though missionary organizations had been providing education earlier than this in the colonies. Colonial education was designed to produce relatively cheap, local manpower for the colonial administration. Rather than being a right for all children, accessing formal education during the colonial days was often only possible for the children of the local elites—those working for the colonizers or the sons and daughters of chiefs and rich merchants. After independence from the European colonial powers, access to schooling only slowly became available for all people, enabling the ruling elites to reproduce their status and to justify the dominance of certain educated groups in society. Elite control was further retained by sticking to the colonial languages as the national language (such as English, French, or Portuguese), which were used within the government and the educational system. These languages were (and still are) often not the first language of large sections of the population. In addition, the curriculum (the main instrument for the organization of teaching and learning, to include what knowledge is to be transmitted) was sometimes used to support the idea of an artificial homogenous state, denying the multicultural reality of many postcolonial states. It could sometimes impose a one-sided view of what was worth knowing, deny the recognition of different identities in society, and be used to justify inequalities and to transmit negative stereotypes about certain groups of people, therefore increasing intergroup tensions.

For instance, in Rwanda, a country that experienced civil war and genocide in the 1990s, hateful stereotypes transmitted through the curriculum in conjunction with restricted access to formal schooling directly fed into the levels of hatred behind the 1994 genocide (in which nearly a million Tutsis and moderate Hutus died at the hands of extremist Hutu armed groups).[41] Rwanda is composed of two main ethnic groups: the Hutu and the Tutsi, with the Hutu group comprising the majority of the population (approximately 84 percent), followed by the Tutsi (15 percent).[42] Under Belgian colonial rule (1923 to 1960), the Tutsis were viewed as being superior by the Belgians because they were believed to physically appear to be more "European" than the Hutu. As a result, the Tutsis were favored in access to education, particularly for secondary education, and in access to government jobs in the colonial administration. Where Hutus were allowed into schools, they were given a different, lower-quality education in Kiswahili, while Tutsis were given a superior education in French, the language of the colonial administration, and were taught that Hutus were unintelligent and suited only for manual work.[43] During the postcolonial period, these practices were reversed.[44] These patterns of educational disparities and negative teaching contributed to hardening divisions over time between the different ethnic groups.

In short, education can play a role in the outbreak of war and can be a factor for young people in joining armed groups in several ways: because of grievances related to the unequal distribution of educational opportunities (including formal, non-formal and vocational education), because of resentment over the way in which students are treated at school, because of the dehumanizing character of the knowledge transmitted in schools, or because of the irrelevance of the curriculum in securing employment after graduation. These factors can act, and have acted, as strong motivations for young people in deciding whether or not to join or support an armed faction.

Issues of Identity: Conflict and Education in Thailand and Kosovo

Education can be a highly political, contentious social institution and is among the root causes of many armed conflicts around the world, particularly when it is misused to polarize and exaggerate issues of identity. Two conflicts in very different parts of the world highlight how conflicts over identity are intensified within the education system and have moved center-stage within these conflicts.

A low-intensity conflict has been ongoing for many years in Southern Thailand between Muslim Malay separatists and the Thai government, with violence escalating in recent years. The repression of Malay identity is a core issue at the heart of the conflict, and the education system is contested ground in this respect. Many Malay people view the education system as a vehicle for the total assimilation of Malays through its propagation of Thai culture and language. Calls for the Malay language to be used as the language of instruction for Southern Thai primary schools have been made since the 1940s, but the Thai government has been reluctant to concede to these demands. Consequently, the escalation of violence in 2004 has resulted in government teachers and school officials in Southern Thailand being threatened and killed. Additionally, schools have been closed because of security problems and in some cases burned down during outbreaks of fighting and violence.[45]

Kosovo recently emerged as a self-declared independent state out of Serbia, which itself emerged out of the former Socialist Federal Republic of Yugoslavia, which dissolved in 1992. In its struggle for independence, the Kosovars used the education system as a tool of resistance against the increasingly repressive Serbian rule (which, among other things, enforced the use of Serb-only language of instruction in schools and universities) during the 1990s. War broke out between the Kosovo Liberation Army and the Serbian government in 1996, ending in 1999. In response to Serb repression and to the subsequent war, Kosovar Albanians, who form the majority of the mixed Albanian and Serb population in the country, started to run a parallel education system. Separate schools were established at all levels for Albanian pupils and students, with instruction provided in the Albanian language. New textbooks were produced, while others were smuggled into Kosovo from Albania. Education provided a platform for questioning the legitimacy of the Serbian state. It strengthened the demand for the establishment of a separate Kosovo state by breaking down any connection with the Serbian education system, and by asserting the separate identity of Kosovo as a non-Serbian state.[46]

The Costs of War: The Economic Impacts of War on Young People

Since the end of World War II, armed conflicts have been occurring primarily in poor and lower-income countries. The most conflict-prone regions in the world are sub-Saharan Africa, Asia, Latin America and Central America, the Middle East and North Africa, and countries in Eastern Europe and the former Soviet Union.[47] Academics have debated intensively as to why this is the case, and there is now a general consensus that poverty is a risk factor for the outbreak of violent conflict. Poverty often has different causes, but where high levels of corruption and an unfair political economy are part of these causes, it is likely that these create widespread grievances which can be mobilized into armed opposition. At the same time, armed conflict also increases the level of poverty among the population.

War has therefore been labeled as "development in reverse," because of its negative economic effects. The longer a conflict is ongoing, the greater the risk for the creation of a so-called "conflict trap," as described in the 2003 World Bank publication "Breaking the Conflict Trap: Civil War and Development Policy."[48] The authors of this publication argue that where socioeconomic development fails, countries can become trapped in a vicious circle: war wrecks the economy and increases the risk of further war. The reasons for the increased risk of a conflict reemerging in a country that has experienced conflict are threefold. First, people may still want to take revenge for atrocities committed during the war, in particular if these went unpunished or unaddressed in the postwar setting. Second, war can be a profitable business for some players, creating particular ways and opportunities for making money which do not exist during peacetime. Third, the same reasons why people decided to take up arms may still be present, if not worsened, in a postwar setting.[49]

Armed conflict is an important determinant of poverty, particularly in Africa[50], costing billions of dollars a year. A recent report by the British charity Oxfam estimated that between 1990 and 2005, the cost of armed conflict to Africa's economic development has been 284 billion dollars—around $18 billion dollars a year.[51] This sum of money is equivalent to the amount of aid that international donors allocated to the continent during the same time period to improve the living conditions of many of the poorest people.

For children and young people, the economic consequences of conflict are wide-ranging and are manifested in both the short and the long-term. As mentioned before, the economic decline and sometimes complete collapse of the economy, in combination with the reallocation of scarce state resources toward military defense, entails deterioration in the education and health sectors, which are critical to the development of young people into adults. And when employment and income-earning opportunities—such as farming, selling goods in the market, or finding formal or informal wage employment in the private sector— dry up due to the violence and insecurity of a conflict, families have less money to pay for schooling, food, clean drinking water, shelter, clothing, and other basic necessities for children. Lowered or lost family income results in increased poverty, which can result in children and young people being required to assume new economic responsibilities such as income-earning roles. This, in turn, prevents them from going to school—an investment which generally helps individuals to achieve higher socioeconomic status in the future.

Forced Displacement in Uganda

The conflict waged by the Lord's Resistance Army in northern Uganda has internally displaced over 1 million people since the 1990s. Many of these people live in crowded camps that are characterized by high levels of poverty. There are few employment and income-earning opportunities for the IDPs, there is limited access to land and markets to sell agricultural goods, movement is restricted in the area and around the camps due to security concerns, and displaced persons receive little financial assistance from relatives living abroad.

Displacement has had significant economic consequences for young IDPs. Farming is the traditional livelihood of the people living in northern Uganda (the Acholis) and the cultivation of land is a key, defining role for young people in the social customs of the Acholis, allowing young people to earn a living but also giving them a sense of pride and self-esteem. But the inability of young people to access land entails that they are unable to learn farming skills. The lack of farming skills, combined with a lack of educational opportunities, also complicates the prospect of returning to their home communities when the conflict ends.[52]

How War Impacts Family and Community Structures

Children and young people do not grow up or live in a vacuum. They are raised by families and they live in communities, which normally take the responsibility for the well-being and development of young people physically, psychologically, and intellectually. Within this setting, young people are socialized, learning about the beliefs and values prevalent among the group. They are also socialized into the adult roles that they will eventually assume.

One manifestation of the enormous impact that war has on society is the scattering and separation of families and communities. Families in many societies include members of the extended family (such as aunts, uncles, cousins, and grandparents, in addition to parents and siblings) rather than just members of the nuclear family (two parents and their children), a concept that predominates in Europe and North America. The extended family often plays an integral role in the rearing of children and young people in many societies. The targeted destruction of homes and villages and massive displacement make it extremely difficult to retain some form of normality and to raise and socialize young people. The transmission of culturally-specific knowledge and practices (such as knowledge about how to grow and prepare food, and the history and folklore of a group of people) is often disrupted by war and can thus fail to be passed on to younger generations. In some cases, these practices are replaced by more violent versions, such as when the widespread cultural practice of initiation rites, which regulate the transformation from childhood into adulthood, is adapted by armed militias to transform abducted children into loyal fighters. Respect for the ancestors, the gods, and the elders are often ridiculed by armed fighting groups. In short, armed conflict often brings social reformulation and reordering, with social structures, positions, identities, and ideas contested and changed.[53] While this does not always have to be a negative thing—some social change can be good—the most extreme forms can be very damaging and can frustrate postwar reconstruction and reintegration.

If children are separated from their parents, they may be forced to look after themselves or even their siblings as well. These so-called "child-headed households" face significant challenges. For example, the 1994 Rwandan genocide resulted in many child-headed households because the parents and family members of young people died during the conflict or were imprisoned as a result of their participation in the genocide. Many turned toward their extended family members for help, stretching this social system to the limit (against the background of an HIV/AIDS pandemic which already had killed many adult members of the society). Four years after the genocide, a UNICEF study estimated that approximately 300,000 children were living in child-headed households, with many of the heads of households being girls.[54] These young people are responsible for caring for other children in the house (for instance, cooking and cleaning and fetching water, food, and firewood), and to earn money (in some cases through prostitution), leaving them with little means or time to go to school or to engage in the activities of childhood such as play.[55] But children in Rwanda have also been separated from their parents for another reason: because the children have been accused of participating in the genocide. Around 2,000 children were imprisoned after the genocide, as the box below explains.[56]

Genocide in Rwanda and Perspectives on Culpability for Children

During the Rwandan genocide (which took place between April and July 1994), approximately 800,000 Tutsis and moderate Hutus were killed by Hutu extremists. The genocide occurred largely because of the long-standing inequalities and historic hostilities between the two main ethnic groups in Rwanda, the Hutu and Tutsi.

Children and young people were both participants in and victims of the genocide. Young people killed and were killed, raped and were raped, looted and had their possessions looted. Thousands of young people between the ages of 14 and 18 were arrested and prosecuted for their participation in the genocide, with many sent to prison.

In 1995, a year after the genocide, Save the Children USA and three Rwandan NGOs initiated a study to gain insights into Rwandan perspectives on culpability and punishment for children convicted of crimes associated with genocide. One of the reasons for the research was the fear that "the application of legal justice might not serve the requirements of the social justice expected at the popular level" (SCF USA: 1995:4), which could endanger the reintegration process of these children. One of the findings of the study was that many respondents defined childhood by the extent of social maturity, rather than using age-based legal definitions: once a person was able to assume certain responsibilities and make independent judgments, he or she was no longer a child. Most respondents considered 14 or 15 years of age as the point where children become adults. In response to the question of whether or not children (as legally defined) can be held culpable for acts of genocide, nearly all respondents felt that they can and therefore should be punished. Moreover, the respondents felt that these children committed the atrocities out of their own free will. While under normal conditions the kind of punishment for children differs from that of adults and also varies with age, the respondents said that those children convicted of murder during the genocide should receive the death penalty. Some respondents added that if the state would not execute them, they themselves would do it.[57]

The Health Consequences of War for Young People

Physical Health

War has a significant impact on the physical health of both children and adults. Both adults and children fall victim to the direct effects of conflict if they are killed or injured as a result of fighting. They can be killed by gunfire, bombs, or land mine explosions, or slaughtered by machetes. As mentioned before, between 90 percent and 95 percent of the victims and casualties of post-Cold War armed conflicts have been civilians, with young people making up perhaps half of all war casualty numbers.[58]

Many thousands of children are injured, maimed, and in some cases permanently disabled by land mines or unexploded ordnance. Land mines are a persistent, hidden threat, as they can lie dormant for years in fields or in areas where children play, walk to school, or collect firewood or food or fetch water. Land mine explosions can cause children to lose their sight, hearing, or one or more limbs, permanently disabling them. This reduces their mobility and affects their ability to go to school and eventually acquire employment, make a living, and to marry or have children. This is the result of a combination of shame associated with disabilities in many societies and the lack of facilities that are accessible to disabled people.

Children and young people are more likely to die or be more seriously injured by a land mine explosion because they are smaller and thus physically more vulnerable than adults to the effects of land mine explosions. Certain types of land mines are designed to "jump up" when triggered and explode at about a meter's height, which is likely to wound an adult but kill a child. Other types of land mines look like toys—sometimes deliberately—and are therefore easily picked up by children. Even in cases where young people survive a land mine explosion, it can take many years for a child to get a prosthetic arm or leg due to poverty and the lack of adequate health care. Land mine disabilities have long-term consequences, necessitating many years of care for child victims as prosthetic limbs must be refitted as their bodies grow over time. This represents a significant burden for poor families.

When adult family members become disabled during a conflict, this can impact their children as well. Disabilities incur significant economic costs—not only in terms of lost incomes when a breadwinner is disabled, but also in the costs of caring for a person with disabilities. Young people may be required to, for instance, drop out of school to care for the disabled person or help contribute to the family income. Disability can even result in family fragmentation when disability results in divorce and abandonment, again with negative consequences for children.[59]

Weapons of War that Injure and Kill

- *Small arms* include guns, automatic rifles, assault rifles, submachine and light-machine guns, shotguns, pistols, and other firearms that are designed for individual use, and which an individual can transport.

- *Light weapons* include heavy machine guns, grenade launchers, portable antiaircraft guns, antitank guns, antitank missile and rocket systems, and mortars. These weapons can be transported by a person or an animal, but often require multiple persons working together to operate them.
- *Ammunition and explosives* include ammunition, shells, and missiles for small arms and light weapons, as well as grenades, land mines, and explosives.
- *Land mines* are explosive devices laid in the ground that are intended to detonate when a person, animal, or vehicle comes into contact with them, or when an operator detonates them. They include antipersonnel mines and antitank mines. A 1997 international treaty known as the "Ottawa Treaty" or the "Mine Ban Treaty" officially bans the production and development of land mines, and requires signatory countries to clear their countries of mines and to destroy all mines in their possession. However, this goal is far from a reality and today many children continue to live in countries affected by the presence of land mines, such as in Eritrea, Angola, Colombia, Kosovo, and Afghanistan.
- *Unexploded remnants of war* (also known as unexploded ordnance) are explosive weapons such as grenades, bombs, rockets, cluster munitions, or anti-vehicle mines that remain after the end of a war. These weapons were either abandoned, or did not explode when they were originally deployed, but they are at risk of exploding and thus pose a constant danger to people.[60]

Many more young people die or are permanently injured as a result of the indirect effects of conflict, which include malnutrition, increased risks of diseases, and a lack of access to health care services.[61] Very young children are at the highest risk of dying during a conflict, primarily from the indirect effects of conflict. The highest rates of children who die before reaching their fifth birthday are found in countries that are currently experiencing war or that have recently emerged from war, such as Sierra Leone, Liberia, Chad, Guinea-Bissau, Angola, the Democratic Republic of Congo, and Afghanistan.[62] In the Democratic Republic of Congo, for example, nearly half of the estimated 5.4 million deaths that have occurred during the conflict and violence in that country since 1998 have been children under the age of five; the vast majority of these children died due to malnutrition and disease.[63] More broadly, it is estimated that as many as 95 percent of all child deaths in recent African conflicts have been the result of starvation or illness.[64]

Poor nutrition due to a lack of food, the lack of access to clean drinking water, the lack of access to health care services such as vaccinations and to live-saving medicines, and the lack of adequate shelter and proper sanitation during times of war increases the chances for the outbreak of epidemics of diseases such as cholera, malaria, measles, tuberculosis, meningitis, and diarrheal diseases. High levels of violence, including rape and gender-based violence against girls and women, facilitate the spread of sexually transmitted diseases such as HIV/AIDS. Refugee populations—cramped together in camps—are equally at risk.[65] For example, one-third of Rwandan refugee children who fled the 1994 genocide to refugee camps in the Congo, then known as Zaire, died as a result of respiratory infections.[66]

Armed conflict negatively affects the ability of a country to produce food and drives up rates of malnutrition. Food distribution systems, including markets and transportation networks, are disrupted by fighting, and food production stops when farmland is burned or filled with land mines by fighting groups, or when farmers are killed or flee to other areas for safety. Food aid rations, provided by international organizations like the United Nations, are in many cases just enough to survive on, and all too often, the population in need cannot be reached or are reached too late because of the fighting, or supplies are confiscated by armed groups to feed their combatants. Small food rations can directly contribute to high levels of malnutrition and poor health among the displaced, particularly among children as malnourished mothers may find it difficult to breast-feed infants and children may not be given sufficient food rations.

As a result, children and young people living in war zones often have little food security as the quality and quantity of available food declines. The effects of malnutrition are devastating and long-term for young people, having an impact on their physical and intellectual development. A recent study about the impact of conflict on Rwanda found that the average height of young children was negatively affected by the country's 1990 civil war, an indication of chronic malnourishment.[67]

Mental Health

It is not only the physical health of children and young people that is affected by war, but also their psychological health and well-being. Armed conflicts are generally characterized by high levels of physical violence, and young people may themselves experience serious injury, abuse, harassment, or combat at close range, or witness atrocities and violent acts such as the death, injury, or torture of family members and friends. For instance, one study revealed that in a refugee camp in Macedonia where refugees from Kosovo had fled during the war, 55 percent of the refugee children reported having seen the torture of a family member during the conflict.[68] Likewise, 90 percent of children who lived in areas of former Yugoslavia which experienced high levels of violence during the armed conflicts there in the 1990s witnessed and experienced extremely traumatic events, such as the violent death or injury of family members.[69]

Exposure to the violence and socioeconomic deprivation caused by war, such as the lack of clothing, adequate food, shelter, medicine, and access to education, can create negative psychological responses in young people. These kinds of traumatic experiences often manifest themselves in the behaviors and attitudes of young people and create feelings of alienation, fear, powerlessness, and sadness and increase levels of anxiety, depression, and post-traumatic stress disorder (PTSD).[70] Symptoms of PTSD include insomnia and nightmares, aggression, an inability to concentrate in school, and feelings of guilt and worry. The consequences of unaddressed psychological distress are long-term, acting as a potentially strong contributing factor in the development of negative behaviors such as alcoholism, violent or criminal behavior, and low self-esteem in adulthood.[71]

Yet it is not only the mental health and well-being of young people that is affected by war; the adults who care for children are affected as well, such as teachers and parents, and as a result they can be unable to provide sufficient care and support for young people. In times of conflict, the level of violence within the family, such as child abuse, can increase, as the trauma and physical violence that people experience in society can act as a trigger of further violence in the home.[72]

Health Care Systems

The negative consequences of war on mental and physical health are compounded when health care delivery is either reduced or stopped altogether. Armed groups may attack the health care system directly by destroying hospitals and clinics, looting supplies and equipment, and by killing trained medical personnel or making them flee. The breakdown of the health system in a country at war means that it may be impossible to treat diseases or provide any kind of preventative care against their outbreak, while at the same time the loss of incomes due to war prevents families from purchasing medicine for sick or injured children, if these are still available. The diversion of national spending to the military and away from social sectors such as health care leads to the deterioration of health care services, as it has in Iraq, a country that at one time had a well-functioning health care system, but which has seen its health care infrastructure destroyed by war with Iran from 1980 to 1988, by the Gulf War in 1991, and most recently by ongoing violence after the American invasion of Iraq in 2003. There is a chronic lack of medical staff and supplies and people are often too afraid to leave their homes to receive medical care.[73]

Many recent armed conflicts were fought in rural areas. As a result, social services such as education and health care are concentrated in the safer urban areas, which may be difficult for rural populations to access if they cannot afford to pay for transportation, or if it is too insecure to travel. Rural areas thus become deprived of health care provision. This has been the case in Nepal, where a 10-year Maoist rebellion had a major impact on the delivery of health care in rural areas. Health care workers were unwilling to travel to Maoist-controlled villages, leaving the rural population with few options other than to make the expensive, long, and dangerous journey to urban areas to seek medical care.

Conflict, Health Care, and Young People in Afghanistan

Afghanistan has experienced conflict at varying levels of intensity for many years. A coup in 1978 brought a pro-Soviet regime to power that tried to institute unpopular social reforms, which provoked armed opposition. The Soviet Union invaded the country in 1979 and installed a new president even more favorable toward the Soviet Union, and it became heavily involved in the country's politics and administration. As a response to the Soviet invasion of the country—these were the days of intense

Cold War competition—the United States started funding the armed opposition to the government, largely composed of Islamic fundamentalists who would later evolve into the Taliban. A civil war ensued in which thousands of Afghans were killed or forced to flee. The Soviets withdrew from the country in 1989, but fighting continued through the 1990s between various armed groups. In 1996, the Taliban seized Kabul and gradually exerted control over the country. But Taliban rule was marked by the imposition of strict Islamic rule which among other things forbade women and girls from working or attending school. Following the September 11, 2001 attacks in New York and Washington, D.C., the United States entered Afghanistan and aided anti-Taliban militias to overthrow the Taliban regime for its role in harboring Osama bin Laden and the Al-Qaeda group. This, however, has not ended the existence of the Taliban, who continue to launch armed attacks in the country.

Many years of conflict have had a tremendous impact on the health of children and young people in Afghanistan. Millions of land mines were laid during the period of the Soviet occupation and subsequent civil war, while large quantities of unexploded ordnance (UXO) were left after the American intervention of 2001. Children constitute half of all victims of land mine and UXO explosions, with boys making up the majority of victims, and the long years of fighting have resulted in many young people suffering from post-traumatic stress disorder. Second, accessing medical care during the Taliban period was difficult for girls and women, as male health care providers were not able to examine female patients without a male chaperone present (and women were largely prohibited from working, even as health care providers). Moreover, girls and women were forbidden to be treated in most hospitals in Kabul, the capital city. With girls and women forbidden from receiving formal education after the age of eight, the education and training of new female health care personnel became difficult. In more recent years, the killing and abduction of health care workers in the southern and eastern provinces of the country by Taliban fighters and other armed groups has forced health care providers to shut down their facilities in these areas. Attacks on health care workers by the Taliban have in some instances been used as a weapon of war. For example, in March 2007, the Taliban abducted a number of health care workers and demanded the release of Taliban fighters from jails in return for the release of the kidnapped health care workers. And while the infant mortality rate has declined since the Taliban regime has been removed, the lack of access to health care due to the ongoing violence impedes carrying out immunization services and has resulted in increased levels of certain diseases and illnesses such as diarrhea, polio, and acute respiratory infections, which particularly affect children.[74]

Child Clubs and the Children as Zones of Peace Campaign in Nepal

Let us end this chapter with a more positive example of what children and youth can do during times of war, and examples of wartime organizational initiatives that have made improvements in the lives of conflict-affected children.

In 1996, civil war broke out in Nepal between the Government of Nepal and a Maoist armed opposition group. The Nepalese conflict was fought largely about the large-scale socioeconomic inequalities that characterize the country, such as deeply rooted discrimination in terms of gender, ethnicity, region, and religion. The conflict ended in 2006 with a peace agreement and elections, bringing the Maoists into power.

During the conflict, several initiatives were undertaken by civil society groups during the war to help mitigate the impact of war on young people. These initiatives were part of the so-called Children as Zones of Peace (CZOP) campaign, which propagated the establishment of child clubs and the introduction of child-friendly codes of conduct in schools. These initiatives were instrumental in helping young Nepalese people to deal with the trauma and violence of the war around them. In addition, the conflict made people question certain values and traditions—part of the rebels' agenda was to end caste (a system of dividing up social status and labor tasks in the Hindu religion) and gender discrimination, two deeply rooted forms of inequality in Nepal—and created a window of opportunity for civil society groups to pressure communities and the government to change the ways in which children are treated—for instance, by pressuring schools to eradicate corporal punishment practices.

The CZOP campaign, initiated in 2001 in Nepal by Save the Children Norway, advocates for children's rights to survival, development, and protection during times of conflict. The campaign stresses that the warring parties of the conflict should not use children in fighting forces and that they should not interfere in children's access to schooling, health care, water supply, and sanitation. Before, schools were closed and teachers and students kidnapped and used as combatants by the Maoist armed opposition. Instead, schools should be seen as zones of peace rather than as arenas for conflict, and the children should be provided with skills to promote peace in their communities.

The formation of child clubs has also been actively encouraged by Save the Children to improve children's participation and empowerment at school and in their communities.[75] Children's clubs provide a network and an environment for children to discuss the effects of war and a way for children to support each other. Children in these clubs have organized themselves to conduct information campaigns about the 2006 peace agreement within their local communities, and have conducted advocacy campaigns to encourage parents to send their children to school.

Save the Children also introduced the use of "codes of conduct" at schools; these codes are guidelines on behavior for both students and teachers and are designed to reduce harassment, discrimination (particularly in terms of gender and caste), exploitation, and other negative behaviors at school. This is a mechanism to both mitigate the impact of conflict on children, but also to begin to address the inequalities which were among the root causes of the civil war in Nepal.

While there is still a long way to go in terms of young people recovering from the effects of the war in Nepal, campaigns such as these can help to strengthen children's resilience and coping mechanisms and to start instituting larger society-wide changes that open space for the broader participation of young people.

Conclusion

Children and young people bear the brunt of the impact of armed conflict. War destroys the social and economic infrastructure and foundations of society needed for children to grow up into healthy and productive adults. The effects of war on young people are multiple and wide-ranging: they can be separated from their families and communities, they may become unable to access schooling and health services, and they suffer from trauma as the result of witnessing or sometimes participating in atrocities. The increased levels of poverty that are caused by war often entail that young people may be forced to assume new roles, such as income earners or household heads. This in turn has further consequences since children who need to work or take care of siblings lack the money or time to go to school.

At the beginning of this chapter, we met Peter, a young Sudanese refugee who had experienced many of the problems faced by children and young people living in war-affected countries. But what will Peter's future bring? Would there be any possibility for him to return to his home village after the signing of the Comprehensive Peace Agreement in 2005 that ended the North-South civil war in Sudan? And what about the young people who became combatants in the SPLA/M—what kind of experience did they have, and what will their future hold now that the north-south war has ended? The next chapter will discuss issues regarding these young combatants.

Notes

1. This is a fictional story, based on details taken from news reports about the Lost Boys.

2. Ibid, 209.

3. United Nations High Commissioner for Refugees (UNHCR), *Statistical yearbook 2006: Trends in displacement, protection and solutions* (Geneva: United Nations High Commissioner for Refugees, 2006).

4. Norwegian Refugee Council, "Internal Displacement: Global Overview of Trends and Developments in 2008" (Geneva: Internal Displacement Monitoring Center, April 2009).

5. The only existing present policy framework regarding IDPs are the *Guiding Principles on Internal Displacement* (see http://www.idpguidingprinciples.org).

6. UNHCR, "The World of Children at a Glance," accessed at http://cvt.hutman.net/files/pg102/The%20World%20of%20Children%20at%20a%20Glance%20Word%20updated.pdf.

7. Elizabeth G. Ferris, "Refugees," in *Encyclopedia of Government and Politics*, ed. Mary Hawkesworth and Maurice Kogan (London: Routledge, 1992): 1360–1373.

8. Barbara E. Harrell-Bond, *Imposing Aid: Emergency Assistance to Refugees* (Oxford: Oxford University Press, 1986).

9. Dennis Gallagher, "The evolution of the international refugee system." *International Migration Review*, 23, no. 3 (1989): 579–598. See also Graça Machel, *The Impact of War on Children* (London: Hurst & Company, 2001).

10. UNHCR, *Refugee Children: Guidelines on Protection and Care* (Geneva: UNHCR, 1994), accessed at http://www.unhcr.org/protect/PROTECTION/3b84c6c67.pdf. See also Machel 2001.

11. Jeff Crisp, "A State of Insecurity: The Political Economy of Violence in Kenya's Refugee Camps," *African Affairs*, 99, (2000): 601–632.

12. Human Rights Watch, "Sexual Violence and Its Consequences Among Displaced Persons in Darfur and Chad," 2005, accessed at http://hrw.org/backgrounder/africa/darfur0505/.

13. UNHCR, "Sexual Violence Against Refugees: Guidelines on Protection and Care," (Geneva: UNHCR, 1995), accessed at http://www.reliefweb.int/rw/lib.nsf/db900sid/LGEL-5N8HEN/$file/unhcr-violence-mar95.pdf?openelement.

14. See the following sources: BBC News, "Child Refugee Sex Scandal," (26 February 2002), accessed at http://news.bbc.co.uk/2/hi/africa/1842512.stm; UNHCR, "Extensive Abuse of West African Children Reported," accessed at http://www.unhcr.org/cgi-bin/texis/vtx/news/opendoc.htm?tbl=NEWS&id=3c7bf8094.

15. UN News Center, "Child Recruitment Continues in Over One Dozen Countries, Reports Ban-Moon," (29 January 2008), accessed at http://www.un.org/apps/news/story.asp?NewsID=25440&Cr=child&Cr1=soldier.

16. Vera Achvarina and Simon F. Reich, "No Place to Hide: Refugees, Displaced Persons, and the Recruitment of Child Soldiers," *International Security*, 31, no. 1 (2006): 127–164.

17. Sarah Kenyon Lischer, "Collateral damage: Humanitarian Assistance as a Cause of Conflict," *International Security*, 28, no. 1 (2003): 79–109.

18. Mary B. Anderson, *Do No Harm: How Aid Can Support Peace—Or War* (Boulder: Lynne Rienner Publishers, 1999).

19. Human Rights Watch, "Colombia: Displaced and Discarded, The Plight of Internally Displaced Persons in Bogotá and Cartagena," 2005, accessed at http://www.hrw.org/reports/2005/colombia1005/5.htm.

20. Save the Children Canada, "School Link: Focus on Colombia," accessed at http://www.savethechildren.ca/canada/resources/school_link_colombia.html.

21. Rachel Brett and Irma Specht, *Young Soldiers: Why They Choose to Fight* (Boulder: Lynne Rienner Publishers, 2004).

22. See the following sources: Phillip H. Coombs and Manzoor Ahmed, *Attacking Rural Poverty: How Non-Formal Education Can Help* (Baltimore: John Hopkins University Press, 1974); Francisco O. Ramirez and John Boli, "The Political Construction of Mass Schooling: European Origins and Worldwide Institutionalization," *Sociology of Education*, 60, no. 1 (1987): 2–17; Anthony Giddens, *Sociology*, 4th ed. (Cambridge: Polity Press, 2001).

23. Thomas Jackson et al., *Who Takes the Bullet? The Impact of Small Arms Violence*, Norwegian Church Aid: Understanding the Issues 3 (2005), accessed at http://www.prio.no/NISAT/Publications/Who-Takes-the-Bullet-The-impact-of-small-arms-violence/.

24. International Save the Children Alliance, *Last in Line, Last in School: How Donors Are Failing Children in Conflict-Affected Fragile States* (London: International Save the Children Alliance, 2007). See also UNESCO, *Education For All By 2015: Will We Make It? EFA Global Monitoring Report* (Oxford: Oxford University Press, 2007).

25. There are eight Millennium Development Goals which UN member states and the international community have agreed to reach by the year 2015. These goals include eradicating hunger and extreme poverty, achieving universal primary education, reducing child mortality, improving maternal health, and the promotion of gender equality and the empowerment of women, among other things. See http://www.un.org/millenniumgoals/.

26. Brendan O'Malley, *Education Under Attack: A Global Study on Targeted Political and Military Violence Against Education Staff, Students, Teachers, Union and Government Officials and Institutions* (Paris: UNESCO, 2007). See also Brian Lai and Clayton Thyne, "The Effect of Civil War on Education, 1980–1997," *Journal of Peace Research*, 44, no. 3 (2007): 277–292.

27. José Marques and Ian Bannon, "Central America: Education reform in a post-conflict setting, opportunities and challenges" (Washington, D.C.: The World Bank, Environmentally and Socially Sustainable Development Network, Paper No. 4, 2003).

28. John Edwards, "Guatemala Poverty Assessment (GUAPA) Program Technical Paper 3: Education and Poverty in Guatemala" (Washington, D.C.: The World Bank, 2002).

29. José Marques and Ian Bannon, "Central America: Education reform in a post-conflict setting, opportunities and challenges" (Washington, D.C.: The World Bank, Environmentally and Socially Sustainable Development Network, Paper No. 4, 2003).

30. Klaus Seitz, "Education and Conflict: The Role of Education in the Creation, Prevention, and Resolution of Societal Crises—Consequences for Development Cooperation" (Eschborn, Germany: Germany Technical Cooperation, 2004).

31. Save the Children UK, "Out of School in Iraq: Barriers to Enrolment and Attendance in Primary Schools" (London: Save the Children, 2006).

32. UNESCO Institute of Statistics in Brief, "Iraq," accessed at http://stats.uis.unesco.org/unesco/TableViewer/document.aspx?ReportId=124&IF_Language=eng&BR_Country=3680. See also Central Intelligence Agency, "Iraq Economic Data," accessed at https://www.cia.gov/library/reports/general-reports-1/iraq_wmd_2004/chap2_annxD.html.

33. UNICEF, "Iraq's Schools Suffering From Neglect and War," accessed at http://www.unicef.org/media/media_23630.html.

34. Women's Commission for Refugee Women and Children, *Global Survey on Education in Emergencies* (2004), accessed at http://www.womenscommission.org/pdf/Ed_Emerg.pdf.

35. Government of Sierra Leone, "New Education Policy for Sierra Leone" (Freetown: Department of Education, 1995). See also Government of Sierra Leone, "Poverty Reduction Strategy Paper Education Sector Review" (Freetown: Government of Sierra Leone, 2004).

36. Ibid.

37. See http://www.internal-displacement.org

38. Pamela Baxter and Carl Triplehorn, "Protecting to Learn or teaching to protect?," *Refugee Survey Quarterly*, 23, no. 2 (2004): 38–71. See also Seitz 2004.

39. Jane Lowicki, "Missing Out: Adolescents Affected By Armed Conflict Face Few Educational Opportunities and Increased Protection Risks," *Current Issues in Comparative Education*, 2, no. 1 (1999): 4.

40. See the following: UNRWA, "Education," accessed at http://www.un.org/unrwa/programmes/education/; Salah Alzaroo and Gillian Lewando Hunt, "Education in the Context of Conflict and Instability: The Palestinian Case," *Social Policy & Administration*, 37, no. 2 (April 2003): 165–180.

41. Elizabeth King, "Educating For Conflict or Peace: Challenges and Dilemmas in Post-Conflict Rwanda," *International Journal*, LX, no. 4 (2005): 904–918; see also Seitz 2004.

42. Central Intelligence Agency, "The World Factbook: Rwanda," accessed at https://www.cia.gov/library/publications/the-world-factbook/geos/RW.html.

43. See the following sources: Mahmood Mamdani, *When Victims Become Killers* (Princeton: Princeton University Press, 2001); Kenneth Bush and Diana Saltarelli, "The Two Faces of Education in Ethnic Conflict: Toward a Peacebuilding Education for Children" (Florence: UNICEF Innocenti Research Centre, 2000).

44. John Rutayisire, John Kabano, and Jolly Rubagiza, "Redefining Rwanda's Future: The Role of Curriculum in Social Reconstruction," in *Education, Conflict and Social Cohesion*, eds. Sobhi Tawil and Alexandra Harley (Geneva: UNESCO International Bureau of Education, 2004), 315–374.

45. International Crisis Group, "Thailand: Political Turmoil and the Southern Insurgency," Asia Policy Briefing no. 80, 28 August 2008, accessed at http://www.crisisgroup.org/home/index.cfm?id=5640&l=1.

46. Marc Sommers and Peter Buckland, *Parallel Worlds: Rebuilding the Education System in Kosovo* (Paris: UNESCO International Institute for Educational Planning, 2004).

47. James Fearon and David Laitin, "Ethnicity, Insurgency, and Civil War," *American Political Science Review*, 97, no 1 (2003): 75–90.

48. Paul Collier et al., *Breaking the Conflict Trap: Civil War and Development Policy* (Washington, D.C.: The World Bank, 2003).

49. Ibid.

50. Bernadette A. M. O'Hare and David P. Southall, "First Do No Harm: The Impact of Recent Conflict on Maternal and Child Health in Sub-Saharan Africa," *Journal of the Royal Society of Medicine*, 100 (December 2007): 564–570.

51. Oxfam International and International Action Network on Small Arms, "Africa's Missing Billions". Briefing Paper No. 107 (2007).

52. See the following sources: Morten Bøås and Anne Hatløy, "Northern Uganda Internally Displaced Persons Profiling Study," Volume I (Kampala: Government of Uganda Office of the Prime Minister, and UNDP, 2005), accessed at http://www.fafo.no/ais/africa/uganda/IDP_uganda_2005.pdf; see also Integrated Regional Information Networks, "Youth in Crisis: Coming of Age in the 21st Century" (February 2007), accessed at http://www.irinnews.org/pdf/in-depth/Youth-in-crisis-IRIN-In-Depth.pdf.

53. Morten Bøås, "Marginalized Youth," in *African Guerillas: Raging Against the Machine*, ed. Morten Bøås and Kevin Dunn (Boulder: Lynne Rienner Publishers, 2007), 39–53.

54. Cited in Susanne Schaal and Thomas Elbert, "Ten Years After the Genocide: Trauma Confrontation and Posttraumatic Stress in Rwandan Adolescents," *Journal of Traumatic Stress*, 19 (2006): 95–105.

55. Human Rights Watch, "Lasting Wounds," accessed at http://hrw.org/reports/2003/rwanda0403/.

56. Jeff Drumtra, "Life After Death: Suspicion and Reintegration in Post-Genocide Rwanda," accessed at http://www.africaaction.org/docs98/rwan9802.1.htm.

57. Save the Children Federation USA, "Children, Genocide and Justice. Rwandan Perspectives on Culpability and Punishment for Children Convicted of Crimes Associated With Genocide (1995).

58. Barry S. Levy, "Health and Peace," *Croatian Medical Journal*, 43, no. 2 (2002): 114–116.

59. UNICEF, "Impact of Land mines on Children in the East Asia and Pacific Region" (Bangkok: UNICEF East Asia and the Pacific Regional Office), accessed http://www.unicef.org/emerg/files/regional_assessment_final.pdf.

60. Definitions are taken from the following sources: Jackson et al. 2005; United Nations Institute for Disarmament Research, "Scoping Study on Mine Action and Small

Arms Control Within the Framework of Armed Violence and Poverty Reduction" (Geneva: UNIDIR, 2006); Camille Pampell Conaway, "Small Arms, Light Weapons, and Landmines" in *Inclusive Security, Sustainable Peace: A Toolkit for Advocacy and Action* (London: International Action, and Washington D.C.: Women Waging Peace), accessed at http://www.huntalternatives.org/pages/87_inclusive_security_toolkit.cfm; and the web site of the International Campaign to Ban Landmines at http://www.icbl.org.

61. Edward Goldson, "The Effect of War on Children," *Child Abuse & Neglect*, 20, no. 9 (1996): 809–819.

62. United Nations Children's Fund. *The State of the World's Children 2008: Child Survival*. (New York: United Nations Children's Fund, 2008).

63. Benjamin Coghlan, et al., "Mortality in the Democratic Republic of Congo: An ongoing crisis" (New York: International Rescue Committee, 2007).

64. R. Albertyn, et al., "The effects of war on children in Africa," *Pediatric Surgery International*, 19 (2003): 227–232.

65. O'Hare and Southall, "First Do No Harm," 564–570.

66. See the 1996 Graça Machel report on the Impact of Armed Conflict on Children.

67. Richard Akresh and Philip Verwimp, "Civil War, Crop Failure, and the Health Status of Young Children," University of Sussex Households in Conflict Network, Working Paper 19 (September 2006).

68. Árpád Baráth, "Children's Well-Being After the War in Kosovo: Survey in 2000," *Croatian Medical Journal*, 43, no. 2 (2002): 199–208.

69. Árpád Baráth, "Psychological Status of Sarajevo Children After War: 1999–2000 Survey," *Croatian Medical Journal*, 43, no. 2 (2002): 213–220.

70. Ulrich Laaser et al., "Public Health and Peace," *Croatian Medical Journal*, 43, no. 2 (2002): 107–113; see also Albertyn et al. 2003.

71. David Satcher, Sharon Friel, and Ruth Bell, "Natural and Manmade Disasters and Mental Health," *Journal of the American Medical Association*, 298, no. 21 (2007): 2540–2542. See also Laaser et al. 2002.

72. Jane Salvage, "'Collateral Damage': The Impact of War on the Health of Women and Children in Iraq," *Midwifery*, 23, (2007): 8-12.

73. Medact, "Rehabilitation Under Fire: Health Care in Iraq 2003–7," accessed at http://www.medact.org/content/violence/MedactIraq08final.pdf.

74. See the following sources: Integrated Regional Information Networks, "Afghanistan: Over 360,000 Affected By Reduced Health Services," accessed at http://www.irinnews.org/Report.aspx?ReportId=78185; 2008 Land mine Monitor Report for Afghanistan at www.icbl.org/lm; Zulfiqar Ahmed Bhutta, "Children of War: The Real Casualties of the Afghan Conflict," *British Medical Journal*, 324, no. 7333 (9 February 2002): 349–352; Michele Heisler, Zohra Rasekh, and Vincent Iacopino, "Health and Human Rights of Adolescent Girls in Afghanistan," *Journal of the American Women's Medical Association*, 54, no. 3 (Summer 1999): 155–157.

75. Jason Hart (with Chandrika Khatiwada), "Participation of Conflict-Affected Children in Humanitarian Action: Lessons From Nepal" (Oxford Refugees Studies Center, 2003).

CHAPTER 3

The Recruitment and Roles of Children and Young People in Fighting Forces

It is March 1991. A few hundred rebels of the so-called Revolutionary United Front have just entered a small West African country, Sierra Leone, from neighboring Liberia. Government soldiers, sent to the border region to fight off the rebels, pass through Samuel's village. Samuel is a small boy, about 10 years old, who lives with his family in a mud-brick house with a roof of zinc plates. Although Samuel attends the local school, he is keener to ride a bicycle with his best friend or build toy cars from sticks and pieces of rope. Samuel's father always tells him that he will become an engineer once he is older.

On that morning, the boy witnesses the soldiers passing through his village and then hears the distant sound of guns and bombs. In the evening, the soldiers return, clearly on the retreat. Samuel's father decides to quickly pack their most valued belongings, put them on the tops of their heads, and head for the safety of the jungle. Later, they follow the narrow footpaths to the nearest town, about 12 miles by foot. They arrive safely, but Samuel's father decides that it is better for his sons to be farther away from the frontline. So he and his older brother are sent to live with a relative in the provincial headquarter town, another 50 miles away.

Their uncle welcomes the boys and arranges a place for them at a local school. Samuel enjoys his new school—it is much better than the old village school with its leaking roof and slates for writing on—and he even gets a double promotion. But the following year his uncle cannot afford to pay the school fees and Samuel has to leave school. One year passes, and another one; Samuel feels that he is wasting his time, away from his parents. Then, one day, he decides to join the army, which has a military base near to the town. Other boys have done it before

WEST AFRICA

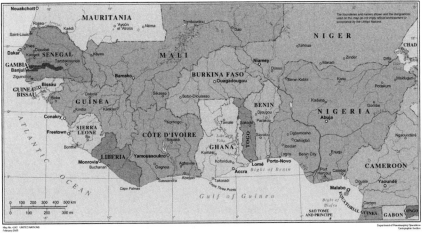

Figure 3.1. Map of West Africa, United Nations Cartographic section, map no. 4242, rev. 10. © United Nations, 2005.
Reprinted with the permission of the United Nations.

him and they are wearing uniforms and some even carry a weapon. They are hanging out with the big soldiers and eating rice from the same pot. They are fighting the rebels who are responsible for Samuel's deplorable situation.

After two weeks of training, Samuel gets a weapon and is sent to the war front. For the first time in nearly two years Samuel is back in the area where he grew up. He and his unit manage to recapture his old village and other places. But soon a new offensive by the rebels is launched and Samuel and his fellow soldiers have to retreat. Later, Samuel and his commander are ordered to defend the highway, running between two provincial headquarter towns which have become a target for frequent ambushes by the rebels, making any journey upcountry a dangerous endeavor. Samuel does not like this mission since he feels that they are an easy target in their army trucks. One day, while driving in a convoy, they are ambushed and Samuel's best friend—another child soldier—is shot and dies on the spot.

Child Soldiers: A Recent Phenomenon?

It is estimated that during the armed conflicts of the late 1980s and 1990s, at any one time there were about 300,000 children active as child soldiers. From the start of the new millennium this number has gone down slightly, and has now been put at around 250,000. But the active involvement of those under the age of 18 in armed conflict has occurred in all times and places. In ancient Greece, young people under the age of 18 were enlisted by both the Athenians and the Spartans. Tens of thousands of children participated in the Children's Crusade of 1212 to fight against the Moors in Jerusalem, although most were sold into slavery at the Mediterranean

Sea ports. Arguably the most famous female underage soldier of all times was Joan of Arc, who, at the age of 16, successfully led the French forces to victory against the English in 1429. She was later burned at the stake, accused of being a witch. Napoleon used children in his campaigns, with some of the "drummer boys" being as young as 12. In fact, the word "infantry" derives from the French word "enfant" meaning "child." And more recently, the First and Second World Wars witnessed many underage conscripts, including the infamous "Hitler Jugend" ("Jugend" is German for "youth"), who were sent to frontline positions toward the end of WWII, when Germany was desperately short of manpower.

Around the same time Samuel's fried is killed, the military government in Sierra Leone agrees to demobilize all their underage combatants. Samuel ends up at a demobilization and reintegration camp for ex-child soldiers on the outskirts of Freetown, the capital of Sierra Leone. The staff of the reintegration project has to deal on average with 50 to 100 demobilized young combatants at any one time in the camp and help them to forget about their military lives and army routines. Days are filled with school, vocational training, games and sport, and counseling. After about six months, Samuel is discharged from the project and is placed with a foster family in Freetown; the whereabouts of his family are unclear. Samuel goes to school but struggles with his drug habit, a leftover from his army years.

Unfortunately, within a year, a recently-elected government is overthrown by the army, which subsequently invites the rebels to take part in a new junta government. Samuel flees to neighboring Guinea, but without any support or person to look after him, he decides to reenlist with the army, to fight again against the rebels in Sierra Leone and some of his now ex-army comrades. When a new peace-accord is signed in 1999, Samuel is still with the soldiers, hardly able to imagine a life without or beyond the army. However, the peace deal envisages the creation of a new army, absorbing fighters of all the warring factions. These include Samuel's former enemies; the rebels and renegade soldiers. He does not feel safe anymore in the army and decides to leave the country to await better and calmer times. He travels to Ghana, a nearby and peaceful English-speaking country, and applies for refugee status while making a living by doing day-to-day jobs.

In 2002, Samuel returns from Ghana to Sierra Leone and joins the army again. The following year he leaves his army unit and joins temporarily with LURD, a rebel group in Liberia, to participate in the attack against the forces of Liberian President Charles Taylor. Taylor has always been a supporter of the rebels in Sierra Leone. But rather than by politics, Samuel is motivated by the possibility to link up with LURD commanders. They may become powerful players if indeed the LURD rebels succeed in taking over the capital of Liberia. Moreover, the prospects for looting are good as well. After Taylor is granted asylum in Nigeria and leaves the country, it looks like the region is heading for better times. Still, many experienced, hardcore fighters from Sierra Leone and Liberia try to link up with the armed factions in the Ivory Coast, which has its own crisis, but the majority of fighters are trying to make a peaceful living. Samuel's fighting days are over, although he stays in the army. With over 10 years of active duty, Samuel could rightly be called a war-veteran. But he is just 23 years of age.

Child Soldiers in a Complex Humanitarian Emergency

Armed conflicts are seldom of a straightforward "good" against "bad" nature. Instead, they often involve multiple players, shifting alliances and, all too often, widespread human rights violations and atrocities by all parties involved. A closer study of the conflict in Sierra Leone makes clear why contemporary armed conflicts are referred to as complex humanitarian emergencies.

Sierra Leone gained independence from Britain in 1961. The Sierra Leone Peoples Party (SLPP) won the first election but lost the next election in 1967 to the rival All Peoples Congress (APC) party. However, before the APC could assume power, a military coup took place. The following year, after another military coup, Siaka Stevens—the APC's leader—was granted victory as the country's new president. But under his rule, government corruption increased rapidly and power became highly centralized. In 1978 Stevens declared Sierra Leone a one-party state and it remained so for the next 14 years, while the authoritarian rulers let the country go bankrupt.

In March 1991 the Revolutionary United Front (RUF) entered Sierra Leone from neighboring Liberia. The rebels claimed that their aim was to overthrow the oppressive APC government and to restore democracy. Among the rebels were troops sent by Charles Taylor, a Liberian warlord who had started a war in his own country on Christmas Eve 1989 and who had nearly captured all of Liberia. After a year of fighting in Sierra Leone, army units from the frontline came down to the coastal capital to complain about the lack of support and equipment by their government, and successfully staged a coup. The new military regime, the National Provisional Ruling Party (NPRC), governed Sierra Leone for the next four years. Both the rebels and the NPRC forces rapidly expanded their forces by enlisting young and underage people. Samuel was one of them. Others—mainly Liberian refugees who stayed in Sierra Leone, including many children—joined the United Liberian Movement for Democracy (ULIMO), to fight against the RUF—Taylor's ally—and ultimately against the forces of Taylor himself in Liberia. Meanwhile, many Sierra Leonean government soldiers seemed to be more interested in looting civilian properties than in protecting them. Civilians accused them of being "sobels," that is, soldiers by day, and rebels by night. In a response to the lack of protection by the army, civilians started to organize themselves into civil defense forces. These militias were based on old (game) hunter guilds, with the most famous one called the "Kamajors." Many young and underage people considered it their duty to their family, community, and their village chiefs to serve in these units.

Nevertheless, the RUF continued to pose a threat to the country. Approximately one-third of the population of Sierra Leone became internally displaced or were living as refugees. The RUF also posed a threat to the government's income from diamond mining. The NPRC hired a South African mercenary firm, Executive Outcomes, to repel the RUF from the diamond mining areas and paid the mercenaries in diamond concessions. The RUF was successfully pushed back, and the NPRC—after another palace coup in early 1996—agreed to the first elections in decades, which saw the SLPP presidential candidate taking office. Peace negotiations with the RUF, started under the NPRC, were continued and in November 1996 a peace-accord was signed between the RUF and the SLPP. But in May 1997, army soldiers, disgruntled over the fact that they were sidelined by the SLPP which put its trust and support in the Kamajors instead of the army, staged another successful coup. The mutineers called themselves the Armed Forces Revolutionary Council (AFRC) and invited the RUF to join them in a power-sharing deal. For nine months the AFRC and RUF controlled the capital and other major towns, but they were in the end repelled by the combined forces of the Kamajors and the regional —but Nigerian dominated—peacekeeping force ECOMOG (Economic Community of West African States Monitoring Group). However, the RUF and AFRC regrouped and launched a deadly attack on Freetown on 6 January 1999. Although ECOMOG troops held firm, it was now clear that a military victory was not possible for either side. Peace negotiations started again, and in July 1999 a peace-accord was signed which allocated several cabinet posts for the RUF and, controversially, a blanket amnesty for all the fighters. ECOMOG troops were to be replaced by UN peacekeepers, which effectively became the biggest UN peacekeeping mission ever, with about 17,500 personnel.

Disarmament and demobilization of the armed factions was, however, slow, and in May 2000 the RUF took 500 UN peacekeepers hostage. Additionally, British soldiers were also taken hostage by a splinter faction of the former AFRC, named the "West Side Boys." The United Nations and British commandos reacted firmly, making it clear that all factions had to obey to the peace agreement. The following year more than 40,000 fighters were demobilized, bringing the total number of demobilized fighters close to 75,000. Among these were thousands of child soldiers and thousands of fighters who joined as children but who became adults while in the army. In January 2002, the president declared the end of the war, and the immense task of rebuilding the country was about to start. Hundreds of thousands of young people had known nothing other than war.

You can learn more about child soldiers and youthful combatants and the war in Sierra Leone through the following sources:

On child soldiers in Sierra Leone:

- Web site: *What is going on? Child Soldiers in Sierra Leone.* http://www.un.org/works/goingon/soldiers/goingon_soldiers.html.
- Autobiographical work: Ishmael Beah, *A Long Way Gone: Memoirs of a Boy Soldier* (New York: Sarah Chrichton Books, 2007).
- Academic article: Krijn Peters and Paul Richards, "Why We Fight: Voices of Under-Age Combatants in Sierra Leone," *Africa: Journal of the International African Institute,* 68 no. 2 (1998): 183–210.

On the conflict in Sierra Leone:

— Film: *Cry Freetown* (1999) by Sorious Samora.
— NGO report: "Youth, Poverty and Blood. The Lethal Legacy of West Africa's Regional Warriors," Human Rights Watch (2005) http://www.hrw.org/reports/2005/westafrica0405/.

— Book: Paul Richards, *Fighting for the Rainforest: War, Youth and Resources in Sierra Leone* (Oxford: James Currey, Ltd., 1996).
— Book: David Keen, *Conflict and Collusion in Sierra Leone* (New York: Palgrave, 2005).

Why They Join: Examining the Factors Which Make Young People Vulnerable to Conscription

Why is it that young and underage people become involved in armed conflict in the first place? Why do they end up as child soldiers, young rebels, or underage militia fighters? The story of Samuel gives some clues in helping to answer this important question. Although each and every life story of a young person caught up in armed conflict is unique, there are also common features to it.

But before we examine Samuel's story in more detail, it is important to underline that the majority of children and young people in conflict zones do not become soldiers or fighters. Such young people are equally affected by the conflict; many leave their homes to, for example, live with relatives in safer areas or to live in internally displaced camps or even outside the war-affected country as a refugee in a neighboring country. Many experience more or less the same events which in the end influenced Samuel to decide to join the army, and noncombatant children find themselves in more or less similar situations. Therefore, while researchers and practitioners agree on several risk factors which make young people more vulnerable to conscription or likely to join an armed group, these can never be considered as a simple sum, where conscription will take place once a certain number of these factors or events have happened. Personal factors, such as the character of the child and his or her capacity to overcome difficult circumstances, often referred to as "resilience," also play an important role. There is often also a unique and direct trigger that makes people join a fighting group, such as an army truck passing and offering a ride; a soldier who needs someone to carry goods; or witnessing an act of violence that creates feelings of revenge. Nevertheless, it is useful to know what general factors make young people more vulnerable to military recruitment, to try to prevent conscription or re-conscription. Let us therefore examine Samuel's motives.

In early 1991 Samuel finds himself living in what has become a war zone. He hears the sounds of gunshots and exploding bombs, witnesses soldiers passing and civilians running for their lives; soon he is on the run himself. It is widely agreed that if a child is from a conflict zone, it is more likely that he or she will become a child soldier.[2] This may sound obvious, but there are also young people who join or are enlisted (often with government forces), who are not from the war zone. In addition, many contemporary conflicts are characterized by highly defuse and shifting frontlines—or no frontlines at all—with rebel units using ambushes and hit-and-run actions as their main fighting tactics. A military coup can also bring the war to previously relatively peaceful places; many of the demobilized child soldiers in Freetown, including Samuel, reenlisted after the 1997 coup.

Right at the beginning of the war, Samuel becomes separated from his parents, which is another major risk factor. Separated children will have to look for food, protection, and shelter themselves. Many are taken up by other refugees or helpful strangers, while others turn to each other for protection and group together, forming street gangs of youths.[3] A small but significant part will end up with the soldiers or fighting forces, which often have food and shelter, and can provide some protection for the young people . In other cases, it is not the separation of the family but rather the presence and encouragement of family members that influence young people to join. Some young people come from families whose members have joined an armed faction before, making it more or less normal that they too join. Other young people are encouraged by their families to join to fight for a just cause or to safeguard the family or village, since a son or daughter with the army or rebels can help to prevent these factions from attacking a village.

Strategies to Prevent the Conscription of Underage Combatants

The saying that "prevention is better than cure" is equally valid for the child soldier phenomenon. Over the years, organizations helping children have identified various strategies and approaches to make children in war situations less vulnerable to armed conscription. But one of the main insights is that there are no blueprint strategies; each preventive action should be based on a detailed understanding of the children's situation and the wider context in which recruitment takes place.

A second important insight is that, where possible, communities should be actively involved in preventing conscription. The Don Bosco football program in wartime Liberia is a good example of this. This program helped young people to set up community-based football teams. If one of the children did not turn up for the daily training sessions, his peers would inform the NGO workers and community authorities, who would then go to the local police and/or army commander to find out if the child had been conscripted. The "release" of an underage fighter is easier if he or she is with an armed faction for only a few days, but it becomes more difficult once the child has become fully trained and indoctrinated.

To some extent, Samuel was lucky in the beginning , since he was taken care of by a relative. However, this took place in the context of prewar but conflict-exaggerated chronic poverty. Poverty is a third major risk factor for conscription. Child soldiers overwhelmingly come from poor backgrounds. In contrast, young people from rich backgrounds seldom become fighters, even if there is universal conscription.[4] Samuel experiences the effects of poverty when his uncle is not able to afford the school fees of all the children under his care and has to take Samuel out of school. Being out of school—either because of poverty or because schools have closed because of the war—is often given as a reason by young ex-combatants for why they joined an armed faction. Education, even if it is of poor quality, provides hope for the future and helps to give a day-to-day purpose and structure for young people. Samuel's story underlines this point, since from the moment he is not allowed to attend school anymore, he starts to feel that he is wasting his time, hanging out on the street for most of the days. If he joins the soldiers he at least learns the skill of warfare—skills that are particularly useful in a conflict-ridden country.

Added to these reasons is the image of friends and other young people who join the military and are wearing uniforms and carrying arms, patrolling in heavy vehicles and commanding civilians. For Samuel, some level of peer pressure, machismo, and self-protection also seems to be involved in the decision to join the soldiers. In contrast, there does not seem to be any political or ideological motivation in his choice, only that he has some desire to take revenge for the havoc the rebels caused and for the deplorable situation he finds himself in as a result of that. This fits with a widespread belief that children and adolescents are too young to join for political or ideological reasons and that these, if still expressed, are the result of indoctrination and brainwashing. This belief is further bolstered by the fact that adolescence is a time in which people are particularly perceptive to other ideas and to opposing established structures, and in search of an identity. These factors can all be fostered by joining an armed faction.

Female Child Soldiers in the Struggle Against the Derg Regime in Ethiopia

The Tigrayan People's Liberation Front (TPLF) successfully fought against the Derg government forces and in 1991 overthrew Ethiopia's dictator, Mengistu. Approximately one-third of the TPLF fighters were female, a number which included many female children. In contrast to other rebel movements, girls and women in the TPLF were respected and held in high regard. The TPLF's political agenda included equal land and property rights, a ban on early marriages, equal divorce rights, and equitable access to education, including technical training. Many of the underage female combatants joined because friends and family also joined the fight against the oppressive regime. Others joined to escape early marriage; a widespread practice during those days entailed that girls as young as 12 were considered old enough to marry. The years of fighting side by side with men and being treated equally resulted in a rather emancipated and outspoken generation of females who were prepared to challenge the more traditional feminine values of Ethiopian society.[5]

Samuel's decision to join the Liberian LURD fighters in their push toward the Liberian capital Monrovia is also not motivated by political ideals (for instance, to help overthrow Liberian dictator Charles Taylor and restore genuine democracy), but by opportunities for financial gain and perhaps to build up relations with powerful people. Linking up with commanders or warlords-cum-politicians can provide some form of immediate livelihood security as well as longer-term security. Many child combatants hope that the commander they have served during the war will reward their loyalty after the war with support for their education or by providing a job for them. These patron-client-structured relations are a common feature of the political landscape of many developing countries, both in peacetime and during times of war. For young people from poor backgrounds, with limited prospects for proper education and a decent job, joining an armed group and building up these patron-client relations is often one of the few ways to progress on the socioeconomic ladder.[6] Throughout Samuel's years in the army he is constantly for the lookout for those people who can help him with food, some money, and support for the future.[7]

A closer study of Samuel's case has brought to light some of the most significant factors that made Samuel and tens of thousands of other child combatants vulnerable to armed conscription. Some were circumstances much beyond Samuel's capacity to do something about—he had to run for his life when the rebels came to his village (although others stayed behind and joined the rebels), and he had to leave school once his uncle was not able to pay the fees anymore. But in other cases Samuel made a more conscious choice—for instance, when he decided to hang out on the street and to spend time with people closely connected to the military. The next section will look more closely into this issue and discusses voluntary and forced conscription.

Voluntary, Coerced, and Forced Enrollment of Children into Armed Forces

Above, several factors were discussed which provide a context in which it becomes more likely that young people will end up joining an armed faction, sometimes as the result of a deliberate choice by the young person. In the context of war, joining an armed faction may be the least bad alternative among several bad options. Moreover, war in general and conscription in particular can also provide opportunities for young people. Children and youngsters from poor backgrounds and with limited educational and employment opportunities have the chance to become someone by joining, perhaps even to be a commander in control of people who may be older and/or more educated.

The spoils of war may also result in young people having access to items which they likely couldn't have obtained in more peaceful times. Others may join to escape a boring life in a small village or to escape an early marriage with a partner who is not of their choosing. While many join voluntarily, other children are conscripted as the result of more coercive factors such as family or peer pressure. Sometimes young people are so convinced about the righteousness of an armed uprising that they want to join. If this conviction is the result of clear indoctrination or even brain-washing—for instance by fundamentalist religious leaders—it is problematic to view this as voluntary conscription and it would be more appropriate to label it as coercive conscription. Beside voluntary and coerced conscription, the literature also distinguishes a third form of conscription, namely forced conscription. In fact, for a long time it has been assumed that the majority, if not all, underage soldiers were forcibly conscripted. More recently however, it has been found that in many cases young and underage fighters are not forcibly conscripted, but have joined more or less voluntarily, as is illustrated by the story of Samuel.[8]

Modes of Conscription

— **Voluntary conscription** is joining an armed faction (government army, militia, or rebel faction) out of one's own and free choice, without the explicit use of force or coercion by the armed faction.
— **Coercive conscription** is joining an armed faction as a result of pressure to do so mainly by family, relatives, religious leaders, etc., but without explicit use of force. Propaganda and indoctrination can be used as means for coercive conscription.
— **Forced recruitment** is conscription into an armed faction against one's will or choice, with the use of threats, force, or violence. Forced recruitment occurs through:
  o **Quota systems** are sometimes put in place by militias, rebels or governments and require each family or community to present a certain number of recruits.
  o **Abduction** is the kidnapping of children who are then forced—sometimes under gunpoint—to join.
  o **Press-ganging** is the raiding by government soldiers or rebels of places where many potential recruits are (such as in school), who are then rounded up and conscripted.

You can find more on the different ways children end up with armed factions in:

— Isobel McConnan and Sarah Uppard, *Children, not Soldiers: Guidelines for Working with Child Soldiers and Children Associated with Fighting Forces*, The Save the Children Fund, 2001. Accessed at http://www.reliefweb.int/library/documents/2002/sc-children-dec01.htm.
— Rachel Brett and Irma Specht, *Young Soldiers: Why They Choose to Fight*, (Boulder: Lynne Rienner Publishers, 2004).
— Michael Wessells, *Child Soldiers: From Violence to Protection*, (Cambridge, MA: Harvard University Press, 2007).

To what extent voluntary conscription by young and, in particular, underage people should be considered as truly "voluntary" has caused heated debate among scholars and practitioners. Charities and nongovernmental agencies working with war-affected children, including ex-child combatants, have long stressed the vulnerable character of these children and perceived them mainly as victims of the war in general and of unscrupulous warlords in particular. In addition, what is proclaimed to be "voluntary conscription" by child soldiers often turned out to be "forced by circumstances" or "lack of any other choices" after more careful consideration. If one is without food or shelter, lacking a job and in poverty, joining the army or a rebel group can be a pure survival strategy, and not something that one really wants. In such a (common) scenario, children join without coercion or the use of force, but can it be considered as genuinely voluntary? Few children who "volunteer" understand beforehand what combat actually entails and that it may be quite different from what they may have seen in Hollywood action films. Nor do most realize beforehand that joining often means "once in, never out" and that their choice is irrevocable.

But some scholars[9] have criticized the "victimization" of young people affected by war, arguing that it denies their "agency."[10] Many of the young people interviewed by these researchers showed a remarkably accurate understanding of the conflict and its causes, and stressed that their decision to join was a voluntary, deliberate, and conscious choice. Goodwin-Gill and Cohn (1993) state that "a very fuzzy line is often all that separates voluntary from coerced participation, and it is impossible to know precisely at what age or development stage a young person is capable of 'volunteering' in the way we would accept of an adult."[11] However, it is also argued by scholars that we should be careful in applying Western perceptions of childhood and children's developmental stages in non-Western settings: " ... ideas about when children become adults vary quite widely across cultures, and a practical (through not always *de jure*) 'adulthood' (i.e. material self reliance) often arrives early—especially for children from poor families, on a continent [Africa] where half the population is below eighteen."[12]

But why is it so important to know if children joined voluntarily or if they were forced to do so? Conscription of children into armed forces is almost always a violation of international human rights law and humanitarian law, and most people have strong moral objections to it as well. Brett and Specht (2004) identify two important reasons why it is important to know whether or not underage people have joined voluntarily:

> The first one is practical. If youngsters have chosen to become involved and the circumstances that led to that decision have not changed significantly, they are more likely to return—even if they are demobilized—than those who were abducted or physically forced into military service. The second aspect is the legal one, and concerns the international instruments that apply to the military involvement of young people.[13]

Demobilization and reintegration programs (see the next chapter) offer ex-child combatants shelter, food, skills training, counseling, and recreational activities. But they do so only for a limited time (typically 6 to 9 months). After that, reintegration support is limited; in some cases school or apprenticeship fees are paid by the program, but at some point most ex-child combatants find themselves without any support. Even if family reunification has been successful, the young people who live with their parents are likely to be worse off than before the war. In those cases where lack of education or poverty has been a driving factor for joining, there is a real chance that in the end the ex-child soldier reenlists because the circumstances that led to that decision to join in the first place have not changed significantly. Reenlisting and re-conscription are even more likely to happen with ex-child soldiers as compared to adult ex-soldiers, since the demobilization and reintegration of ex-child soldiers often already takes place while the conflict is still going on, making it easier to join again since the same factors that influenced a child to join (for example, coming from a conflict zone) are still present.

Brecht and Specht (2004) also identify a legal reason for why it is important to know if an underage combatant has joined voluntarily or has been forced to do so. There are four bodies of international law that are of relevance to the phenomenon of child soldiers, namely: international human rights law, international humanitarian law, international criminal law, and international labor law. Between these, there is a series of international human rights declarations which prohibit the conscription and use of underage combatants. Most have been signed and ratified by the majority of the countries in the world.[14] Still, the rights of children—most often defined as all those below the age of 18, unless national law states differently—are not equally covered. Forced conscription of people below the age of 18 is never allowed, neither in international treaty law nor in international customary law, but international law is less firm where it concerns the voluntarily conscription of children of 16 years and older.[15] The Optional Protocol to the Convention on the Rights of the Child on Involvement of Children in Armed Conflicts allows for voluntary recruitment of 16– and 17–year-old children in government armed forces[16] (but not in any other armed forces, such as militias or rebel movements). Where it concerns the conscription of 16- and 17-year-old children, it is stipulated that they are not allowed to take part in active combat. Some countries, however, made certain reservations when they signed and ratified these treaties, stating for instance that in situations of national threat or emergency, children of 16 and 17 years of age can be allowed to take part in active combat.[17] In short, while child soldiering, from a legal perspective, is increasingly condemned and made illegal, international treaties and conventions still do not cover all situations. And reality has shown that signing and ratifying these treaties and protocols is one thing (and a relatively easy thing to do), but living up to the commitment is something else. Rebel factions, although also bound to obey these treaties, may in particular feel less obliged to follow them, since it is the government which signed up to these in the first place.

Still, the increasing body of international treaties and conventions in relation to the conscription of underage combatants can only be appreciated (as long as the international community does not feel that it therefore has done enough). Now that national, hybrid, and international war tribunals and the International Criminal Court (ICC) in The Hague are becoming increasingly effective in prosecuting warlords and military commanders, these legal provisions acquire extra significance. For instance, all those indicted by the Special Court for Sierra Leone were charged with the forcible conscription of underage people, and have been found guilty for it. Additionally, Ugandan and Congolese commanders have been charged and found guilty by the ICC for using child soldiers, and former Liberian president Charles Taylor has been charged in connection with the use of child soldiers in the Sierra Leonean conflict.

Induction into the Army or Rebel Forces

Once children are conscripted, either forcibly or voluntarily, they likely go through an induction process. During this induction period, all new recruits receive some kind of military training in which they are taught about the weapons they will be using and about military orders, ranks, and fighting tactics. This training can be extremely limited in duration, perhaps one or two weeks, after which the recruits are sent to the war front, sometimes ending up as cannon fodder. For example, children who were used for human wave attacks and as minesweepers during the wars between Iran and Iraq in the early 1980s received very limited training, but more often than not they received no training at all. The length of the training depends on how urgently new manpower is needed; press-ganging and limited training seem to be the norm in times of manpower shortages.

But the induction process entails more than just military training. It also includes explicit and implicit strategies to make conscripts loyal and/or to prevent defection. Some of these strategies have been notoriously cruel while others work on a more subtle level. During the 1975–1992 conflict in Mozambique, immediately after the country's seven-year-long independence struggle from Portugal by the Liberation Front of Mozambique (FRELIMO), the rebel Mozambican National Resistance (RENAMO)—which was supported by the South African apartheid regime—forced captured children to kill their family members in front of their whole village. Not only did these children have no direct family to return to if they managed to escape from the rebels, but they were also unlikely to be accepted by extended family members and villagers. Through this forced act of execution, defection became much more difficult, and many young people in the end did not see any other possibility than to stay with the RENAMO forces. In general, any attempt to escape from rebel forces in particular is heavily punished, and new recruits are often forced to witness the execution of a captured defector or must carry out the execution themselves. Exposure to active combat and forced participation in executions can be used to "normalize" violence and death, so that child recruits quickly overcome their fear and more easily adapt to their new roles and lives. Interviews with ex-child combatants from many different conflicts suggest that many still remember their first killing, but also state that killing soon became normal and there was no longer a reason to try to get away from it by escaping.

Other, less horrifying means of induction are also used. Many recruits, including underage recruits, receive some kind of ideological training. Most rebel organizations claim to fight for societal change and/or to overthrow an oppressive regime. Hence, the new child recruits are taught to believe that they are fighting for a higher and better purpose; they are "freedom fighters" or "revolutionaries."

While the extent to which these claims represent a genuine agenda can in many cases be questioned, this does not however entail that ideological training and indoctrination are any less effective. Many child soldiers who were abducted and forcibly conscripted have turned into loyal fighters, partly because of the effectiveness of ideological training. Alternatively, children conscripted by government forces are often told that they are protecting their families, homes, and fatherland against rebels who have no right to challenge the government. In such cases, indoctrination in the army can often be the continuation of propaganda by the government in schools and in daily life.

The effects of indoctrination are further strengthened by the separation of the recruits from civilians and the outside world. Recruits and soldiers live in military barracks, which they are not allowed to leave without the consent of a superior. Where it concerns the recruits of rebel organizations, isolation can be even more fundamental. Children who have been conscripted by rebel organizations such as the FARC in Colombia, the LRA in Uganda, or the RUF in Sierra Leone have spent years without seeing their families or parents, and in some cases find it hard to imagine a functioning world outside of their bush and jungle camps. On top of the physical isolation—due to the location of these camps in terrain that is difficult to access—this also fosters mental isolation. Because of the fact that they are young, they have a much shorter memory of pre-conscription civilian life.

The Lord's Resistance Army and the Need for More Research

The so-called Lord's Resistance Army in Uganda has been portrayed by the Western media as a highly irrational and barbaric guerrilla force, terrorizing Northern Uganda while abducting small children who are subsequently forced to commit unthinkable atrocities against their own families to induct them into the movement. Joseph Kony, the LRA's leader, is alleged to want to rule the country by the Ten Commandments. Or so anecdotal evidence and messages sent out by the Ugandan government seem to suggest. With the emerging peace, access to larger groups of former fighters is possible. The media images can now be tested and some prove to be exaggerated or even wrong. For instance, the LRA appears to be a much more conventional military organization, and many of its actions make strategic sense rather than being irrational or "spiritually" guided. Recruiting by abduction is even more widespread than previously thought, but appears to focus more on young adolescents than small children. Moreover, Blattman and Annan (2008) found that of 462 abductees whom they interviewed, more than three-quarters stayed with the LRA for less than a year.[18]

You can find more on the LRA in:

— *The Lord's Resistance Army: War, Peace and Reconciliation*, by Tim Allen & Koen Vlassenroot, eds. (London: James Currey, forthcoming).
— Peter Eichstaedt, *First Kill Your Family: Child Soldiers of Uganda and the Lord's Resistance Army* (Chicago: Lawrence Hill Books, 2008).

Cut off from their parents, families, and civilian life, child soldiers are likely to substitute these relationships by building up relations with their fellow fighters and commanders. The army or rebel organization becomes their new family; a commander may become a substitute father or mother. This psychological process is referred to as the "Stockholm Syndrome"[19], wherein the conscript starts to experience feelings of loyalty and obedience to his or her abductor or commander, because he spares and protects him or her while others are killed (for instance, for attempting to defect) or exposed to rape (as a punishment).

Punishments—if rules are broken—are a common way to compel loyalty, or at least obedience. But rewards—material privileges or an early promotion—are equally effective to promote the loyalty of conscripted children toward their commanders and the army or rebel organization. In the end, it is often a combination of the above mentioned factors which make new conscripts turn into combatants who have some level of loyalty toward the faction they are fighting for. Organizations that want to help young ex-combatants in their transition process from military to civilian life have to find ways for each child to overcome and counterbalance the effects of the above factors, as will be discussed in more detail in the next chapter. But first, we look further into the different roles and tasks underage combatants have in the army or rebel organization.

Roles of Young People in Fighting Forces

Child soldiers are not only those underage people who have weapons and are actively involved in combat. Instead, the most widely accepted definition on child soldiers states that

> A "child soldier" is defined as any child—boy or girl—under 18 years of age, who is part of any kind of regular or irregular armed force or armed group in any capacity, including, but not limited to: cooks, porters, messengers, and anyone accompanying such groups other than family members. It includes girls and boys recruited for sexual purposes and/or forced marriage. The definition, therefore, does not only refer to a child who is carrying, or has carried weapons.[20]

One of the reasons why the definition of a child soldier includes those children who do not carry weapons is that children who are cooks or porters can equally find their lives in danger by military actions. They too are exposed to the negative emotional and mental impact of being part of an army unit or rebel group. In some cases, children who are active fighters and carry weapons may be better off than those who are in more subordinate roles, since the first group is more likely to have at least some level of power and control, which can positively affect their coping strategies and increase their resilience. It is also important to realize that children may have multiple roles; they can be porters of ammunition during attacks and between frontline positions but once they return to the base, they can take on the role of cook or cleaner. And in many cases, children start with supportive roles but after several months become fighters, sometimes at their own request.

The Kalashnikov

Technical progress is partly responsible for the high numbers of children actively involved in combat. In the past, weapons were too heavy to be carried by children and too expensive to be entrusted to them. These days, small arms like the AK-47 (Kalashnikov) assault rifle, are light—a loaded AK-47 weights approximately 5 kg (11 pounds)—, easy to use and maintain, are cheap, and have an immense amount of firepower compared to earlier weapons. In many war-affected countries, an AK-47 can be bought for the price of a goat or chicken. There are about 500 million small arms in the world and many circulate in developing countries and regions experiencing armed conflict. More than 90 percent of the conflicts which took place during the 1990s involved only small arms and light weapons.[21] While the wide availability of small arms is unlikely to be a cause of armed conflict, it can catalyze it and make it more deadly.

You can find more on the role of small arms and light weapons (SALW) in contemporary conflicts in:

— Mike Bourne, *Arming Conflict: The Proliferation of Small Arms* (Hampshire: Palgrave MacMillan, 2007).
— "The Impact on Children of Illicit Trafficking of Small Arms, Landmines and Unexploded Ordnance," accessed at http://www.un.org/children/conflict/english/smallarmslandmines.html.

While they are all labeled as child soldiers, one can distinguish between the more supportive roles of children in armed forces, such as cooks, domestic servants, porters, medics, and sex slaves, and the more active roles which include children who actually fight and guard checkpoints and those who act as bodyguards and spies. One of the reasons why over the last two or three decades an average of 200,000 to 300,000 children have been active as child soldiers around the world at any time is because they are capable of performing such a wide range of combat or combat-related activities, sometimes even better than adults can. After all, who will be suspicious of an "innocent" child hanging around at a military base in search of food, when in reality he or she is spying on the soldiers in order to brief the rebels about their movements? And which soldier can compete with a child soldier who attacks (almost) without fear, where the older soldier may be reluctant because of a more mature understanding of the risks and dangers of a certain mission? Contributing to their popularity among commanders is the fact that children are cheap—they do not ask for a wage—and they are more easy to recruit—they are often vulnerable and in need of food and shelter because of family separation—and they are more easy to indoctrinate. In other cases, children may free up adult fighters from long hours of duty, such as guarding checkpoints or making long journeys to deliver messages between different camps. Where it concerns more supportive roles, children in many developing countries are expected to help the household with chores, such as carrying water, washing clothes, cleaning, and cooking from a much younger age than their counterparts in the Western world. They continue to do this in an armed group, but now for their surrogate family; the commander (and his wife). Obviously, some of the supportive roles children perform in an armed faction have no cultural resonance, for example where children are forced to provide sexual services to the commander and fighters.

While children are likely to have a less developed understanding of the risks and dangers of combat and fighting, at least initially, they too experience fear and can be paralyzed by it. To prepare soldiers, including child soldiers, for battle and to force them to overcome their fear, different methods can be used by the armed faction. Many ex-child soldiers reported that they took—or were forced to take—drugs prior to going to the war front. Smoking marijuana is commonly reported. Others are provided with amphetamines, and in some cases, with heroin and (crack) cocaine. Armed groups can access these drugs through plunder (of hospitals or health clinics) and through trade. Several armed factions are actively involved in the production and trade of illegal drugs, such as the Mujahideen in Afghanistan and the FARC rebels in Colombia. Survivors of army or rebel atrocities often indicate that the child soldiers involved in the attack seemed to be high on drugs during the attack. Other ways to make child soldiers less fearful is by offering spiritual "protection." By undergoing certain rituals, often rooted in traditional beliefs, child soldiers are made to believe that they have become invincible. Underage fighters of the Kamajor militia in Sierra Leone believed that by undergoing certain traditional rituals and not breaking certain taboos—such as eating meat or coming close to a woman—they would become invisible and thus be able to approach the enemy without being seen. Others wear "bulletproof" jackets, woven of traditional country cloth, which are supposed to deflect the enemy's bullets. Some ex-child combatants in, for example, Liberia and the Congo, indicated that they drank the blood or ate the hearts of their victims to overcome fear and possess their enemy's courage.

The Gender Dimension

Attention to the issue of child soldiers by scholars, NGOs, and international organizations is a relatively recent phenomenon, with the first significant reports appearing in the mid–1990s. Focus on female child soldiers is even more recent. For some time, scholars and practitioners did not explicitly distinguish between boy and girl fighters, having boy soldiers in mind almost by default whenever they used the term "child soldiers." This was particularly worrying where it concerned the planning of the disarmament, demobilization, and reintegration of underage combatants; the first DDR programs had few, if any, facilities for female child soldiers (see next chapter) if they were identified by the DDR officers in the first place. It was also assumed that if girls were with the army or rebels at all, they were much more likely to have more supportive roles rather than active combat roles. But our understanding of the gender differences with regards to underage conscription has changed over the last few years, due to an increasing body of research and experiences with female ex-child soldiers. It has become clear that female child soldiers are actively fighting in frontline positions and that in a good number of cases they have commanding positions, which increases their power and decreases any vulnerability normally associated with girls within armed factions. More generally, it has become clear that an armed conflict and military conscription impacts the two genders in different ways.[22]

"Black Diamond"

"Black Diamond" is the *nom de guerre* of one of Liberia's best known female commanders. "Black Diamond" joined the LURD (Liberians United for Reconciliation and Democracy) armed faction in its struggle against the government forces of warlord-turned-president Charles Taylor in 1999, after she was gang-raped by government soldiers. While only 17 or 18 years of age, her fighting skills and bravery soon resulted in a commanding position. She headed her own rebel unit, called the Women's Artillery Commandos (WAC), which was highly regarded by male commanders for its discipline and ability to carry out missions. Being stronger, better, and more ruthless than male fighters can help female and girl soldiers to protect themselves and to survive the war.

For more about Black Diamond, see for instance:

— "Liberia's Women Killers": http://news.bbc.co.uk/1/hi/world/africa/3181529. stm.
— "Rory Carroll Meets One of Liberia's Most Formidable Rebel Fighters": ——http:// www.buzzle.com/editorials/8–25–2003–44587.asp.

Part of the lack of focus on female child soldiers in the past can be explained by a bias in research and attention, based on (wrong) assumptions about who are fighting and who are not. Government armies have, in general, fewer female and girl soldiers in their ranks than rebel movements. And among the total number of females in armed opposition groups, a relatively high percentage are underage. But female child soldiers are in many cases less visible than their male counterparts. Commanders who have female child soldiers among their ranks may not want to reveal this after demobilization since these girls may still be of use to them as their wives or domestic servants, whereas male ex-child soldiers can be a burden to the commander after demobilization. In other cases, female ex-child soldiers do everything possible to keep their pasts hidden after demobilization. Most cultures associate violence with men and find it more appropriate for males (including boys) to involve themselves in fighting than for women, let alone girls, to do so. It is also often assumed that girls who have participated in fighting groups have been sexually active, thus compromising their chances for a future marriage. This makes it easier for boys to be forgiven by the community once they return than it is for girls who clearly broke a cultural taboo by actively fighting. Postwar community reactions to female ex-child soldiers are all too often ones of rejection or accusation.

In many cases girls are recruited or join an armed group for the same reasons as boys. Girl soldiers may even be preferred by commanders, as while boy child soldiers who are sent out to spy raise little attention, girl child soldiers on the other hand do not raise any suspicion at all. But a more horrifying reason for the conscription of young and ultra-young girls into armed forces is also known. Against the background of an ever growing HIV/AIDS pandemic, male fighters and commanders want girls who are still virgins to satisfy their sexual needs. A part of the girls conscripted or abducted by armed opposition groups solely provide domestic and sexual services. Rape can also be used to punish girls (and boys) for not following orders or for trying to escape. As a way to protect themselves from being indiscriminately raped and/or gang-raped, some girls try to establish a relationship with a specific commander so that they can guarantee some degree of protection (and perhaps some privileges as well) for themselves and are only forced to have sex with one man.

Still, one should be careful not to generalize and subsequently stigmatize, by assuming that all female ex-child soldiers have been victims of rape and sexual exploitation. There are armed groups—the Kurdistan Workers' Party (PKK), the Liberation Tigers of Tamil Eelam (LTTE) in Sri Lanka, or the various armed groups in the Philippines—with female child soldiers among their ranks, which do not have a record of widespread or systematic sexual exploitation. And not all relations between girls or young women and male fighters or commanders have to be of an unequal or coercive nature. Young women may choose to marry a soldier or rebel fighter of more or less their age, rather than becoming the third or fourth wife of a village notable who may be twice or three times their age.

Further resources on female child-soldiers:

- Web site: *What is going on? Child Soldiers in Sierra Leone.* http://www.un.org/works/ goingon/soldiers/goingon_soldiers.html.
- Monograph: *Africa's young soldiers: the co-option of childhood.* (Afua Twum-Danso, 2003).
- Book: *Where are the girls? Girls in fighting forces in Northern Uganda, Sierra Leone and Mozambique: Their lives during and after war.* (Susan McKay and Dyan Mazurana, 2004).

Conclusion

The involvement of children in warfare is not a recent phenomenon, nor has it in the past been limited to a few countries or a specific continent. But the number of underage people who were part of government or opposition groups in post-Cold War conflicts has been unprecedented, and the African continent has born most of the brunt.

The study of the child soldier phenomenon—the reasons for their conscription, their roles inside armed movements, and the effects of long-term exposure to a conflict environment—has resulted in the gaining of insights. We now have a better understanding of these issues, not in the least through listening carefully to ex-child combatants, and this is crucial for developing strategies to prevent armed conscription of underage people. These insights are also essential for helping young people in their transition process from a fighter's life to that of an ordinary civilian. This transition process is known as the disarmament, demobilization, and reintegration process, and it will be the focus of the next chapter. To get a child out of the war is one step, but an equally important step to be followed is to get the war out of the child.

Has the war been taken out of Samuel, the child soldier introduced at the beginning of this chapter? Probably not. Clearly, he is not a child anymore, nor is he involved in combat. But six years after the end of the war in Sierra Leone, Samuel is still a soldier, although he now spends his days in the barracks rather than at the war front. He is fed up with the army, but like so many other child soldiers, Samuel fought for many years without an official army number and as a result does not have many financial entitlements if he wants to end his time in the army. Leaving the army would mean that he must give up his poor but regular income and his monthly bag of rice. For Samuel, some of the same reasons that made him join the soldiers in the first place are still keeping him in the army, many years after the peace-accord was signed to end Sierra Leone's civil war.

Notes

1. This is a true story. More details, including an interview with Samuel, can be found in: Krijn Peters and Paul Richards, "Jeune Combatants Parlant de la Geurre et de la Paix en Sierra Leone," *Cahiers d'études africaines*, 38 no. 2–4 (1998): 581–617; see also Krijn Peters, "Reintegrating Young Ex-combatants in Sierra Leone: Accommodating Indigenous and Wartime Value Systems," in *Vanguard or Vandals: Youth, Politics, and Conflict in Africa*, eds. Jon Abbink and Ineke van Kessel (Leiden: Brill, 2005): 267–297.

2. Cf. Rachel Brett and Margaret McCallin, *Children: The Invisible Soldiers*, 2nd ed. (Stockholm: Save the Children Sweden, 1998); Graça Machel, *The Impact of War on Children* (London: Hurst & Company, 2001); Rachel Brett and Irma Specht, *Young Soldiers: Why They Choose to Fight* (Boulder: Lynne Rienner Publishers, 2004).

3. Ishmael Beah, the author of an autobiographical book about his years as a child soldier in the Sierra Leonean conflict, grouped together with other children after he was separated from his parents but before his group joined the soldiers. See Ishmael Beah, *A Long Way Gone: Memoires of a Boy Soldier* (New York: Sarah Crichton Books, 2007).

4. Rachel Brett and Irma Specht, *Young Soldiers: Why They Choose to Fight* (Boulder: Lynne Rienner Publishers, 2004).

5. Angela Veale, *From Child Soldier to Ex-fighter: Female Fighters, Demobilization and Reintegration in Ethiopia*, Monograph No. 85 (Pretoria: Institute for Security Studies, 2003).

6. For an example of the role of patrimonial relations in wartime, see for example Henrik Vigh, *Navigating Terrains of War: Youth and Soldiering in Guinea-Bissau* (Oxford: Berghan Books, 2006).

7. Peters 2005.

8. Dumas and de Cock (2003) found that two-thirds of the underage combatants they interviewed in four different war-affected countries indicated that they had joined voluntarily. See Laetitia Dumas and Michaëlle de Cock, *Wounded Childhood: The Use of Child Soldiers in Armed Conflict in Central Africa* (Geneva: ILO, 2003).

9. See for instance Brett and Specht 2004, and Angela McIntyre, *Invisible Stakeholders: Children and War in Africa* (Pretoria: Institute for Security Studies, 2004).

10. "The notion of agency attributes to the individual actor the capacity to process social experiences and to devise ways of coping with life, even under the most extreme forms of coercion. Within the limits of information, uncertainty and the other constraints (e.g. physical, normative or politico-economic) that exist, social actors are 'knowledgeable' and 'capable'. They attempt to solve problems, learn how to intervene in the flow of social events around them, and monitor continuously their own actions, observing how others react to their behavior and taking note of the various contingent circumstances." From Norman Long and Ann Long, *Battlefields of Knowledge: The Interlocking of Theory and Practice in Social Research and Development* (New York: Routledge, 1992): 22–23

11. Guy Goodwin-Gill and Ilene Cohn, *Child Soldiers: The Role of Children in Armed Conflict* (Oxford: Oxford University Press,1993): pp. 23–24.

12. Paul Richards, "Militia Conscription in Sierra Leone: Recruitment of Young Fighters in an African War," in *The Comparative Study of Conscription in the Armed Forces*, Lars Mjoset and Stephen van Holde, eds. (Oxford : Elsevier Science Ltd., 2002): 255–276.

13. Brett and Specht 2004, 105.

14. All countries in the world, except for the USA and Somalia, have signed and ratified the UN CRC.

15. The USA, the UK, and the Netherlands are examples of countries where children ages of 16 and above can join the army. But African countries which have signed and ratified the African Charter on the Rights and Welfare of the Child are required to "take all necessary measures to ensure that no child [everyone below the age of 18] shall take a direct part in hostilities and refrain, in particular, from recruiting any child" (ACRWC, Article 22).

16. The Protocol requires the following cumulative conditions; 1) conscription is genuinely voluntary; 2) with the informed parental or guardian consent; 3) based on full information of duties and 4) only if there is reliable proof of age. If one or more of these conditions are not met, the recruit under the age of 18 should be considered as forced, even if he or she indicates to have voluntarily joined (Brett and Specht: 2004, 115). It is self-evident that in many countries with poor birth records or in cases of armed conflict causing parents to become separated from their offspring, these conditions are unlikely to be met.

17. As an example of such a reservation: "The United Kingdom understands that article 1 of the Optional Protocol would not exclude the deployment of members of its armed forces under the age of 18 to take a direct part in hostilities where: a) there is a genuine military need to deploy their unit or ship to an area in which hostilities are taking place b) by reason of the nature and urgency of the situation: i) it is not practicable to withdraw such persons before deployment; or ii) to do so would undermine the operational effectiveness of their ship or unit, and thereby put at risk the successful completion of the military

mission and/or the safety of other personnel." See http://www.unhchr.ch/html/menu3/b/treaty17.htm.

18. Christopher Blattman and Jeannie Annan, "On the Nature and Causes of LRA Abduction: What the Abductees Say," forthcoming book chapter, 2008, accessed at http://www.chrisblattman.org/BlattmanAnnan.LRA.pdf

19. In 1973 bank robbers in the Sweden capital Stockholm held four people hostage. Grateful that they were not killed, the hostages started to develop feelings of gratitude to the robbers, or "Stockholm Syndrome."

20. From the 1997 Cape Town Principles (see the appendix of this book).

21. Bernadette A. M. O'Hare and David P. Southall, "First Do No Harm: The Impact of Recent Armed Conflict on Maternal and Child Health in Sub-Saharan Africa," *Journal of the Royal Society of Medicine*, 100 no. 12 (2007): 564–570.

22. See the following sources on female child and adult combatants: Dyan E. Mazurana et al, "Girls in Fighting Forces and Groups: Their Recruitment, Participation, Demobilization, and Reintegration," *Peace and Conflict: Journal of Peace Psychology*, 8 no. 2 (2002): 97–123; Michael G. Wessells, "The Recruitment and Use of Girls in Armed Forces and Groups in Angola: Implications for Ethical Research and Reintegration," Ford Institute for Human Security Working Papers, 2007, accessed at http://www.fordinstitute.pitt.edu/pub-workingpapers.html.

CHAPTER 4

The Disarmament, Demobilization, and Reintegration of Young Ex-Combatants

The Transition from Combatant to Civilian

The population of a state emerging from armed conflict faces enormous challenges, as it must rebuild the country after years or sometimes decades of war. There is an urgent need to rehabilitate and reconstruct buildings such as schools, hospitals, and government offices and to repair roads, bridges, and dams. The national energy grid may have been heavily damaged, as oil and gas pipes and electricity cables are easy targets for the fighting parties. Civilians who have fled the fighting and have been internally displaced or lived outside the country as refugees will return once the situation is considered safe—sometimes before the official peace agreement has been signed. As a result, huge population movements take place with hundreds of thousands of people returning home, or to what remains of their dwellings. In some cases, people's homes or land are occupied by other people, which can give rise to significant tensions during the often fragile early days of the postwar period. But people do not only need to have a house to live in, they also need to start working again. So, abandoned and overgrown fields have to be put into production again, craftsmen's shops rebuilt and reequipped. In fact, it might be the case that the whole local and national economy has to be kick-started again. Local and international companies which closed during the war and which may have had their stock and equipment completely looted have to start operating again to offer people employment opportunities outside the agricultural subsistence sector.

Taking into account that the vast majority of the armed conflicts which have taken place over the last few decades happened in the world's least-developed countries with already weak economies prior to the outbreak of the conflict, one can easily imagine that postwar reconstruction is an immense task. In addition, these countries have to find a way to make a peaceful transition from combatant to civilian possible for the tens of thousands, or sometimes hundreds of thousands, of soldiers and fighters. Failing to do so will pose a direct threat to the recently achieved peace since disgruntled ex-combatants may start to cause mayhem or even take up (secretly hidden) arms again. Former combatants may be unwilling to completely disarm or demobilize when they know that there are no proper disarmament incentives or reintegration prospects in place. The highly fragile situation of countries which have recently moved out of war is illustrated by the finding that these countries have a 40 percent chance for conflict to reemerge within five years after the end of hostilities, with each subsequent year of peace lowering this chance by 1 percent.[1]

It has now become standard practice that peace-accords include provisions for a so-called "Disarmament, Demobilization and Reintegration" (DDR) program. Such a program will have to stipulate how the fighters and commanders of the armed factions will be disarmed, when this should start and in what time frame the whole process should be completed, who will be responsible and actually execute the disarmament, and who will organize and implement the various reintegration projects.

Recently, the United Nations established a special UN Disarmament, Demobilization and Reintegration Resource Centre, which has formulated a comprehensive set of policies, guidelines, and procedures on DDR: the Integrated DDR Standards (IDDRS).[2] The formulation of these standards underlines again the extent to which DDR programs have now become a standard and important part of the postwar transition process. The official UN definition[3] of each of the stages of DDR is as follows:

Disarmament

Disarmament is the collection, documentation, control, and disposal of small arms, ammunition, explosives, and light and heavy weapons of combatants and often also of the civilian population. Disarmament also includes the development of responsible arms management programs.

Demobilization

Demobilization is the formal and controlled discharge of active combatants from armed forces or other armed groups. The first stage of demobilization may extend from the processing of individual combatants in temporary centers to the massing of troops in camps designated for this purpose (cantonment sites, encampments, assembly areas, or barracks). The second stage of demobilization encompasses the support package provided to the demobilized, which is called reinsertion.

Reinsertion

Reinsertion is the assistance offered to ex-combatants during demobilization but prior to the longer-term process of reintegration. Reinsertion is a form of transitional assistance to help cover the basic needs of ex-combatants and their families and can include transitional safety allowances, food, clothes, shelter, medical services, short-term education, training, employment, and tools. While reintegration is a long-term, continuous social and economic process of development, reinsertion is a short-term material and/or financial assistance to meet immediate needs, and can last up to one year.

Reintegration

Reintegration is the process by which ex-combatants acquire civilian status and gain sustainable employment and income. Reintegration is essentially a social and economic process with an open time-frame, primarily taking place in communities at the local level. It is part of the general development of a country and a national responsibility, and often necessitates long-term external assistance.

Since DDR programs are often part of the peace-accord, they normally are implemented after it is signed.[4] During the war, government and armed opposition forces are unlikely to voluntarily participate in an exercise which reduces their number of fighters and thus their military strength. However, where it concerns those under the age of 18 who are part of the military forces or rebels, this is not the case. Since it is a crime under international law to have children participating in armed combat, governments and rebel organizations should actively support the disarmament and demobilization of these children. Hence, DDR programs for child soldiers sometimes start to run while the conflict is still going on. Nevertheless, the reluctance of commanders to give up their fighters, even child soldiers, remains. Those advocating for the disarmament and demobilization of children that are a part of the fighting forces thus have to find ways to pressure the government and the rebels to give up these children. One way is to expose governments who have children in their army; "naming and shaming" can be an effective tool, particularly if a government is looking for the goodwill and support of the international community and donors. This is one of the functions of the UN Special Representative of the Secretary-General for Children and Armed Conflict. Another body that is mandated to do this is the UN office for the High Commissioner for Human Rights. In addition, for those countries that have signed and ratified the UNCRC, the UN Committee on the Rights of the Child will monitor its application, including optional protocols (if signed and ratified). This committee is an independent body of 18 experts elected by the state parties to the UNCRC. The UNCRC presents a new generation of human rights treaties which clearly identify the state parties as duty bearers. As duty bearers, they have the obligation to respect, protect, facilitate, and provide children's rights.

Transitional Justice and Child Combatants

As part of the transition from violent conflict or authoritarian regime toward democracy, societies can choose to undertake a range of judicial and nonjudicial approaches to address past human rights abuse. This is normally referred to as "transitional justice." So-called "Truth and Reconciliations Commissions" (TRC) and "War Tribunals or Courts" are two of the most widely used approaches implemented by post-conflict countries. The question of whether or not underage combatants who committed atrocities and war crimes and who may even have held commanding positions should be held accountable for their actions (and ultimately be tried for them) has caused heated debates. The consensus that has emerged is that ex-child soldiers can be asked to give testimonies in (closed) TRC hearings; this is also because the willingness to participate in these hearings gives a positive signal to the wider community the child will be reintegrating into. However, indictments of underage ex-combatants by War Tribunals is not considered good practice, and in the rare cases where underage ex-fighters are tried, the sentences should be restorative-oriented rather than retributive (such as imprisonment or the death penalty).

You can find out more about Transitional Justice through the following sources:

— International Centre for Transitional Justice, at http://www.ictj.org.
— "Expert Discussion on Children and Transitional Justice" (2008) at http://www.unicef-irc.org/knowledge_pages/resource_pages/trans_justice/.

Rebel organizations often prove less sensitive to the above mentioned practice of "naming and shaming." Almost by default, rebel organizations cannot be supported by other countries, or at least not overtly, since this would violate the sovereignty principle of a country.[5] Hence, it makes little sense to threaten the withdrawal of support for rebel groups who use child combatants. And some rebel organizations—such as the RUF in Sierra Leone and the LRA in Uganda—operate in near-complete isolation and/or are supported by dubious regimes, and thus seem to have little concern about what the outside world thinks of them and whether they are condemned or not. This makes it difficult for those advocating for the release or demobilization of child soldiers at a more grass-roots level. Practitioners working for organizations such as UNICEF, Save the Children, the International Committee of the Red Cross, or the International Rescue Committee visit military barracks and talk to commanders to explain the law and demand the release of children. In such cases, approval to do so is often already given by the Ministry of Defense or commander in chief.

However, entering rebel territory may be an extremely dangerous endeavor, in particular since the impartial and neutral principles of these organizations are not always respected anymore.[6] In addition, command structures can be much more fluent in a rebel group; child-focused agencies may pass a rebel checkpoint without problems only to be turned back at the next one because a different commander is in charge, not fully recognizing the authority of the first. In such cases, NGOs have to come up with more creative ways to facilitate the demobilization or self-demobilization of child soldiers. One way can be to work with other service providers. Perhaps health workers are allowed to enter rebel territory, and can beforehand be asked to be on the lookout for underage conscripts. Perhaps civilians have access to the rebel territory, such as market women or traders, and they can be of help. At least they may be able to give a better idea of the situation and number of underage conscripts in rebel-held territory.

Another method of encouraging the demobilization and self-demobilization of child conscripts in both the army and armed opposition forces is the use of informative messages during radio broadcasts of popular (music) programs. Pointing out that conscription of underage combatants is a violation of a series of international laws and subject to punishment may help, but equally or more helpful is providing accurate information to fighters about what will happen if they (self-) demobilize. A child soldier may be reluctant to self-demobilize (escape) or ask to be demobilized, because he or she is afraid of what will happen to him or her; will she or he punished or even executed, and will she or he have to care for her- or himself, looking for food and shelter? Once child combatants are aware that they will not be punished or put in jail and that in fact a program is awaiting to assist them in demobilizing, a program in which they would receive food, shelter, education, and skills training, many young combatants will be more likely to look for an opportunity to leave the army or rebel movement.

But while a considerable part of the total number of child combatants will disarm, demobilize, and reintegrate before the end of the war, the majority will demobilize at the end of the conflict, at the same time as the adult fighters.

The Disarmament of Child Soldiers in Liberia

Liberia was one of the few countries in Africa that was never colonized by a European country. However, it maintained strong links with the U.S., since former slaves in the U.S. who wanted to return to Africa were supported to settle down in Liberia. Until 1980, Liberia was ruled by the "True Whig Party", an elite party protecting the interests of the minority, so-called "Americo-Liberians," against the indigenous population that made up more than 95 percent of Liberia's inhabitants. In 1980 Samuel Doe, a member of the Krahn ethnic group, staged a successful coup and became the first indigenous president of the country. Politics became increasingly ethnic-based, and in 1989 the Americo-Liberian Charles Taylor invaded the country from neighboring Ivory Coast, soon gathering support from the Mano and Gio ethnic groups which were oppressed by the Doe regime. An armed conflict started which continued for more than 13 years.

All the factions involved in the fighting, sometimes more than six or seven at one time, had underage fighters among their ranks. In 1997, with Taylor's NPFL as the dominant force, elections were held, and under the slogan "He killed my ma, he killed my pa, but I'll vote for him," Taylor won. Although the elections were considered fair by international observers, it was widely believed that not voting for Taylor would reignite the war, something that happened anyway in 2000. A DDR program was implemented toward the end of 1996, but there were no special provisions in the peace-accord for underage fighters. NGOs working with children lobbied intensely to put the issue of child soldiers on the agenda of the Liberian government and of those in charge of the DDR process (ECOMOG and UNOMIL). One of their successes was that underage fighters did not necessarily have to present a weapon at a DDR site to be accepted as an ex-combatant and to benefit from support. This was crucial, as in many cases commanders would confiscate the weapons beforehand to hand them over to older fighters or sell them to anyone who considered it beneficial to register as an ex-combatant.

About 4,000 child soldiers passed through the DDR program (out of a total number of 20,000 fighters). A considerable number of these 4,000 child soldiers may not have been genuine fighters at all, but children who wanted to benefit from the DDR provisions. On the other hand, it was estimated that for each child soldier passing through DDR, another three or four did not do so and rather informally demobilized themselves, making the actual number of children involved in the conflict much higher. It is important to realize that up to the moment of physical separation (and in many cases after that as well) the commander had considerable power over his or her child soldiers. Deliberately misinforming or making children afraid of the DDR program can easily be done by a commander, if it works to his advantage.

Seven steps to disarmament were distinguished in the Liberian case and are presented in Table 4.1.[7] These are illustrated by comments of the ex-child soldiers in the right-hand column.

Conflict started again in Liberia in 2000 and final peace did not come before President Taylor stepped down in 2003. The 2003 Comprehensive Peace Agreement included a program of cantonment[8], disarmament, demobilization, rehabilitation, and reintegration (CDDRR). UNICEF coordinated the process for underage combatants. More than 10 percent of the 100,000 combatants that were disarmed were children, with spontaneous disarmament of child soldiers already going on before the final peace agreement. Nearly a quarter of the demobilized child soldiers were girls.[9] Within a year of starting of the disarmament process, nearly all former child soldiers had been reunited with their families.

Contrary to the 1996–97 DDR program, underage combatants going through disarmament received a US $300 safety-net (demobilization) allowance, just like the adult ex-fighters. This made some ex-child soldiers vulnerable to exploitation by their former commanders, since the already rapid demobilization process did not always sufficiently break the links between former commander and ex-child combatant. On the other hand, some of the ex-child soldiers who did return to their communities later reunited with their commanders anyway, because the commanders were able to provide them with food, protection, and shelter in the difficult postwar reconstruction period.[10]

The Reinsertion Process

Once underage combatants have disarmed and been demobilized—that is, physically been separated from their units and commanders—those who design and implement the DDR program for underage fighters are confronted with a dilemma. A part of the ex-child combatants may be aware of the whereabouts of their family and could thus reunite with them without many problems. Being with family or relatives is normally considered to be "in the best interest of the child", or at least preferable to being away from and staying with strangers or in an institution. On the other hand, and it is here where the dilemma becomes clear, many ex-child soldiers are traumatized and need some assistance in adapting to a civilian life again.[11] Family reunification straight after demobilization may put both the ex-child combatant and his or her family under enormous pressure, which can result in the child running away from home to live on the street or rejoin his or her former comrades in arms.

Obviously, one cannot generalize, and each case should be assessed on an individual basis. Some ex-child soldiers are deeply traumatized, while others seem to have come out of the conflict more or less unaffected. Some struggle with a drug habit or are easily triggered into violent behavior, while others are not. In addition, the social and economic situation of the receiving family may frustrate an otherwise smooth reintegration process. If only some family members have returned to their place of birth, struggling to meet their daily needs in a village damaged by years of fighting, it is not unthinkable that the young ex-combatant may decide to leave his or her place of birth and subsequently drift back to the army or rebel movement. Another factor which influences the success level of self reintegration—which refers to those who only go through disarmament and demobilization and do not receive any reinsertion or reintegration support, or to those who do not even go through official disarmament and demobilization—is the popularity of the fighting faction that the ex-child combatant belonged to.

Those who fought with a faction perceived by civilians as "good"—because they protected civilians and their belongings—may be welcomed back by their families and communities and supported in the reintegration process. But those who were affiliated with the "bad" faction—one that committed atrocities and harassed civilians—may encounter a high level of overt and covert resistance by the community in the reintegration process. In such cases, it can be helpful if NGO or Community Based Organization (CBO) workers advocate on behalf of these ex-child combatants. And even with the efforts of these social workers, there is still a fair chance that self-demobilized child soldiers, as well as those ex-child soldiers who received reinsertion support, who belonged to infamous government or rebel organizations will end up away from their families, reintegrating in urban settings or mining camps where they can live more anonymous lives.

Table 4.1 Seven Steps of Disarmament

Step 1	Fighters, both children and adults, arrived at the disarmament site—often a schoolbuidling or military barracks—with their weapons. Their commander was likely to be with them.	We were with 36 soldiers. We lined up and disarmed voluntarily.
Step 2	Those with weapons handed these over to the peace-keeping forces (in this case ECOMOG forces) who checked whether or not the weapon was serviceable. Child soldiers did not need to present a weapon to qualify.	I gave my weapon to the commander and he gave it to the ECOMOG soldiers. I was afraid to carry my gun to ECOMOG because they were our enemy
Step 3	Name and age were documented and a picture was taken for an identity card. But social workers indicated that it took days, if not weeks before children really trusted the NGO staff and started to give the correct information.	I refused to let them take my picture. But they gave me provisions.
Step 4	UNICEF staff conducted another interview after which Save the Children staff interviewed each child soldier to gather information for the family tracing teams and to identify those who were in need of special protection in the meantime.	He [social worker] asked questions about my parents and if I missed them during the war. I had enough time to express my problems and I trusted the person.
Step 5	Adult and child fighters underwent a quick medical check in a special room	He [the nurse] gave me a tablet.

(continued)

| Step 6 | The ex-child combatants received coupons which were supposed to be exchanged for education or vocational training. Due to lack of donor commitment the funds to make this happen were never put in place. All fighters were supplied with 25kg (55 lbs) of bulgur [wheat] and a gallon of vegetable oil, but the children often received less and/or had to hand it over to their commander. | We were taken to the demobilization site by the ECOMOG soldiers. We had to stand in line, and we gave in our weapons. They took a photograph for the ID [identity] card. Then we were given a bag of bulgur wheat, oil and some other provisions. |
| Step 7 | Those who knew the whereabouts of their relatives could use (in theory) UNOMIL trucks to get home. But since there were only a few trucks available, many ex-child combatants in the end returned to their commanders. The more determined ones had to sell their DDR provisions to get money for private transport. | Some boys went straight home but others went straight back to their commanders. |

Krijn Peters and Sophie Laws, "When Children Affected By War Go Home: Lessons Learned from Liberia," Save the Children report. © Save the Children, 2001. Reprinted with the permission of Save the Children.

Residential Care

It is partly for the above mentioned reasons that it is now common practice to provide institutionalized care for ex-child combatants for a certain period of time. So-called "Interim Care Centers" (ICCs) or "Transit Centers" (TCs) have been established by a number of local, national, and international NGOs and international organizations—or in some cases by the army itself—during and after a conflict. These centers aim to provide a safe environment in which the ex-child fighters are helped with their transition from a fighter's life to that of a civilian. The time spent in these centers can vary, but on average it is about six to nine months. During this time, the ex-child soldiers receive education and skills training and enjoy recreational activities, which will be discussed in more detail below. They are provided with shelter, food, and medical care, and they often take part in formal and informal counseling activities, which help them to overcome the traumatic experiences that many have had. The overall aim of these activities is to bring some structure and routine back into the lives of these young people, since their days within the army or rebel movement were often character-ized by irregular hours of work, wherein weeks of relatively little activity were fol-lowed by intense periods of fighting. All of the above listed activities are helpful in bringing back a more normal daily rhythm, which in return helps the young ex-combatants to deal with their psychological and mental issues.

Residential or Community-Based Care?

While interim-care centers clearly offer advantages—more equal and standardized support, low logistical demands, a special environment offering protection to heavily traumatized children, etc.—there are also some problems with residential care. Care centers do not reflect the common living situation of a child (which is with a family), and they often provide better living conditions than what is the norm outside the center, making children less willing to leave and even attracting non-ex-combatant children. They can also be an attractive target for militias in search of new man-power, since the center's residents have per definition experience with serving in an armed faction.

Different child organizations have experimented with alternative forms of care, mainly small-group living in the community and foster parent care. Successes have varied, and it seems that residential care will still be needed, in particular where large groups of underage combatants disarm in a short time frame and are unlikely to be aware of the whereabouts of their family.

You can find more on residential care in the following source:

• Glenn Miles and Paul Stephenson, *Children in Residential Care and Alternatives. Children at risk guidelines*, accessed at http://tilz.tearfund.org/webdocs/Tilz/Topics/CareENG_full%20doc(1).pdf.

If a clear need is identified to have residential care provided to ex-child combatants, a series of issues has to be dealt with. To start with, the physical location of the center—or, more likely, centers—has to be decided upon; obviously, if it is too close to the war front (if the war is still going on) or in an instable region, this might put the life of the children in the center at risk. But a location that is too far away from the place where the children originate from may hinder their reintegration process as they may be unfamiliar with the language or customs in the community in which the center would be located. Related to the issue of the center's location is the relationship of the center with civilian communities. Although locating the center far away from a town may be preferred by the inhabitants of the town who are likely not too eager to have a group of ex-child combatants as their next-door neighbors, remoteness will again negatively affect the reintegration opportunities of these young people, since they will then have fewer opportunities to interact with civilians. This is also the reason why these centers should not be fenced, which, if done, would make daily interaction with civilians more difficult and will stigmatize the ex-child combatants even further.

As far as the building itself, it has to be sufficiently large, with separate rooms for daily activities and classes and sufficient dormitories—enabling boys and girls to sleep in separated rooms. There should be a kitchen area, toilets and washing facilities (again separated for boys and girls) and staff offices. Rather than having these centers purposely built, they tend to be located in temporarily unused school buildings, council structures, barracks (abandoned by the military or belonging to scouts groups) or even in abandoned hotels—likely to have closed because of the war anyway.

Let us now have a closer look at the activities that take part in these centers—or, in the case of nonresidential care, are provided within the community—aimed at helping children to deal with their past lives and prepare them for their future lives.

Catch-Up Education

Few child soldiers benefitted from formal education while they were with the army or in an armed faction, although in some cases child soldiers may still have received some education. This might have occurred if they served in shifts, being at the war front for some time and then in safer camps or territories at other times where they may have benefitted from education, particularly if it is part of the political or ideological agenda of the armed faction. But even in this scenario, the amount of education received is likely to be limited. Thus, in general, each year spent as a child soldier is a lost year as far as education is concerned. Some child soldiers may spend five or ten years within a faction, and only demobilize once the conflict ends. In addition, most armed conflicts in which child soldiers fight occur in poor countries with already weak educational provisions. Likely, the war will only worsen the educational situation when schools are attacked, abandoned by their teachers or left without government funding. As a result, many child soldiers may have only spent a few years in school at best, of which most is likely be forgotten by the time they come out of the armed faction. So, a 16-year-old ex-child soldier can have the educational level of an eight-year-old civilian child.

But for understandable reasons, it is considered problematic to enroll a 16-year-old boy or girl in year two or three of a primary school. He or she has to sit together with very young children, which is likely to be experienced as being rather embarrassing. And although the 16-year-old's reading, writing, and arithmetic skills may be of a low level, the former child combatant is socially and emotionally much older than the eight-year-old child. Consequently, the ex-child soldiers in ICCs are provided with a so-called "catch-up education" or "accelerated learning program" (ALP). This is a compressed curriculum, designed to quickly bring them to a level more in line with their age. Although no wonders can be expected from this special form of education, the lower teacher-pupil ratio can be very effective. It is well possible that after 6 to 12 months of "catch-up education" the ex-child soldier may enroll at a normal school, in a class close to his or her age group.

Vocational Training

Basic literacy and numeracy skills are important for everyone. But the reality for many ex-child combatants is that they have missed so many years of education that it is unlikely that they will have an "academic" career, exceptions excluded. Continuing their education will mean that they remain dependent on sponsors willing to pay their school fees and provide for their daily needs for many years after they leave the ICC. Some indeed try to continue their education, often with intervals in which they look for some work to earn enough to pay for another semester or year in school. But the majority of the slightly older ex-child soldiers usually prefer to be trained in a vocational skill, with the expectation that they will be able to make a living out of their training once they have returned to their communities or places of reintegration.

In general, the most common skills which are made available to ex-child combatants when they are in an ICC are carpentry, tailoring, and masonry. Popular among girl ex-combatants in particular are skills like hairdressing and soap-making. Obviously, one expects that the skills offered reflect the most common skills practiced in a country, and thus one should account for national or regional differences. Other popular skills that are sometimes offered are car mechanics or computer skills.

The daily vocational training can be given in the ICC, with special craftsmen or women coming in to teach the children, or it can be provided outside the center, perhaps at a vocational training institute or at a crafts place, where the young ex-combatants become apprentices. The advantage of the external training is that it facilitates the reintegration process since the ex-child combatants will mix with other children and apprentices. But where training in the center is chosen, the center can still allow civilian children (from the neighborhood, for example) to participate in the sessions to promote reintegration.

While it seems that the youthful ex-combatants stand a better chance to gain some sustainable income in the future if they decide to learn a skill, rather than continuing their formal education, there are nevertheless several difficulties associated with skills training. First, some skills may be appropriate, but only in a certain context. An ex-child combatant may learn how to repair automobiles, but if he or she originates from a small village where only a handful of cars pass each day, it is unlikely that the skill will be of any use, unless he or she leaves the village and settles down in an urban center. Other skills may be much preferred by the young people since they are associated with modern life, but the overall demand is likely to be low. For instance, ex-combatants who were trained in computer skills in Sierra Leone were in the end extremely unlikely to find a job in the country's tiny information technology sector. For other skills, such as carpentry or tailoring, there is a much greater demand. Here however, the ex-child combatants have to compete with craftsmen who have been carpenters or tailors for many years and who are much more skilled. Six or nine months of skills training in an ICC will teach the basics, but it does not turn one into a fully-trained and skilled craftsman. Thus, partly-trained ex-combatants need further training before they are likely to be able to make a living out of their training. Continuing one's skills training in a formal vocational training center is one way, but as with continuing formal education, this requires someone or some organization that is willing and capable to pay fees and a basic living allowance. Becoming an apprentice is another way to further training, and although the apprentices are unlikely to be paid well or be paid at all, their basic needs are taken care of by the master.

Sports and Recreational Activities

Play and sport usually make up an important part of the day in an ICC. Keeping the young people busy is helpful in taking their minds away from the things they did and experienced while they were with the armed group, and it helps them to get rid of extra energy in a nonviolent way. Through sports and games, ex-child combatants also learn how to settle disputes without resorting to force. Peer pressure is helpful in this regard, since the group will not permit one or two children to spoil the game with rough play. Games between ex-child combatants of different factions or between ex-child combatants and civilian children are excellent ways to work toward reconciliation and reintegration. The participation of children of the nearby community in the games is also helpful in encouraging the community to accept the ICC, since it often is an initial source of fear and concern for the community.

Football as Reconciliation

In 1997 a "historic" football match took place in Liberia. Boys (and some girls) from the Virginia center played against those of the Gbarnga center, two Interim Care Centers ran by the Save the Children UK's Liberia program. They were all ex-child soldiers, but the Virginia players were mainly associated with an armed faction calling itself the Liberia Peace Council (LPC) or with the United Liberation Movement of Liberia for Democracy (ULIMO), while the Gbarnga boys were predominately ex-National Patriotic Front of Liberia (NPFL) fighters. Staff of both centers were nervous for days in advance; how would the two former enemies react to each other? When the bus with the Virginia players and supporters arrived at the football field in Gbarnga, one boy took off his white shirt and held it outside the bus window. This triggered a huge round of applause and all the children started to sing, dance and celebrate. The staff was relieved. And although the Gbarnga boys lost the match, it felt like everybody had won that day.

You can read more about ex-child soldiers in Liberia through the following sources:

— G. Schembri, *Liberia's ex-child fighters: a narrative account of the work of SC UK in Liberia*, 1997
— Krijn Peters & Sophie Laws,*When Children Affected By War Go Home: Lessons Learned From Liberia* (Save the Children, 2003), accessed at http:// www.savethechildren .org.uk/en/54_5220.htm.

Counseling and Therapy

The need for some form of counseling or therapy for former child soldiers seems obvious: the majority of ex-child soldiers have experienced multiple and highly traumatic events, during the course of many years. These include the witnessing of and participating in killings, torture, torching of civilians, body mutilations, and rape and gang-rapes, including those of friends or family members. In many cases the children have been victims of some of the above traumatic experiences themselves; many have been tortured, perhaps when they were captured by the enemy or simply if they did not follow orders from their own commander. Others have been raped repeatedly. While most civilians, including children, have been affected by the war, few have been exposed to it as intensely and regularly as former child combatants. The level and amount of traumatic experiences can be so high that one wonders if the children can ever again live normal lives, where their lives are not dominated by terrible memories of the past.

Post-Traumatic Stress Disorder (PTSD)

Reactions to traumas, such as being tortured or having to torture someone else or witnessing the killing of a person or killing a person oneself, can be neurological, evoking anxiety and intense fear; somatic, resulting in stomachaches and headaches; mental or psychological, causing nightmares or flashbacks; and social, for instance resulting in fighting or social isolation.[12]

In the 1980s and 1990s, programs working with children affected by war increasingly started to use expatriate consultants who provided therapy. These therapeutic sessions were typically based on psychiatric models from the West. The majority of young people in war situations (child soldiers and internally displaced and refugee children) were diagnosed as suffering from post-traumatic stress disorder (PTSD), a disorder first diagnosed among American Vietnam War veterans.

However, halfway through the 1990s the first criticism of this model—developed in a Western context but universally applied—started to emerge. It is now more widely acknowledged that the social and cultural context is of great importance in shaping a child's experience of suffering and his or her response to it. Moreover, not all traumatic effects necessarily have to be attributed to the war experiences. And PTSD only captures a specific part of the problems and worries of children. Too much focus on trauma can divert attention from a child's wider needs, which can be psychological but equally very practical in nature: acquiring a daily meal, good shelter, protection, or school fees.

You can find more on war-affected children and trauma in

— Patrick J. Bracken and Celia Petty, eds. *Rethinking the Trauma of War*, London: Save the Children with Free Association Books, 1998
— Alcinda Honwana, *Child soldiers in Africa*, Philadelphia: University of Pennsylvania Press, 2005

Nevertheless, many former child combatants seem to live normal lives and do not seem to be troubled by their past, or at least not to the level that it affects their daily functioning. How do they cope with their past and how were they helped in coping with this?

To begin with, it is important to realize that not all child soldiers have been exposed to the same kind and level of traumatic experiences. Some child soldiers who predominantly carried out domestic tasks for commanders and remained in the barracks might have witnessed few traumatic events, while others who operated on the frontlines fought and committed atrocities. There can also be huge variations in the length of exposure—some child combatants have been with the fighters for only a few days or weeks, while others have been part of an armed faction for many years. Both these variables will affect the level and the extent to which a child is traumatized by his or her past experiences. But there are other factors which influence the level of trauma developed that are not directly related to wartime experiences. For instance, the genetic makeup of a child plays a role, as does the social network he or she has access to and his or her coping strategies. These are all factors which contribute to a child's "resilience", which refers to the ability of children to "bounce back" from traumatic events and experiences.

Nevertheless, many programs helping ex-child soldiers with their transition to civilian life include some form of counseling or therapy. These can vary from structured one-on-one sessions with a psychologist or psychiatrist to group sessions wherein through means of drama or creative arts, ex-child combatants are encouraged to reflect on their past lives and subsequently to focus on their strengths and the future.

There is now an emerging understanding that counseling or therapeutic sessions have to have some resonance with practices of healing and helping that are common in the specific culture. As with so many programs that aim to help people, Western blueprint approaches are not always helpful, and can even be counterproductive.

Family Tracing and Reunification

An armed conflict often creates large population movements as people flee from their place of birth because it has become too dangerous and look for refuge within or outside the country. Often, displaced people and refugees will stay in more than one camp during the course of the war, perhaps because a specific camp becomes too close to the frontline or because refugees find out that other camps are better protected or catered for. Against this background, ex-child soldiers, who may have spent five or even ten years with an armed faction, away from home and relatives, then have to find their parents or family members after being demobilized. It is no small wonder, then, that a considerable percentage of former child combatants need help with this. Even those who, upon disarmament, clearly state that they know the location of their village or the whereabouts of their relatives may find it difficult to locate their families, exactly because of the above mentioned effects of armed conflicts: a village may be abandoned, and relatives may not yet have returned or even have been killed.

Child agencies helping ex-child soldiers can establish so-called Family Tracing and Reunification (FTR) teams. These teams try to gather as much information as possible from former child combatants in order to locate their family and home town. Sometimes children know very few details, particularly if they have been abducted or joined an armed group at a very young age. They may even have forgotten their real name, only knowing their *nom de guerre*. But from bits and pieces of information, such as language and ethnic markers, the moment of conscription and by which faction, or specific characteristics of the landscape around the village or town (a river, bridge, or dam, for example) some idea about the location of their place of birth can be gained. At the same time, the FTR teams can use the large database often established by UNHCR in a conflict-affected country which documents missing persons. Most internally displaced and refugee camps have a special wall of an office or building which shows hundreds if not thousands of pictures of people who have lost and are looking for someone. If all agencies work together, a large network is created in which cases of separated family members are often solved.

Although it may sound strange, not all ex-combatants provide the FTR teams with the information they need. Sometimes the young people deliberately withhold information about the likely whereabouts of their parents or the location of their village. An obvious reason is that they just do not yet trust the people involved in the FTR. But even when the young people know that they have nothing to fear from these social workers, they can still withhold information. To understand this

Figure 4.3. Drawing by a Former Child Soldier in Sierra Leone Reprinted with permission of Krijn Peters.

Figure 4.2. Drawing by a Former Child Soldier in Sierra Leone Reprinted with permission of Krijn Peters.

93

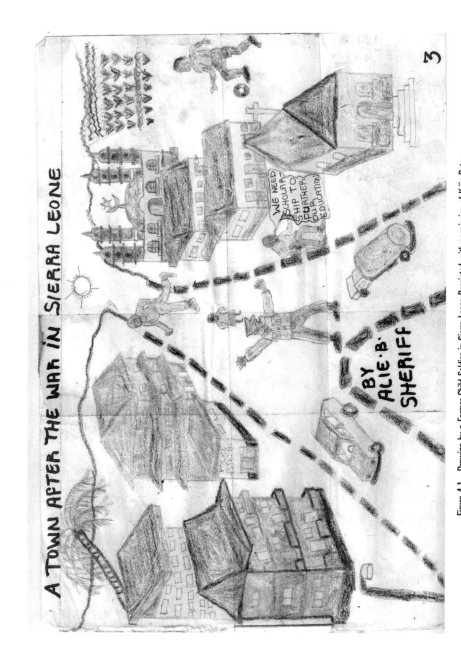

Figure 4.1. Drawing by a Former Child Soldier in Sierra Leone Reprinted with permission of Krijn Peters.

we have to recall the reasons why some of the underage people decided to affiliate themselves with an armed faction in the first place. Some people joined because they had no or limited access to education, no job prospects, or because they came from very poor backgrounds. Going back home means that they return to this situation and likely to an even a worse one because of the destruction of the war. However, if they can frustrate the family tracing process, they can stay longer in the ICCs, benefiting from all the provisions offered, such as education, vocational training, shelter, and two or three meals a day. In addition, the ICCs are often located in or near a town or urban area, which can be much more attractive to these youngsters than a rural village with no running water or electricity.

Stuck in the Center?

The overwhelming majority of ex-child combatants who stay in an ICC are in the end reunited with their parents or extended family. But there will always be a small group of children whose families cannot be identified. These children are the true war orphans. They are likely to stay in the ICC much longer than the average child, perhaps moving from one center to the other as they start to close down, but at some point even the last ICC will close. What to do next? One option is to find foster parents. Another option, more suitable for the slightly older ex-child combatants, is group home living, which entails a small number of boys and girls (typically between 5 and 10) living together under the supervision of a social worker.

Sometimes ex-child combatants withhold information out of fear of being reunited with their families. Some of the ex-child combatants have been forced to commit atrocities in their village of birth, such as killing community members or even family members. These children probably fear the moment they return to their place of birth and are afraid to be refused to resettle or even to be avenged, despite the fact that they have been forced to commit these atrocities. One can imagine that it takes weeks, if not months, of trust-building between an ex-child combatant and staff member of an ICC before this kind of information is revealed. And it may take an equally long period of time to convince the child that it is safe to return to the place of birth, despite his or her fears.

This last point brings us to the actual reunification process. The majority of children will be happy to be reunited with their parents and family members, and vice versa. But even in the case where a smooth, problem-free reunification is foreseen, it is important that the FTR teams assess the situation beforehand rather than turning up unexpectedly with the child at his or her parents' front door. Obviously, this is even more important when it is known that the child has committed atrocities in the village or community. In such cases, meetings with the parents, family members, community members, traditional leaders, religious leaders, schoolteachers, etc. can be held to inform and explain that although the child in question has committed atrocities, he or she was forced to do so.

A major concern of the community is often whether or not the child is of any danger to the peace in the community: does he still have "rebel blood" in him, or is his heart peaceful? A community can suggest to conduct a purifying or "cleansing" ritual, if this is part of its culture to do so. Such a ritual can entail that upon being received by the community, the child is asked to take off his military clothes (or clothes associated with his or her past), which are then burned. The child is then provided with a new set of civilian clothes and is welcomed back in the community. Sometimes the child is required to fast for a certain number of days or to perform some rituals or services in order to make him or her a full member of the community again. While in general these traditional rituals should be considered as supportive of the child's reintegration process, reintegration rituals which inflict physical pain or which are emotionally or psychologically damaging should be discouraged by the FTR teams.

Reintegration: A Diverse Reality

The reinsertion process, including the time spent in an Interim Care Center, is only the first step on the long road toward full community reintegration. The catch-up education, the counseling, and the vocational skills training are all aimed at helping the young people in their long-term reintegration process. The concept of reintegration is an important one, but it is equally very complex. Evidence gathered over a number of years shows clearly that only a part of the ex-child combatants will return and stay with their parents after they have been demobilized. Others will live with friends or relatives, for instance in urban or mining centers. There is even a group who will continue to stay with their commanders in a postwar setting. For instance, research conducted in Liberia in 2000 found that 27 percent were living with their parents, while 23 percent were living alone or with friends. Most (33 percent) were living with extended family members.[13]

The idea that successful reintegration equals reunification and living with one's parents is too limited. In many developing countries not experiencing conflict, it is common practice for adolescents to temporarily leave their parents' house or village of birth to live with family in urban areas where they can attend secondary schools or take up apprenticeships. Young people of poor households are expected or required to leave to look for some way to earn cash by working on a plantation or in a mining area or in town. In short, a young person living away from his or her parents is not an abnormality in developing countries. Moreover, ex-child combatants present a special category since in many cases they have been exposed to an urban life already and have travelled widely during their years within the army or armed faction. While being with the armed faction, they have experienced a very different life than what they would have experienced if they had continued to live in their village, and it is much more difficult to adapt to such a life again after the war. Some ex-child combatants claim that they miss the excitement of the war years, and the least likely place to encounter some of that excitement is in a remote village where one almost by default has to engage oneself in farming. It is therefore of little surprise that many of the older ex-child combatants in particular do not return to their families, or leave them after a short period of time, to look for a different and more exciting lifestyle.

Research on the medium- and longer-term reintegration of ex-child combatants is still limited. Child agencies are often overstretched and as a result focus mainly on lessons learned about the disarmament and demobilization of child soldiers, the functioning of Interim Care Centers, and the reunification process. Sometimes, a follow-up visit with the ex-child combatant by an NGO takes place, but since the needs are often overwhelming in post-conflict countries, priorities are likely to be given to other issues. Many NGOs decide to leave a postwar country after two or three years and move on to the next humanitarian emergency. And many of the child combatants have moved on themselves, making it much more difficult to locate them.

Nevertheless, it seems that the majority of the ex-child combatants do reintegrate, whether this means living with their parents or family or living away from them, and they are not worse off than their counterparts who have not actively participated in the conflict. This is quite an achievement and testimony of the remarkable resilience of these young people, taking into account the intense and prolonged trauma many of them must have experienced. But how exactly do we know whether or not ex-child combatants have reintegrated? How do we measure "reintegration"?

Social and Economic Reintegration

To start with, we can distinguish between reintegration indicators that are more focused on social aspects and those more focused on economic ones. Some of the indicators which fall into the category of social reintegration include whether the young people live with their parents (or family, if their parents have died). This is generally considered an indication of "successful" social reintegration. If they live together with other youths, on the street, or with their former commanders, this can suggest that they experienced difficulties in being accepted in their home community and have failed to fully reintegrate. As mentioned, cases should not be judged from statistics; it may be perfectly normal that a 16 year old ex-child combatant lives with other young people away from his parents in a mining camp working as a miner. Such a situation has more to do with the fact that this is a common scenario for people from poor backgrounds than with the fact that the child has been a former fighter. Other indicators of social reintegration can be for instance whether or not the ex-child combatant is going to school, is a member of sport team or a youth association, or indicates that he or she has many friends in the neighborhood, in particular if these are non ex-combatant friends. In many cases, a good indication is whether or not the person in question indicates that he or she feels accepted by, and has reintegrated into, the community. This question can also be put to family, friends, religious leaders, traditional authorities, and teachers: do they feel that the young person has reintegrated and is just like any other youth, or is there still something that sets him or her apart which can be related to the child's former life as an ex-combatant?

For those ex-child combatants who are slightly older—around the age of 15 and above—reintegration also has economic aspects to it. Questions to ask include: have they been granted a plot of farmland to start growing their own crops; are they trusted enough to be lent money to; if they want to cultivate a field or build a dwelling, are there people who will support them with the work; and are they still the ones who will take over (part of) the shop or farm once their father or mother has grown old or died? Are they employed—which indicates that their employer trusts them—or are they self-employed?

Conclusion

The disarmament, demobilization, and reintegration of ex-combatants is a complex and difficult process, and it is not any easier where it concerns underage ex-combatants. This chapter has discussed many of the steps that have to be taken to support the transition process from fighter to civilian for young people. Over the years, nongovernmental organizations and international bodies have built up a wealth of experience in helping former child soldiers in this process, and now a series of "best practices" have been formulated. However, helping war-affected young people, including former child soldiers, can never be based on blueprint models. Each and every former child soldier presents a unique history and set of strengths and weaknesses which require individual and tailor-made approaches and support. The challenge, therefore, is to think beyond pre-defined ideas of what children need and what successful reintegration is. Reintegration, including reconciliation, is most likely to succeed if communities are involved. In the end, organizations helping ex-child combatants turn their attention to other children in need in other war-affected countries, and ways to fully reintegrate and live a life like any other child or youth, should be found by the child, his or her family, and the community.

The reintegration of ex-child combatants normally takes place within the context of a countrywide postwar rehabilitation and reconstruction process. Although ex-child combatants may have specific needs during this process, at the same time they share many of their needs with noncombatant but war-affected children and youths. The next chapter will focus on this postwar reconstruction process.

Notes

1. Paul Collier, "Economic Causes of Civil Conflict and Their Implications for Policy," in Chester A. Crocker, Fen Osler Hampson, and Pamela R. Aall, eds. *Turbulent Peace: The Challenges of Managing International Conflict* (Washington, D.C.: U.S. Institute of Peace Press, 2001), 143–162.

2. For the Integrated Disarmament, Demobilization and Reintegration Standards (IDDRS), see http://www.unddr.org/.

3. See the web site of the UN Disarmament, Demobilization, and Reintegration Resource Centre at http://www.unddr.org. UN Disarmament, Demobilization, and Reintegration (DDR) definition © United Nations, 2009. Reproduced with permission.

4. Many countries experiencing armed conflict have signed multiple cease-fire agreements and peace agreements before a final agreement is signed which proves to hold. In such cases a DDR program, started as part of what turned out to be a failed peace-accord, may continue to run during the reemerged period of fighting.

5. Some countries do overtly support a rebel faction in another country, such as Rwanda and Uganda in the Democratic Republic of Congo, claiming that their own national security is in danger if they do not. Covertly, many countries have supported rebel organizations in other countries. Perhaps most illustrative were the considerable number of conflicts in developing countries during the Cold War, where the two Superpowers—the United States and former Soviet Union—supported either the government or the rebels, fighting wars by proxy.

6. For instance, about 500 UN peacekeeping troops were held hostage by RUF forces in Sierra Leone in 2000. In Iraq, the UN headquarters was bombed by militants in 2003 and several NGO workers have been attacked and/or executed over the years.

7. Krijn Peters and Sophie Laws, *When Children Affected By War Go Home: Lessons Learned From Liberia* (Save the Children, 2003), accessed at http://www.savethechildren.org.uk/en/54_5220.htm.

8. Cantonment refers to a process ranging from the processing of individual combatants in temporary centers to the massing of troops in camps designated for this purpose. Cantonment sites can be encampments, assembly areas, or barracks. See the web site of the United Nations Disarmament, Demobilization, and Reintegration Resource Centre at http://www.unddr.org.

9. Report of the UN Secretary-General on Children and Armed Conflict, UN document number A/59/695-S/2005/72, 9 February 2005. Accessed at http://www.unicef.org/emerg/files/SG_report_cac.pdf.

10. Coalition to Stop the Use of Child Soldiers, *Global Report 2008*, accessed at http://www.child-soldiers.org/home.

11. An additional dilemma was introduced when an underage combatant stayed with a commander who was also a relative of the child. In such cases, breaking up the link between child soldier and commander also means that the link between two family members is broken.

12. Michael Wessells, *Child Soldiers: From Violence to Protection* (Cambridge, MA: Harvard University Press, 2006).

13. Peters and Laws 2003.

CHAPTER 5

After the War: War-Affected Young People in Post-Conflict Environments

Guatemala After 36 Years of Armed Conflict

On the evening of 29 December 1996, there were great celebrations with fireworks and parades in Guatemala City, the capital of Guatemala. A peace treaty had just been signed between the Government of Guatemala and the Guatemalan National Revolutionary Unity (UNRG) rebel group, ending the country's 36–year civil war. But, high up in the mountains of Guatemala, rebel combatants—some of whom had joined rebel groups during their adolescent years—were unsure of what this development would mean for them. Would anything change for the better in the country with the ending of the civil war?

The post-conflict challenges in Guatemala were daunting; 36 years of warfare had left a devastating mark on Guatemalan society and its people. The country's civil war had been bitterly fought between the Government of Guatemala on the one side and four left-wing armed opposition movements which eventually came together as a guerrilla umbrella organization, known by the Spanish acronym as the UNRG. The spark for the start of the war and for subsequent years of repressive and abusive military rule was a military coup in 1954 that overthrew the democratically-elected government. Between the 1960s and the 1990s, successive military governments killed thousands of civilians suspected of having links with the guerillas. The military counterinsurgency increased in intensity during the 1980s with a genocide campaign against Guatemala's indigenous peoples, the most violent period of the conflict. By the official end of the war in 1996, tens of thousands of people (primarily indigenous peoples) had been killed, disappeared, tortured, harassed, raped, and forced to flee their homes to live as refugees or IDPs. Young people had missed out on the opportunity to go to school and were in some cases forcibly recruited by the Guatemalan army and the rebel groups.

A cease-fire and several peace agreements were signed during the mid-1990s to bring Guatemala's civil war to an end. Several of these agreements attempted to address the deep-rooted discrimination long suffered by Guatemala's indigenous

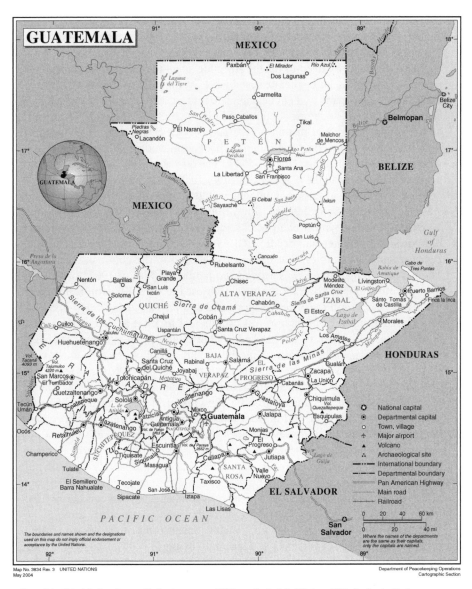

Figure 5.1.   United Nations Cartographic Section, map no. 3834, rev. 3. © United Nations, 2004. Reprinted with the permission of the United Nations.

peoples, as well as the needs and concerns of young people. For instance, some of the agreements called for the reform of the education and health sectors; for improvements in the provision of education; for the eradication of discrimination, poverty, and unemployment in order to improve the quality of life; and for the naturalization of children born in exile. The signing of these agreements was an important first step in bringing the conflict to an end by acknowledging its root causes.[1] But the people of Guatemala—and in particular the war-affected children and young people—faced many recovery and reconstruction challenges after the signing of the final peace treaty in December 1996. Who would help Guatemalan refugees living abroad—the majority lived in neighboring Mexico—to return to Guatemala, to rebuild their homes, and to create sustainable livelihoods? And who would help the rural people—many of them belonging to indigenous communities which had been marginalized for decades—to rebuild their homes and villages? How would former combatants reintegrate into society and become civilians again? Would children and young people be able to attend school again, and would they receive any assistance to reintegrate into Guatemala's formal education system? And would the provisions stipulated in the peace agreements actually be implemented and the root causes of the war be addressed—and who would monitor that?

To support the immediate transition from war to peace, the United Nations authorized the deployment of a peacekeeping force (the United Nations Verification Mission in Guatemala, or MINUGUA) to the country to support a human-rights-monitoring mission that had been deployed in the country since 1994. The peacekeeping mission was active from January to May of 1997 and helped to carry out humanitarian demining activities, the demobilization of former URNG members, and to collect weapons and ammunition. In addition, the Historical Clarification Commission was established in 1994 as part of the peace agreements, with the task to document what had happened during the war, including the numerous human rights abuses and acts of violence.

Yet, despite the fact that the civil war officially ended in 1996, the violence has not. The postconflict period in Guatemala has been characterized by a large increase in violence. Organized criminal networks and gangs have proliferated in the country, and crime and murder rates are high.[2] Continued violence may be due to the large amount of psychological trauma that continues to haunt the war-affected, sometimes causing violent outbursts in people, and to the fact that the problems that led to the outbreak of the war remain largely unresolved, including the gross social inequalities between different groups. Many of the peace agreement provisions have yet to be fully implemented and conditions have improved very little for most of the people in the country, especially those of the indigenous population. Children and young people continue to be affected by the country's high levels of violence, in addition to living with the effects of the long civil war, such as being orphaned. The country is characterized by some of the worst social indicators in the region, including high levels of poverty, child malnutrition—around two-thirds of the country's indigenous children are malnourished[3]—and low levels of formal education.

From Civil Wars to Crime Waves in Central America

Other countries in Central America also experienced civil wars during the 1980s and 1990s, for instance El Salvador and Mexico. While the wars in each of these countries are now over, crime and violence continues to plague the postwar societies of Central and South America, particularly gang and drug-related violence. The high levels of crime and violence and the existence of gangs are in part related to the civil wars: some gang members are former combatants, the children of former combatants, or war refugees who violated the law in their host country (often the United States) and who were deported from prisons in the United States back to their countries of origin. Gangs have been able to entrench themselves due to the high rates of poverty and social exclusion as well as the lack of opportunities for large segments of the population in these countries. The civil wars also contributed to the creation of a climate of impunity and to the normalization of violence.

In Guatemala, thousands of young people are either members of gangs or have some association with gangs. A 2005 report by Amnesty International (see below) on the violence in Guatemala demonstrated that women are one of the primary targets of gang violence in Guatemala. As a result of the high levels of gang violence, the Guatemalan state has diverted state resources into combating the gangs and away from social sectors such as education and health. This continues the climate of violence and militarization between the government and civilians, but also contributes to the deterioration of conditions in the country's social sectors, further widening the gap between rich and poor and fuelling grievances over these inequalities that can entice people to take up arms or encourage them to join a gang.

To access the report by Amnesty International ("No Protection, No Justice: Killings of Women in Guatemala," 2005), go to:

- http://www.amnesty.org/en/library/info/AMR34/017/2005.
- More about gangs in Central America and their impact on the US can be found at http://www.fas.org/sgp/crs/row/RS22141.pdf.

The Transition from War to Peace

Much of this book has been concerned with war, the impact of war on young people, and the roles that young people play in war. While some conflicts, as we have seen, may take years or even decades to be resolved, in the end a peace agreement is often signed between the warring factions to end a conflict. But what is peace? Is peace simply the absence of war? The term for peace as simply the absence of armed conflict and direct violence is called a *negative peace*. On the other hand, a *positive peace* is one which entails the presence and promotion of social justice. This distinction is critical, because it is often social injustice which contributes to the outbreak of conflict in the first place. As the former United Nations Under Secretary General for Disarmament Affairs stated in 2002: "Peace is not simply the cessation of hostilities; it is the dynamic management of human, political, and economic development and change by non-violent means."[4] But how is such a positive peace achieved in the aftermath of conflict, and what role can and do young people play in the consolidation of positive peace in conflict-affected countries?

As the example of Guatemala shows, the transition from war to peace is neither unproblematic nor straightforward. For instance, the end of war does not always mean the end of violence, nor does it mean that the problems that led to the outbreak of the war have been resolved. Conflict can resume after years of no fighting and peace agreements can fail to keep warring parties apart. Even when the fighting does not resume, many new issues emerge in a post-conflict environment that directly impact on and involve children and young people in particular. Among these issues are the process of reconstructing social infrastructure; the type, amount and duration of assistance given to the victims of war; and the creation and implementation of new policies that try to prevent the reemergence of war and improve living conditions for people. Thus, while the postwar period can be a window of opportunity to begin to deal with the damage caused by war as well as to address the root causes of war, it can also be a period of great hardship for many people.

The previous chapter explored the transition from war to peace for young ex-combatants. However, the overwhelming majority of young people in war-affected societies have not been combatants. But, all categories of young people will have been affected by the conflict, and all young people have to find ways to live in post-conflict environments. This chapter will explore some of the characteristics of postwar contexts and the range of issues that generally confront children and young people in societies transitioning from war to peace. Different stages and processes can be distinguished in the transition process from war to peace, including the peacemaking and conflict resolution process, the deployment of peacekeeping troops, and the post-conflict reconstruction and peace-building phases. Each of these stages and processes impact children and young people differently.

Containing Violence Through Peacekeeping: Consequences for Children and Young People

The process of resolving an armed conflict is a multifaceted, multi-phased process, and one which entails that the direct, physical violence of a conflict must be stopped and the warring parties brought together to agree about a peace settlement. In an armed conflict, the use of violence to achieve objectives becomes the norm, and some kind of peacekeeping operation to prevent the resumption of a full-blown conflict is often helpful. Peacekeeping is the insertion of international armed forces into a conflict-affected country with the consent of the concerned parties; the mandate of a peacekeeping operation is often to keep the warring parties apart and to thus facilitate or even enforce peace by preventing violence, creating a space for peacemaking. Peacekeeping missions may also carry out a range of humanitarian activities that are directly or indirectly relevant to the well-being of young people, such as assisting in the organization of elections, in delivering humanitarian aid, and in rebuilding state infrastructure (such as schools, roads, and hospitals).[5]

The number of peacekeeping operations nearly doubled during the 1990s, from 10 operations in 1990 to 17 by 2005.[6] Two of the largest (and most recent) UN peacekeeping operations in the world are the United Nations Mission in Liberia (UNMIL) with approximately 14,000 peacekeepers, and the United Nations Organization Mission in the Democratic Republic of Congo (MONUC) with approximately 17,000 peacekeepers.[7] But the United Nations is not the only organization involved in peacekeeping; for instance the African Union (AU) has joined forces with the UN to carry out a peacekeeping operation in Darfur (UNAMID), while NATO (the North Atlantic Treaty Organization) carried out a peacekeeping operation in Bosnia and Herzegovina during the war in the Balkans region in the 1990s. The European Union and ECOMOG (a West African multilateral armed force) have also been involved in peacekeeping missions.

Contributions to UN peacekeeping troops are made by countries from all over the world, although India, Pakistan and Bangladesh are traditionally the largest contributors.[8] The majority of peacekeeping personnel are military

Figure 5.2.   United Nations Transitional Administration in East Timor peacekeeper with children. UN Photo by Eskinder Debebe. Reprinted with the permission of the United Nations.

troops, but peacekeeping operations normally also include small numbers of police officers, military observers, and civilian personnel. United Nations peacekeeping missions now include civilian child protection advisors and officers; the very first child protection advisor was deployed to the United Nations peacekeeping mission in Sierra Leone (UNAMSIL) in 2000. The responsibility of these advisors is to ensure that the needs of children receive attention and are mainstreamed in peace agreements and in postconflict policies and programs. Child protection advisers also train peacekeeping mission personnel on child rights and protection issues.

Peacekeeping operations can have a direct and positive impact on the lives of young people. An example is the Democratic Republic of Congo, where civil war has raged in different regions of the country since the mid-1990s. A peacekeeping operation was deployed to the country in 1999. Part of the mandate of the mission is to assist in the promotion and protection of the human rights of vulnerable peoples, including children. Peacekeeping troops in the mission have helped to rebuild schools and have organized technical training courses for youths in order to give them a means to earn a livelihood.

But sometimes peacekeeping operations cannot prevent the continuation of negative consequences for young people, such as when peacekeepers fail to protect young people from harm. For example, in 1994, Dutch peacekeepers failed to prevent the massacre of thousands of men and young boys at Srebrenica, Bosnia. In Rwanda, a limited mandate for the UNAMIR mission to Rwanda required peacekeepers to evacuate foreign nationals from the country, but not to halt the wider violence that culminated in the 1994 genocide, which resulted in the victimization and killing of many young people.

Moreover, despite the inclusion of child protection advisors and units in some peacekeeping missions, it is now known that these operations can also have other direct, negative impacts on children and young people. Already in 1996, the UN Study on the Impact of Armed Conflict on Children (see the preface of this book) noted a rapid rise in child prostitution levels associated with the introduction of peacekeeping forces in countries such as Mozambique and Cambodia.[9] A more recent report by Save the Children also highlighted the problem of sexual exploitation and abuse of children by peacekeepers and aid workers in countries experiencing conflict or in a post-conflict phase, including Sudan, Haiti, and Côte d'Ivoire.[10] This report documented instances of children exchanging sex with peacekeepers and aid workers for food, money, or other items and services, and of children and young people being raped or trafficked to other destinations for prostitution or sexual slavery. Among the negative consequences is the fact that young people can contract sexually transmitted diseases—the rapid increase of HIV/AIDS cases in Cambodia, for example, was linked to the start of the peacekeeping mission in that country—, or are unable to marry later in life due to the stigma associated with prostitution. The reasons for the exploitative behavior of some peacekeepers can vary. Peacekeepers are often (relatively) well-paid and have access to scarce resources, putting them in a position of power. High poverty levels and the loss of protective community and family structures because of war may force women and young people to find other ways of survive, for instance through prostitution. In addition, conflict-affected societies have often experienced high levels of sexual violence as an intentional strategy of war and such behavior may have become normalized to some extent. Lastly, a climate of impunity and a sense of powerlessness of the victims may reign in such a context, making it hard to prosecute perpetrators and for young people to report cases of abuse against them.[11]

Peacekeeping: Resources for Further Research

- United Nations Department of Peacekeeping Operations: http://www.un.org/Depts/dpko/dpko/.
- United States Institute of Peace web site on peacekeeping: http://www.usip.org/library/topics/peacekeeping.html.
- Save the Children UK 2008 report on the abuse of children by peacekeepers ("No One to Turn To"): http://www.savethechildren.org.uk/en/docs/No_One_to_Turn_To.pdf.
- Brahimi report on UN peace operations (2000): http://www.un.org/peace/reports/peace_operations/.
- The Annual Review of Global Peace Operations: http://www.cic.nyu.edu/international-security/globalpeace.html.

Ending War Through Peacemaking: How Are the Needs and Concerns of Children and Young People Taken into Account in Peace Agreements?

Wars can end in different ways.[12] One of the warring parties can win a military victory over the other warring party, or the warring parties can simply stop fighting (or stop most of the fighting), without the signing of any formal agreement. Alternatively, the warring parties may agree to a cease-fire, which is an active suspension of hostilities but which does not attempt to address the root causes of a conflict, or the conflict may be ended through a negotiated peace agreement that tries to fully settle the disputes between the two parties.

Peacemaking is the process whereby the warring parties move toward the point where they reach a voluntary negotiated settlement of the conflict in order to end a conflict.[13] Often, a peace agreement is signed—a formal arrangement that is designed to stop violence through a cease-fire and to permanently end a conflict through the establishment of new political, social, economic, and legal structures.[14]

The signing of a peace agreement has become the preferred mode of ending conflicts, and the number of conflicts that end with negotiated settlements has been on the increase in recent years. Between 1940 and 1990, just over half of all conflicts between states (interstate wars) ended through peace negotiations, while only 20 percent of civil wars during the same time period ended in negotiated settlements, wherein the parties signed a peace agreement to end a conflict.[15]

During the 1990s, however, more conflicts ended via negotiated settlements (peace agreements) than in military victory[16], and between 2000 and 2005, nearly all conflicts ended with a peace agreement. This increase in negotiated settlements of conflicts during the post-Cold War period is very likely due to the increased involvement of the international community in peacemaking efforts, particularly by the United Nations.[17]

Despite the fact that more wars are now ending in negotiated settlements, peace agreements are unfortunately more likely to fail than to succeed, resulting in the warring parties reengaging in conflict. In fact, peace achieved through a negotiated settlement is three times more likely to fail than is peace achieved through a military victory. Partly as a result of this, conflicts that end in negotiated settlements last nearly three times longer on average than those that end in military victory.[18] One explanation for this is that the signing of peace agreements between elites may leave wider societal tensions and local-level conflicts unaddressed, leaving the way open for the resumption of conflict.[19] Peacemaking through the signing of a peace agreement is therefore not the same as building a long lasting and sustainable peace in a conflict-affected society by addressing the root causes of a conflict. Therefore, a peace agreement can be viewed as a kind of road map—or a first, but important, step—for postconflict state-building.

For the purpose of this book, it is important to look into the question of how peace agreements address the needs and rights of children and young people. Fortunately, since the end of the Cold War, many peace agreements have specifically incorporated the needs and concerns of young people. Issues around education are in particular frequently incorporated in peace agreements. Some agreements call for the mere resumption of activities in the education sector, while other agreements call for the full reform of education policies and curricula and improved access to formal education opportunities.[20] The peace agreements for Guatemala (1996), the Philippines (1996), and Macedonia (2001) are examples of agreements which lay out plans for a full reform of the education sector as part of a more general commitment to reforming the political, social, and economic structures in these countries—structures which may have been discriminatory in the past and thus contributed to the outbreak of armed conflict. Young people are also addressed in peace agreement provisions for DDR processes, and some agreements state that the warring parties must stop using children in conflict. The 1999 Lomé agreement for Sierra Leone was one of the first peace agreements to explicitly address the issue of child soldiers, and stated that the government should give attention to the issue of child soldiers and mobilize resources to address the needs of young combatants in DDR processes.

Less frequent ways in which the needs and concerns of young people feature in peace agreements include calls for the registration of births and the naturalization of children born in exile (such as refugees), as well as calls for sufficient attention to the needs of young returning refugees and IDPs, including the provision of assistance to returnees, such as in re-accessing education. The peace agreements signed for Guatemala (1996) and Burundi (2000) had articles in them relating to this issue. Several agreements recognize the general impact of war on children and young people and call for measures to ensure the protection, care, welfare, health, and security of young people. They also call for the commitment of all parties to uphold international treaties such as the 1989 Convention on the Rights of the Child and to provide war-affected young people with humanitarian and government assistance, special care, and rehabilitation. Many peace agreements make broad provisions and statements that benefit young people as a part of the war-affected civilian population, including the cessation of violence, resuming social and economic development, improving food security and transportation networks, and rehabilitating damaged infrastructure.

Table 5.1 shows in more detail some of the full and partial peace agreements where issues relevant to children and young people are addressed, including the provisions that are made for them.

Despite the positive examples in the table, the voices and needs of specific groups in society, such as women and children, are often not well represented in peacemaking efforts. Peacemaking is often an elite affair. In addition, each peacemaking process is context-specific and unique, and there is therefore no blueprint for how to address children's issues during peace negotiations. However, the United Nations Office of the Special Representative of the Secretary-General for Children in Armed Conflict has drafted a set of operational guidelines for what and how child-specific issues can and should be addressed in the negotiation and drafting of peace agreements.[21] These guidelines are divided into 12 sections, each addressing the needs of different categories of and issues relevant to children. Below, the most important elements of each of these 12 sections are given:

1. *Implementation:* A child protection expert should be included in any monitoring of the implementation of a peace agreement.
2. *Child soldiers:*
   o The use and recruitment of child soldiers should be considered as a cease-fire violation.
   o The integration of child soldiers into the regular armed forces as part of a DDR program should be prohibited.
   o Priority should be given in a peace agreement for the release of children detained by a fighting group, and the government should be obligated to help reunite these children with their families.
   o Peace agreements should create a commission to locate children disappeared during an armed conflict.
3. *Child DDR:*
   o The warring parties should be obligated to disclose the number, location, and identity of chbld soldiers within their ranks.
   o Child DDR processes should start as soon as possible, be prioritized to receive funding from the international community, and should take place in separate facilities from adults and should last longer than adult DDR.

Table 5.1 Examples of Peace Agreement Provisions Pertaining to Young People

Country and Year of Agreement	Provisions Relating to Children and Young People
Rwanda, 1992	• Assist vulnerable groups such as children • Assist returning refugees to access education and health services
Guatemala, 1994-1996 (multiple agreements)	• Registration of the births of Guatemalan refugees born in exile and register them as native Guatemalans • Recognize the education of uprooted Guatemalans • Reform the education sector • Attention to rural development needs • Reform of the health care sector, especially regarding child health care
Philippines, 1996	• Reform the education sector • Permit the participation of youths in the national Legislative Assembly
Sierra Leone, 1999	• Address needs of children affected by conflict and provide care and protection for them • Address the needs of child soldiers in DDR processes • Provide free basic education
Burundi, 2000	• Reform of the education sector • Children should be protected and not used in conflict • The return of refugees must take into consideration the vulnerabilities of children, and returnee children should be given government assistance and property rights • Government should provide assistance to war-affected children Government should uphold commitments to international legal documents such as the UNCRC • Address needs and issue of child soldiers
Democratic Republic of Congo, 2003	• Reconstruct and reform the education sector • Address the needs of children affected by war • Create a commission for the protection of children • Address the needs of young IDPs • Address the needs and issue of child soldiers
Sudan, 2004	• Comply with and uphold Convention on the Rights of the Child

o Child DDR should be considered as a long-term process and funding should be made available to ensure that children initially excluded from DDR programs are later assisted.

o Child DDR processes should be designed to consider the special needs of girls, the disabled, and other vulnerable children associated with fighting groups.

o Gender-specific services should be provided in DDR programs, and interim care facilities should be located as far away as possible from any areas experiencing fighting so as to avoid the re-recruitment of former young combatants.

o The design and implementation of family tracing and reunification and of vocational training programs should consider the opinion of children.

o The government should establish mechanisms to allow close relatives to adopt or gain custody of orphaned child soldiers.

4. *Violations of international human rights and international humanitarian law:* The violation of child rights should be considered a violation of a cease-fire.

5. *Attacks on schools and hospitals:* Should be considered as violations of a cease-fire, and priority should be given to reconstructing schools and hospitals after a conflict.

6. *Justice and reconciliation / amnesty:* The agreement should not include any amnesty provisions for crimes committed against children.

7. *Land mines:* In clearing land mines, the protection and needs of children should be taken into account.

8. *Refugees and IDPS:* In the return and resettlement of refugees and IDPs:

o Priority access to land should be given to returning families, including female and child-headed families, and equal property rights should be guaranteed for all people, including children.

o The government should recognize education received while in exile, and should expedite naturalization of children born while being a refugee. Displaced children should be assisted to reunify with their families.

Peacemaking: Resources for Further Research

Through the following web sites, you can learn more about peace agreements and access different peace agreements:

- United Nations Peacemaker: http://peacemaker.unlb.org/
- United States Institute of Peace: http://www.usip.org
- United Nations Department of Political Affairs: http://www.un.org/Depts/dpa/
- All Africa's Peace Africa web site: http://allafrica.com/peaceafrica/resources/
- Uppsala University Conflict Data Program Database: http://www.pcr.uu.se/gpdatabase/search.php
- The African Centre for the Constructive Resolution of Disputes (ACCORD): www.accord.org.za
- Beyond Intractability: www.beyondintractability.org/essay/structuring_peace_agree/
- INCORE (International Conflict Research): www.incore.ulst.ac.uk/services/cds/agreements/
- Conciliation Resources: www.c-r.org/our-work/accord/peace-agreements/index.php

Postwar Reconstruction and Peacebuilding Efforts: Impact on and Involvement of Children and Young People

Once a conflict has ended, a country enters—by default—the post-conflict phase. This phase is often marked by the reconstruction of physical infrastructure destroyed during the war, the reestablishment of public services such as education and health, the return of IDPs and refugees, and attempts to reconcile the impact and traumas of war. Peacebuilding activities are also often a part of the post-conflict phase.

Making, Keeping, and Building the Peace

The terms "peacebuilding," "peacekeeping," and "peacemaking" are sometimes used as if they have the same meaning. However, they refer to different activities, taking place at different times in the conflict/post-conflict process:[22]

- **Peacekeeping:** activities carried out primarily by foreign military personnel, usually under the mandate of the UN or a regional security organization, intended to maintain the peace in a postconflict environment.
- **Peacemaking:** a range of political and diplomatic activities intended to halt ongoing conflicts.
- **Peacebuilding:** measures designed to reduce tension or build confidence between opposing states or political, religious or ethnic groups, in order to prevent the start or resumption of armed conflict.

The United Nations (2001), a major actor implementing peacebuilding activities, views peacebuilding as consisting of three key elements: (1) the consolidation of internal and external security; (2) the strengthening of political institutions and good governance; and (3) the promotion of economic and social rehabilitation and transformation.[23] In a 2004 document, the United Nations emphasizes the importance of good governance in building peace, stating that "along with establishing security, the core task of peacebuilding is to build effective public institutions that, through negotiations with civil society, can establish a consensual framework for governing within the rule of law."[24] But peacebuilding is not something that should be concerned only with (good) governance or a focus on the national level. Rather, peacebuilding should and must also work "from below"—that is, by empowering communities that are affected by conflict to actively contribute to the consolidation of peace. The next sections of this chapter will look at the role of young people in aspects of each of these three elements of peacebuilding, as well as in the post-conflict phase more generally.

The United Nations Peacebuilding Commission

In December 2005, the United Nations established the Peacebuilding Commission (PBC). The PBC is an intergovernmental advisory body that is mandated to assist conflict-affected states in the transition from war to peace by:

* Bringing together all relevant actors to mobilize resources and to advise on proposed strategies for post-conflict peacebuilding and recovery;
* Helping to ensure predictable financing for early recovery activities and sustained financial investment over the medium to long-term;
* Developing best practices on issues in collaboration with political, security, humanitarian, and development actors.[25]

Sierra Leone and Burundi, two states that experienced devastating civil wars during the 1990s, were the first two countries placed on the agenda of the PBC at the request of the governments of these countries themselves. Country-specific "integrated peacebuilding strategies" and "priority plans" are designed to bring the governments of these countries together with national and international partners around a shared set of peacebuilding objectives and priorities. Financial support for countries on the agenda of the PBC comes from the United Nations Peacebuilding Fund.

For Burundi , the PBC identified several priorities that should be addressed to build peace in the country, including: the promotion of good governance and the institutionalization of democracy; strengthening the rule of law within the armed forces; the promotion of human rights and justice to combat impunity; implementing economic reforms; resolving land disputes; and reintegrating returned displaced persons. Particular attention was paid to young people in Burundi's peacebuilding plan, which stated plans to target community-based recovery programming toward youth in order to improve social cohesion. For example, calls were made to provide economic alternatives to young people, particularly jobs and income earning opportunities, as well as training and technical support. Further calls were also made for increased focus on assisting conflict-affected and vulnerable youths in both urban and rural areas, such as returned displaced youth and street children.

The first peacebuilding priority that was identified for Sierra Leone in the country's integrated peacebuilding strategy and priority plan is youth employment and empowerment. Addressing the issue of youth is a top priority for building peace in Sierra Leone because, as the peacebuilding strategy documents for the country states, the political and economic marginalization of young people prior to the outbreak of the civil war directly played into the outbreak of the civil war and into how the conflict was sustained. In particular, youth unemployment is identified in the strategy documents as the most serious threat to the country's stability and socioeconomic development. Young people in postwar Sierra Leone continue to experience high rates of joblessness, poor-quality schooling, and few opportunities to fully participate in political processes. Actions taken by the Government of Sierra Leone to address the issue of youth exclusion thus far include the establishment of a youth-focused national ministry and the formulation of a national youth policy, as well as the launch of a Youth Employment Scheme. Three additional priorities complete the list of Sierra Leone's peacebuilding objectives: democracy and good governance; justice and security; and capacity-building in public administration.

You can read more about the PBC and its work in Sierra Leone and Burundi on the following web sites:

- The Peacebuilding Commission: http://www.un.org/peace/peacebuilding
- On the work of the PBC in Sierra Leone: http://www.unpbf.org/sierraleone/sierraleone.shtml
- On the work of the PBC in Burundi: http://www.unpbf.org/burundi/burundi.shtml
- On the United Nations Peacebuilding Fund: http://www.unpbf.org

Addressing the Security Needs of Young People

During times of war, there is often very little security for people, particularly physical security—that is, safety from bodily harm and access to sufficient food and water in order to survive. In fact, war is a direct threat to human security; that is, it is a threat to the security of individuals and communities, to the welfare of ordinary people, and to freedom from threats to rights and to safety.[26]

The previous chapter explored the experiences of young combatants in disarmament processes. Disarmament is one facet of improving the postwar security climate through the collection, removal, and destruction of (light) weapons and small arms in conflict zones. Often, peacekeeping forces are charged with the mandate to disarm warring factions. Disarmament has a military as well as a humanitarian dimension to it, since disarmament has a significant impact on the lives of both combatant and noncombatant young people. When the warring parties put down their weapons, it is a clear signal of their commitment to end the war and consolidate the peace.

Disarmament will help to lower the general threat of postwar armed violence (e.g. armed robberies, kidnapping) in society through the reduction of the number of weapons possessed by individuals. In addition, by reducing the level of expenditures on armed violence and instead increasing expenditure for more productive activities such as rehabilitating physical infrastructure and restarting education facilities, the peace is further strengthened and consolidated. Redirecting spending away from armed violence and into social institutions (the so-called "peace-dividend") will help to demilitarize a society and indicates that the state is committed to the well-being of its citizens.[27] More generally, such state investment creates a stable climate which in turn may encourage foreign investment, of crucial importance to improving war-affected economies.[28]

Moreover, disarmament can ameliorate the conditions that result from armed violence and which negatively impact the quality of children's lives and on a nation's socioeconomic development more generally. For example, the removal of land mines from farmland can contribute to improving food security by reestablishing livelihoods for rural peoples, and can reduce the numbers of postconflict injuries and casualties and thus the number of individuals who will need long-term medical care. Removing land mines makes it safe for children to walk to school, to play, and to do chores such as collecting water and herding cattle.

Removing Landmines in Nagorno-Karabakh: Improving the Lives of Young People After War

Demining for humanitarian purposes—rather than for military purposes—is an important postwar activity in areas where land mines were laid by armed groups. Demining is particularly important for young people in land mine-affected areas, as it is critical for resuming education services, recovering farmland to earn a living from, and reducing the threat of injury and death from land mine explosions. According to the Landmine Monitor Report (http://www.icbl.org), tens of thousands of land mines remain to be cleared in former conflict areas. Children belong to one of the most affected groups, sometimes for years after a war has come to an end, as is for instance the case in Mozambique. For that reason land mines are sometimes referred to as the "silent killer."

Demining activities have taken place in, for example, Nagorno-Karabakh, a heavily-mined region that lies between Armenia and Azerbaijan, countries once part of the Soviet Union. These two countries fought a war between 1991 and 1994 to control the territory of Nagorno-Karabakh, during which thousands of land mines were laid. In Nagorno-Karabakh, children are the primary victims of land mine explosions; while playing, farming, or herding cattle, children are at risk of stepping on or touching unexploded ordnance and land mines.

The Halo Trust, a charity that specializes in the removal of the debris of war, is the only organization that currently carries out demining activities in Nagorno-Karabakh. Halo also operates a mine risk education program in Nagorno-Karabakh in order to alert children to the risks posed by land mines and other unexploded remnants of war. See http://www.halousa.org for more information on demining activities in Nagorno-Karabakh.

Return and Reintegration of Forced Migrants

The international community perceives three acceptable "durable" solutions to end existing refugee and IDP situations: integration into the country or community of asylum, resettlement in a third country or in another part of the home country, and repatriation and return to the country and/or community of origin.[29]

Repatriation is the preferred donor option for ending refugee situations, and it is often claimed that the great majority of today's refugees would themselves prefer to return home once the situation is safe and stable enough in their home country. It is the "ideal solution because it returns refugees to their homeland, to familiar surroundings, to their friends and family—[making them] able to resume normal lives"[30], and it has been a successful solution in a number of cases. Successful refugee repatriation is here defined as there being no further or continued refugee flows out of the country. This does not mean that the repatriation process was without problems or that repatriated refugees do not face hardship or further displacement as IDPs upon their return. However, the choice for repatriation as the preferred solution may also have more to do with the fact that many states today, both developing and developed, do not wish—for economic or political reasons—to integrate refugee populations into their countries.[31]

Repatriation can either be officially assisted by the United Nations High Commissioner for Refugees (UNHCR) or it can be unassisted and spontaneous, often occurring when refugees are tired of camp conditions and know that it is safe to return. The added benefit of repatriating with the UNHCR is the continued reintegration assistance that returnees often receive from the UNHCR in the immediate post-return phase. The UNHCR normally offers incentives to repatriate by providing transportation back to the country of origin as well as money, housing materials, seeds and farming equipment to returning refugees registered with the UNHCR. Other national and international organizations are also involved in assisting refugees and IDPs to return to their countries and communities of origin.

Repatriation of Forced Migrants

According to the UNHCR, over 700,000 refugees returned to their home countries in 2007, with approximately the same number returning in 2006. The largest movement of refugees back to their countries of origin was to Afghanistan, Sudan, the Democratic Republic of Congo, Iraq, and Liberia.[32]

The UNHCR has devoted attention to the issue of ensuring the safety, care, and protection of children and young people during displacement and return. The following documents guide the UNHCR in relation to the repatriation of displaced children (all accessible at http://www.unhcr.org):

- *Refugee Children: Guidelines on Protection and Care* (first publication 1988)
- *UNHCR Guidelines on Determining the Best Interests of the Child* (2008)
- *UNHCR Handbook for the Protection of Women and Girls* (2008)

Once refugees and IDPs have returned to their state or community of origin, the resettlement and reintegration process starts. Reintegration is, for the UNHCR, the goal of refugee repatriation.[33] The reintegration of returning forced migrants is a complex and multidimensional process, encompassing a process of adaptation, as people learn to live together again.[34] Return and reintegration into the home or the local community and/or state can be a long and difficult process. Although violence may have ceased in the country or community of origin, the political situation may not have changed significantly and returnees may be uncertain about what they will encounter when they return. Returnees face major challenges when returning home, including the possibility of harassment and retribution. Other challenges returnees are confronted with include continued displacement if their homes are not yet safe to live in or are occupied by others; the loss of property and land; overgrown farming land and destroyed infrastructure; a lower standard of living than in host states, a lack of sufficient food and clean water supplies, general social maladjustment, few employment opportunities, and difficulty in accessing the social services such as the formal education system.[35]

What do return and subsequent reintegration mean for young refugees and displaced people? For them, the "resettlement" process can be more like "settlement", particularly if they have been in a protracted situation of displacement. In these cases, people have lived for years as refugees or IDPs, and a whole generation of young people has grown up knowing only life in a displacement camp, without any real knowledge of the communities they are supposed to return to, except for the stories of their parents or relatives. In some cases, displaced children may have been schooled in a different language than their mother tongue, and lack both language skills and exposure to and knowledge about local customs back home. Going "home" is not necessarily a process of return for young people, but rather one of adjusting to a sometimes completely new physical setting. The process of "return" and "reintegration" can thus have a profound impact on the psychological well-being of young people. In some cases, children and young people may not return with their families, due either to the fact that their parents have gone home before them (to rebuild the house or initiate income generating activities), or because children and their parents have become separated during flight or due to the death of the parents. In the case of Sierra Leone, some refugee children living in displacement camps in neighboring Guinea were left behind in the camps when their parents returned to Sierra Leone, in order for the children to continue benefiting from education services in the camps. Because repatriation operations were carried out in the middle of the academic year, this disrupted the school year for many children. Some parents thus chose to leave their children behind in the camps so they could finish the schooling they had begun, or because parents felt that the education services were of lower quality or had not yet restarted back in Sierra Leone.

The UNHCR currently advocates for the implementation of so-called "4Rs" programs during the post-conflict period. These programs entail the *repatriation* and sustainable *reintegration* of refugees and IDPs back to the states and or communities of origin, the *rehabilitation* of destroyed social and economic infrastructure in returnee areas (i.e. schools, clinics, houses), and the general *reconstruction* of political order and institutions.[36] 4Rs programs are designed to integrate the needs of returning refugees and displaced persons into national development plans.[37] The intention of these programs is to bring together crisis and development-focused actors and institutions, strengthen the linkages between national governments and local communities, build up the capacity of local government institutions, and help returnees to create sustainable livelihoods through the reconstruction of social services and infrastructure, thus working to ensure that repatriation will indeed be a durable solution (that is, that returning forced migrants do not again become displaced due to a lack of the basic means to build up a livelihood).

While the aim of 4Rs programs is to create a smooth transition from the short-term phase of humanitarian relief to the longer-term development phase, this transition is not always as smooth in reality. The reigning international humanitarian aid paradigm still demarcates between relief and development assistance. Returnees may receive basic immediate assistance after the end of a crisis situation from agencies such as the UNHCR, agencies which focus on the short-term needs of transport and temporary shelter and food support. The government and organizations such as the United Nations Development Program (UNDP), the World Bank, and local and international NGOs which provide long-term development needs such as the rehabilitation of the social sectors which are critical for young people often step in at a later stage.[38] Returnees may sometimes face significant periods of time between the end of the short-term humanitarian support and the start of more development-oriented assistance. Projects that are funded by relief money—but that fit within the mandate of development organizations—sometimes become unsustainable to maintain because these fall in between two different funding streams.[39]

Going "Home"? Repatriation During Times of Continuing Conflict and Violence

The repatriation of forced migrants does not always occur under the most ideal circumstances. Peace, stability, and security may not yet be prevalent and persistent in home countries and communities. This has been the case for example in Iraq and Afghanistan, two countries to which refugees have returned during times of ongoing conflict and violence.

The 2003 U.S.-led invasion of Iraq resulted in the displacement of millions of Iraqis, as internally displaced people as well as refugees to the neighboring countries of Iran, Jordan, Syria, or further abroad. The new Iraqi government has encouraged the return of refugees back to the country and has organized some return trips for refugees with the assistance from United Nations. However, the security situation remains precarious in Iraq, and returnees face many challenges upon arriving in their home country. Young returned Iraqi refugees and their families often experience difficult living conditions, such as a shortage in habitable and safe houses; increased levels of poverty; a lack of jobs; and the poor availability of health services. High levels of violence pervade in certain areas of the country, with bombings and attacks on civilians. Moreover, civilians are kidnapped on a regular basis by the numerous sectarian groups, and young people have been recruited to join armed groups and have served as suicide bombers.

The high level of violence makes it difficult for many children to go to school, as it is neither safe to walk to the school building, nor to be at school, where militants can attack. The general conditions in the classrooms are poor, with a lack of books and supplies. Many Iraqi refugee children still living in exile in countries such as Lebanon already face difficulty in accessing school due to severe poverty, the lack of legal status as a refugee, and the fact that many public Lebanese schools are already overcrowded. Returnee children face further when trying to reintegrate into the Iraqi school system for similar reasons: deep poverty, the lack of proper documentation for school registration, and because returnee students have learned another curriculum in a different language of instruction, impeding a smooth transition into Iraqi schools. As a consequence of the violence in Iraq, nearly a million Iraqi children are currently out of school, some of whom are returnee children and young people.

The following sources give more information about the displacement and the return of refugees to Iraq:

- Newspaper article: Cara Buckley, "Refugees Risk Coming Home to an Unready Iraq," *The New York Times*, 20 December 2007.
- UNHCR, "Preliminary Repatriation and Reintegration Plan for Iraq," April 2003, accessed at http://www.unhcr.org/cgi-bin/texis/vtx/home/opendoc.pdf?tbl=SUB-SITES&id=3ea9554e4.
- Special issue of *Forced Migration Review*, June 2007: "Iraq's Displacement Crisis: The Search for Solutions." Can be accessed at http://www.fmreview.org/mags1.htm.

Addressing Economic Needs and Reestablishing Social Services: Reconstruction and Recovery

The post-conflict period is a time of rebuilding the physical, economic, political, and social infrastructure and foundations of society, often devastated by years of war. Rebuilding these is a critical element of building peace and preventing the reemerging of conflict, but also for helping young people living in conflict-affected countries to resume their pre-conflict lives and to restart the processes critical to their development. Much energy (and money) is spent on the rehabilitation of physical infrastructures, such as health clinics, schools, roads, and other buildings. Everyone traveling in a post-conflict country will notice the many signs indicating another school or community center rehabilitation project by the government (and a foreign sponsor) or by one of the many international nongovernmental organizations present in the country. These rehabilitation projects normally achieve quick, visible, and quantifiable results and there is a great need for them, but they should not come at the cost of neglecting other—non-physical—priorities. Social and economic reforms (such as improved distribution of social goods like education) within a post-conflict society are equally important in achieving a sustainable peace.

Above, we looked at the importance of improving security for peacebuilding and in particular, how important improved security is for the lives of young people living in post-conflict settings. We will now discuss the two remaining elements of the United Nation's peacebuilding triangle, with regards to young people: the strengthening of political institutions and good governance; and the promotion of economic and social rehabilitation and transformation.

Political Transformation: Good Governance

What does "good governance" mean, and how are young people involved in promoting good governance and in strengthening political institutions in a post-war climate? Governance is about the manner of governing and the process of making and implementing decisions, usually within the context of national and/or local government. Good governance is closely related to this, and is about the quality and mechanisms of governance. The UNDP defines good governance as being "about the equal participation of all citizens—men and women, young and old—in public and political life."[40] The United Nations Economic and Social Commission for Asia and the Pacific (UNESCAP) further defines good governance as having the following characteristics: "it is participatory, consensus oriented, accountable, transparent, responsive, effective and efficient, equitable and inclusive and follows the rule of law. It assures that corruption is minimized, the views of minorities are taken into account and that the voices of the most vulnerable in society are heard in decision-making. It is also responsive to the present and future needs of society."[41] However, when the term "good governance" was first introduced in the early 1990s by the World Bank, its meaning was more focused on the relations between the state and the market rather than between the state and civil society. The IMF and World Bank perceive good governance as a means of building institutional capacity to support the development of markets and as a means of strengthening the institutional frameworks of governments by strengthening the rule of law and rooting out corruption.[42]

Child and youth groups and organizations can play an important role in improving political governance and strengthening political institutions in post-conflict countries. Examples of such involvement come from the Democratic Republic of Congo, Guinea-Bissau, and Bosnia and Herzegovina. In 2003, the United Nations organized a Children's Parliament in the Democratic Republic of Congo. The parliament was run by and for children, and the young representatives administered justice by, for instance, mediating family disputes and lobbying to get children out of prison. This has provided young people with the opportunity to promote their own concerns within the national political sphere and to gain experience in administering justice in a country where the justice system is often corrupt and has deteriorated due to years of neglect.[43] Children's parliaments have been instituted in other conflict-affected countries such as Guinea-Bissau, where the children's parliament there has lobbied political parties to integrate the concerns of young people into their campaigns and future governments.[44] In Bosnia and Herzegovina, the Youth Party of Bosnia and Herzegovina has demanded better quality education, accountability, and an end to corruption.[45]

The participation of young people in decision-making processes at national and local levels—such as in school management committees, child clubs, religious organizations, youth parliaments, and political parties, or in youth-focused civil society groups—can be an important element of conflict prevention and peacebuilding. Often, children and young people are not listened to and are among the more disempowered members of society. In conflicts where children and young people have made up a significant amount of the fighting forces, such as in many of the conflicts discussed in this book, it is important to provide opportunities and effective ways for young people to participate and to be included in national and local political processes in order to learn how to solve issues in a nonviolent way.

Good governance, beyond the slightly narrow understanding of some donors such as the World Bank, is also about social justice. For example, it can facilitate the empowerment of women and girls to overcome social inequalities. If women are empowered, it is not only more likely that their experiences during the war and the effects of war on women are acknowledged and addressed (such as large-scale sexual violence and the presence of female combatants), but also that the contribution that women and girls can make in the peacebuilding process is fully acknowledged. To encourage the adoption of a gendered perspective in peacemaking, peacekeeping, and peacebuilding operations and processes, the United Nations adopted Security Council Resolution 1325—outlined below.

A Gendered Peace

On 31 October 2000, the UN Security Council adopted Resolution 1325, which addresses the importance of gender in conflict resolution, peacemaking, peacekeeping, and peacebuilding efforts and operations. The resolution specifically urges UN member states to, among other things:

- Ensure that women are represented in conflict resolution and peace processes;
- Take a gendered perspective when negotiating and writing peace agreements;
- Ensure that women are part of UN peacekeeping missions and of peacebuilding and other field-based operations and that these operations have a gendered perspective;
- Pay attention to the needs of women and girls during repatriation and reintegration operations and during post-conflict reconstruction activities;
- Support local women's peace initiatives, and involve women in the implementation of peace agreements;
- Take special measures to protect women and girls during periods of armed conflict;
- To prosecute acts and war crimes related to violence against women;
- To consider the particular needs of women and girls in the construction of refugee camps, as well as in DDR operations.

> The text of the resolution can be accessed at: http://www.unfpa.org/women/docs/res_1325e.pdf.

But how appropriate is it to talk about a "post-conflict" situation or the "aftermath" of an armed conflict for women and girls affected by conflict? Meintjes, Pillay, and Turshen (2001)[46] argue that there is no "aftermath" for women in a post-conflict situation because the impact and effects of conflict on women are still experienced by them long after the signing of a peace deal. In addition, in several cases, the level of violence against women actually increases after the end of a conflict (such as in Guatemala). For girls in particular, persistent and conflict-deepened poverty often means that they may lose out on the opportunity to go to school since families often use their limited income to send boys to school first. For similar reasons girls may also miss out on health care services.[47] Furthermore, even in cases where gender equality may have been an important aspect of the ideology and practices of particular rebel groups, such as the Tigray People's Liberation Front (TPLF) in Ethiopia, and even where these have been taken on board by the new government after a conflict—the TPLF was victorious—this does not mean that the ideals about gender equality will also automatically change gender roles and perspectives at a local level.[48]

Social Sector Rehabilitation: Rebuilding the Health Sector and Addressing Health Issues

The rehabilitation of the social infrastructure in a post-conflict country entails—among other things—the rehabilitation of the health and education sectors. War-induced damage to these sectors means that it may take many years before they operate anywhere near prewar levels. What may have already been a low-quality health system characterized by unequal access before the war is made much worse by armed conflict, necessitating a response after the war to both conflict-related health issues and to the more general (poverty-related) health issues.[49]

As mentioned before, according to recent statistics from UNICEF[50], out of the top ten countries with the worst under-five mortality rates[51] in the world, six of them are post-conflict countries. As was discussed in Chapter Two, the health consequences of armed conflicts for young people are enormous. Reconstructing the health sector during the post-conflict period is thus critical, to deal with the many health issues present that are the direct and indirect effects of conflict. A first step is to reconstruct health facilities, such as health clinics and hospitals. But equally important is that these health centers should have well-trained personnel such as doctors and nurses. These individuals may have left during the conflict. According to the UNFPA, in Sierra Leone in 2008—six years after the end of the war—there were just six obstetricians, of which only one worked outside of the capital. The United Nations further estimated that there were just 65 trained medical doctors for a country of 5 million people. It is therefore important that a post-conflict country has the capacity to plan, finance, and deliver health care services on a long-term basis.

Additionally, new health issues may emerge in a post-conflict setting for children and young people, as the effects of conflict on children and young people will still be experienced long after the guns are laid down and a peace agreement is signed. For example, a post-conflict situation might be characterized by the rapid spread of sexually transmitted diseases (STDs).[52] STDs such as HIV/AIDS can spread when prostitution rates increase in response to the presence of a peacekeeping mission (as discussed earlier) or when there are few other income-earning opportunities in a war-shattered economy and young people become involved in prostitution to earn money. The presence of large numbers of vulnerable children, such as street children and orphans who have lost their families due to a conflict, entails that such children have less access to health care and fewer means to pay for health care or for good quality food and water that keeps them healthy. Furthermore, land mines and unexploded ordnance remain in the ground for years, posing a long-term public health issue, while mental trauma may persist for years on end. A recent study on the mental health of young people orphaned during the Rwandan genocide of 1994 showed that 10 years after the genocide, nearly 50 percent of the child orphans who took part in the study continued to suffer from post-traumatic stress syndrome.[53] Few survivors of the Rwandan genocide have had access to any kind of mental health care services, such as counseling or therapy—a common scenario in many post-conflict states, including for young people.

Educational Reconstruction, Reintegration, and Reform

As with the health sector, many issues and challenges arise in restarting, rehabilitating, and in some cases, reforming the education sector of a post-conflict country. In the first place, destroyed school buildings and educational infrastructure (such as teacher training colleges and government education sector buildings) must be rebuilt. Furniture and teaching and learning materials such as textbooks have probably been lost during the conflict and need to be replaced. Second, education sector personnel may need to be increased, since teachers and other educated individuals may have been killed or fled the country permanently, requiring the training of new teachers and education officials. Existing personnel may also need to be retrained to deal effectively with the postwar education challenges within schools and government institutions.[54]

Third, large numbers of children must reintegrate, or integrate for the first time, into the formal education system, such as returned refugees and IDPs, former child soldiers, and those who did not have access to the education system due to the war. As was discussed in Chapter 4, various catch-up programs such as Accelerated Learning Programs (ALP) are used in some postwar situations to help overaged children with their reintegration into school, compressing the time that children must spend completing their primary schooling, for instance from six to three years. Eradicating school fees also helps children to access school, as do policies and laws that make universal primary education mandatory. Mass access to education in the post-conflict period can eradicate feelings of social exclusion and thus contribute to sustainable peace, in particular if people have been motivated to participate in the conflict because of lack of access to education in the first place. For instance, after the end of the wars in Liberia and Sierra Leone, primary education was made tuition-free and compulsory for all children. Scholarships provided to girls to pay for textbooks and other supplies in these countries increased the primary school enrollment of this vulnerable group. These measures were important since educational exclusion was among some of the young people's motivations for taking up arms during the civil wars in those countries.[55]

Rebuilding the education sector is particularly vital in rural areas and in areas where refugees and IDPs return to (though much of the reconstruction efforts are often concentrated in urban areas). It plays a critical role in the reintegration of war-affected IDP or refugee children—and can be among the conditions to return in the first place—and in the healing of communities more generally. Refugees and IDPs who may have accessed education during a conflict and who return home can bring new skills and knowledge with them that may contribute to the socioeconomic development of their country and/or community of origin and help prevent further conflicts.[56]

Also, textbooks and the curriculum more generally may need to be redesigned to reflect new knowledge and learning needs such as land mine awareness or to eradicate stereotypes, beliefs, and attitudes that may have contributed to the conflict, as well as to teach children peaceful conflict resolution techniques. For example, in post-conflict Liberia, human rights and citizenship education has been added to the curriculum, while the Guatemalan peace agreements require that bilingual and multicultural education be incorporated into the curriculum in order to rectify the social, political, and economic injustice and marginalization of the country's indigenous majority. Reforming the curriculum can be, however, a contentious matter; in Rwanda, for instance, there has been no teaching of history in schools since the end of the genocide. Before the genocide, history teaching was divisive and taught children to have contempt for other groups in society. Another example of how difficult curriculum reform can be in the aftermath of a conflict comes from Bosnia and Herzegovina, where three parallel curricula emerged during and after the conflict, with "each one purporting to represent the heritage and ideology of one of the country's three constituent peoples— Bosniaks, Croats, and Serbs—and accompanied by deeply entrenched, ideologically based policy positions."[57] Further exacerbating this curricular division is the fact that the education system in Bosnia and Herzegovina is ethnically segregated, prohibiting contact between different groups of children. It is difficult to imagine how such an education system promotes peace in a war-torn country.

Rebuilding the Economy: Jobs, Livelihoods, and Foreign Aid

Education is strongly connected to employment, income generation, and national economic development. There are strong links between (the lack of) economic development and the outbreak of civil war on the one hand, and between education and national economic development on the other. As stated before, civil war and conflict in general predominates in poor, less-developed countries. One explanation for this relationship is that individuals participate in conflict because they have few other income-earning opportunities (or what is termed a "low opportunity cost"). In a poor and less-developed country, low and unequally distributed income creates a pool of impoverished and marginalized young people who may be more easily recruited by rebel groups who promise access to loot, money, and other economic goods.[58] The role of education in peacebuilding becomes clear. In theory, education can play a critical role in giving people the skills to find jobs and other income-earning opportunities—activities which contribute to economic growth. This is the basis of what is called "human capital theory," a theory which emphasizes the importance of the level of workers' skills for their productivity, and thus for the economic growth of a country.[59] Few countries in the world have achieved sustained economic growth without having achieved universal primary schooling first.[60]

However, the reality is that the relationship between education and economic growth, and between the level of economic development and civil war, are not so congruous. Simply providing universal primary education to the population is not enough to avert the outbreak or resumption of a civil war. Several countries with well-educated populations have experienced civil war, such as Lebanon, Georgia, Russia, and Cyprus. Furthermore, education does not always translate into employment, and the failure of education to connect to the labor market can frustrate young people. In the former Yugoslavia, for instance, a country with a highly-educated population, unemployment rates soared immediately before the civil war broke out there, creating massive frustration.[61] Furthermore, education is not the sole cause for economic growth or job creation.[62]

While there has been much focus by NGOs, donor agencies such as the World Bank, and IOs such as the United Nations on creating jobs and income-earning opportunities—particularly for young people—in post-conflict contexts as part of foreign aid packages and programs, it proves to be extremely challenging to create the kind of long-term economic growth and job creation that people desire and need to lift themselves out of poverty. The presence of many NGOs and IOs in an immediate post-conflict environment can result in jobs for some young people, but only on a short-term basis. When the relief stage ends and the development phase begins, most of the organizations reduce their programs or leave altogether. Longer-term job skills can be delivered through vocational training and apprenticeship programs such as those discussed for ex-combatants in Chapter 4 (for example, hairdressing, tailoring, or carpentry), but the demand for some of these services and industries may be limited and young people's lack of experience often results in the employment of older and more skilled and experienced workers. The competition for jobs can be extremely high, in particular in urban areas, which often harbor many people displaced by the conflict from rural areas. Furthermore, the damage that conflict inflicts on the economy makes it even more difficult to create a robust postwar economy that can provide jobs, as the physical capital of the economy is generally ruined (roads, buildings, and farms), and the human capital (educated and skilled individuals) killed, displaced, or disabled. As pointed out before, making the country attractive to foreign investors and thus employers is not easy, because many post-conflict countries struggle with bad postwar security records.[63]

The example of East Timor in the box below provides a glimpse of some of the challenges of job creation for young people in a post-conflict setting.

Youth, Foreign Aid, and Conflict in East Timor

Some of the challenges that can be encountered in a post-conflict situation regarding young people, job creation, the delivery of foreign aid, and fostering economic growth can be illustrated with the case of East Timor (or Timor Leste).

From 1975 to 1999, East Timor fought a long civil war to free itself from occupation by Indonesia. The country finally won its independence in 1999 when Timorese voters chose to secede from Indonesia in a UN-supervised referendum. But violence broke out during and after the referendum, largely instigated by Indonesian-supported militias who wanted to discourage independence. A UN peacekeeping mission was sent to the country to stabilize the situation. However, security deteriorated after the withdrawal of the peacekeeping mission; in 2006, gang violence provoked large-scale civil unrest and displacement, indicating that the country was still extremely vulnerable. As a result, the United Nations decided to send another peacekeeping operation to the country.

The 2006 violence initially began as a reaction to infighting within the Timorese army, when soldiers submitted a petition to the ruling government claiming mismanagement and discrimination within the army ranks. This provoked conflict between and within the police and the military, a conflict which quickly dispersed to the general population after a peaceful protest march turned violent. Violent protests played out for days, with a rebel group of soldiers fleeing to the hills and fighting against the state army while gangs roamed the streets of the state capital, Dili, burning houses and displacing thousands of people.

One factor that contributed strongly to the outbreak of gang violence was the high rate of youth unemployment in the country, especially amongst urban youth, and the failure of economic aid and development programs to reach and benefit young people. While East Timor had been a recipient of large of amounts of foreign aid after achieving independence, this aid did very little to address issues of political exclusion and the lack of economic opportunities for young people, and rather helped to centralize political power and the delivery of social services in Dili. Very small amounts of foreign assistance were channeled into creating job opportunities for youths. As a result, frustrated youths and young members of gangs played out their anger on the streets of Dili in 2006.

You can read more about the 2006 crisis in East Timor and the role of young people and foreign aid in the following sources:

- Report: "Review of Development Cooperation in Timor Leste: Final Report." Oslo: Scanteam, 2007. Accessed at http://www.scanteam.no/reports/2007/Timor%20Cooperation%20-%20Report.pdf.
- Report: James Scambary, "A Survey of Gangs and Youth Groups in Dili, Timor Leste," report commission by AUSAID, 2006. Accessed at http://www.etan.org/etanpdf/2006/Report_Youth_Gangs_in_Dili.pdf.
- Report: Richard Curtain. "Crisis in Timor Leste: Looking Beyond the Surface Reality for Causes and Solutions," working paper presented to seminar organized by the State, Society, and Governance in Melanesia Project at the Australian National University, 27 July 2006, accessed at http://rspas.anu.edu.au/papers/melanesia/working_papers/06_01wp_Curtain.pdf.

Conclusion

As this chapter and the previous one have illustrated, a post-conflict context has many challenges for young people. Conflict has long-ranging consequences for young people which, if not addressed after the official end of fighting, can result in the resumption of violence. This was illustrated by, among other things, the outbreak of fighting and political divisions in 2006 in East Timor, and by the high levels of gang violence in Guatemala. Therefore, there is—unfortunately—little reason to assume that a post-conflict period is a smooth, linear transition from war to peace. Rather, the post-conflict phase is a fragile period that is as fraught with danger and insecurity. While holding great potential for improvements in the lives of young people, the ending of a conflict pushes new issues and needs to the fore, such as the resumption of social services, the return of young displaced persons to their villages and communities of origin, and the rebuilding of society more generally.

Young people are affected by, but are also important players in, the war-to-peace continuum. They play and should play a role in peacemaking, peacekeeping, peacebuilding, and reconstruction and rehabilitation efforts, particularly so because young people are so important to the future of societies. This makes issues pertaining to young people in war-affected countries that much more important, for what kind of society will emerge after a war that has not included a large segment of its population in peacebuilding efforts?

Notes

1. Ralph Lee Woodward, *A Short History of Guatemala* (Antigua, Guatemala: Editorial Laura Lee, 1992); Susanne Jonas, *Of Centaurs and Doves: Guatemala's Peace Process* (Boulder: Westview Press, 2000); Susanne Jonas, "Democratization Through Peace: The Difficult Case of Guatemala", *Journal of Interamerican Studies and World Affairs* 42, no. 4

(2000): 9–38; Trish O'Kane, *Guatemala: A Guide to the People, Politics, and Culture* (New York: Interlink Books, 2000).

2. Human Rights Watch, "Universal Periodic Review of Guatemala" (May 4, 2008), accessed at http://www.hrw.org/en/news/2008/05/04/universal-periodic-review-guatemala.

3. UNICEF, "At a Glance: Guatemala", accessed at http://www.unicef.org/infoby country/guatemala.html.

4. Jayantha Dhanapala, "Making Peace Last: Disarmament as an Essential Element," speech given for the DPI/NGO Conference at the United Nations on 10 September 2002, accessed at http://www.wwan.cn/disarmament/HomePage/HR/docs/2002/2002Sep10 _NewYork.pdf.

5. Alex Bellamy, Paul Williams, and Stuart Griffin, *Understanding Peacekeeping* (Cambridge: Polity Press, 2004). See also Oliver Ramsbotham, Tom Woodhouse, and Hugh Miall, *Contemporary Conflict Resolution*, 2nd ed. (Cambridge: Polity Press, 2005).

6. The World Bank and the Human Security Report Project, *Mini Atlas of Human Security* (Brighton: Myriad Editions, 2008).

7. See the web site of the United Nations Department of Peacekeeping Operations for troop numbers: http://www.un.org/Depts/dpko/dpko/.

8. The World Bank and the Human Security Report Project, 2008.

9. Sandra Whitworth, *Men, Militarism, and UN Peacekeeping: A Gendered Analysis.* Boulder: Lynne Rienner Publishers, 2004).

10. Save the Children U.K., "No One to Turn To: The Underreporting of Child Sexual Exploitation and Abuse by Aid Workers and Peacekeepers," (2008), accessed at http://www.savethechildren.org.uk/en/docs/No_One_to_Turn_To.pdf.

11. Vanessa Kent, "Protecting Civilians from UN Peacekeepers and Humanitarian Workers: Sexual Exploitation and Abuse," in *Unintended Consequences of Peacekeeping Operations* Chiyuki Aoi, Cedric de Coning, and Ramesh Thakur, eds. (Tokyo: United Nations University Press, 2007): 44–66.

12. Christine Bell, *Peace Agreements and Human Rights* (Oxford: Oxford University Press, 2000); Peter Wallensteen and Margareta Sollenberg, "Armed Conflicts, Conflict Termination, and Peace Agreements, 1989–1996," *Journal of Peace Research* 34, no. 3 (1997): 339–358; Barbara Walter, "The Critical Barrier to Civil War Settlement," *International Organization,* 51, no. 3 (1997): 335–364.

13. Ramsbotham, Woodhouse, and Miall 2005.

14. Bell 2000; Christine Bell, "Peace Agreements: Their Nature and Legal Status," *The American Journal of International Law* 100, no. 2 (2006): 374; John Darby and James Rae, "Peace Processes From 1988–1998: Changing Patterns," *Ethnic Studies Report* 18, no. 1 (1998): 45–59.

15. Walter 1997.

16. Human Security Centre, *Human Security Brief 2006* (University of British Columbia, 2006).

17. Timothy Sisk, "Peacemaking in Civil Wars: Obstacles, Options, and Opportunities." Kroc Institute Occasional Paper 20:OP:2, 2001.

18. Human Security Centre, 2006.

19. Jonathan Goodhand, *Aiding Peace? The Role of NGOs in Armed Conflict* (Boulder: Lynne Rienner Publishers, 2006); Jeremy Ginifer (with Mike Bourne and Owen Greene), "Considering Armed Violence in the Post-Conflict Transition: DDR and Small Arms and Light Weapons Reduction Initiatives," University of Bradford Centre for International

Cooperation and Security Briefing Paper (September 2004), accessed at http://www
.brad.ac.uk/acad/cics/publications/AVPI/briefing/AVPI_DDR_Briefing_Paper.pdf.

20. Kendra Dupuy, "Education in Peace Agreements, 1989–2005," *Conflict Resolution Quarterly* 26, no. 2 (2008), 149–166.

21. Office of the Special Representative for Children in Armed Conflict, "Operational Guidance Note on Addressing Children's Issues in Peace Agreements", accessed at http://peacemaker.unlb.org. © United Nations, 2009. Reproduced with permission.

22. The World Bank and the Human Security Report Project, 2008.

23. United Nations Security Council, "No Exit Without Strategy: Security Council Decision-Making and the Closure or Transition of United Nations Peacekeeping Operations," Report of the Secretary General, April 20, 2001.

24. United Nations, "A More Secure World: Our Shared Responsibility," Report of the Secretary General's High-level Panel on Threats, Challenges, and Changes," (2004: 72) accessed at http://www.un.org/secureworld/report2.pdf.

25. Taken from the web site of the UN Peacebuilding Commission at http://www.un
.org/peace/peacebuilding/.

26. Roland Paris, "Human Security: Paradigm Shift or Hot Air?" *International Security*, 26, no. 2 (2001): 87–102.

27. Clayton Thyne, "ABC's, 123's, and the Golden Rule: The Pacifying Effect of Education on Civil War, 1980–1999," *International Studies Quarterly* 50, no. 4 (2006): 733–754.

28. Paul Collier et al., *Breaking the Conflict Trap: Civil War and Development Policy* (Washington, D.C.: The World Bank, 2003).

29. Elizabeth G. Ferris, "Refugees", In Mary Hawkesworth and Maurice Kogan (eds.), *Encyclopedia of Government and Politics* (London: Routledge, 1992): 1360–1373); David Korn, *Exodus Within Borders: An Introduction to the Crisis of Internal Displacement* (Washington, D.C.: Brookings Institution Press, 1999); W. R. Smyser, *Refugees: Extended Exile* (New York: The Center for Strategic and International Studies, 1987).

30. Smyser, 1987: 32.

31. Iris Teichmann, "Asylum Seekers, Refugees, and Racism," in Gerard McCann and Stephen McCloskey (eds.), *From the Local to the Global: Key Issues in Development Studies* (Sterling, VA: Pluto Press, 2003): 199–216; B. S. Chimni, "From Resettlement to Involuntary Repatriation: Towards a Critical History of Durable Solutions to Refugee Problems," *Refugee Survey Quarterly* 23, no. 3 (2004): 55–72.

32. See the UNHCR Statistical Yearbook for 2007, accessed at http://www.unhcr.org/statistics/STATISTICS/4981b19d2.html.

33. Jesse Newman, "Narrating Displacement: Oral Histories of Sri Lankan Women", University of Oxford Refugee Studies Center Working Paper No. 15 (October 2003), accessed at http://www.rsc.ox.ac.uk/PDFs/workingpaper15.pdf.

34. Oladele O. Arowolo, "Return Migration and the Problem of Reintegration", *International Migration* 38, no. 5 (2000): 59–82.

35. Mulenga Nkula, "Refugees and Durable Solutions: The Case of Mozambique and Kosovo" (2004), accessed at http://www.fiuc.org/esap/ZAMB/ZAMB7/General/refugees1.pdf; John R. Rogge and Joshua O. Akol, "Repatriation: Its Role in Resolving Africa's Refugee Dilemma," *International Migration Review* 23, no. 2 (1989): 184–200

36. UNHCR, *Handbook for Repatriation and Reintegration Activities* (Geneva: UNHCR).

37. Betsy Lippman and Sajjad Malid, "The 4R's: The Way Ahead?" *Forced Migration Review* 21, (2004):9–11

38. Nkula 2004.

39. Patricia Weiss Fagen, "Post-Conflict Reintegration and Reconstruction: Doing it Right Takes a While," in N. Steiner, M. Gibney, and G. Loescher (eds.), *Refugee Protection: Ethical, Legal, and Political Problems and the Role of UNHCR* (New York: Routledge Press, 2003); Dana Burde, "Weak State, Strong Community? Promoting Community Participation in Post-Conflict Countries," *Current Issues in Comparative Education* 6, no. 2 (2004): 73–87.

40. UNDP Sudan, "Good Governance and Equity in Political Participation in Post-Conflict Sudan," accessed at http://www.sd.undp.org/projects/dg1.htm.

41. United Nations Economic and Social Commission for Asia and the Pacific, "What is Good Governance?", accessed at http://www.unescap.org/pdd/prs/ProjectActivities/Ongoing/gg/governance.asp.

42. Martin Doornbos, "'Good governance: The rise and decline of a policy metaphor?'" Journal of Development Studies, 7: 6 (2001): 93–108.

43. Stephanie McCrummen, "'Children's Parliament' Sets High Bar in Congo," *The Washington Post*, August 11, 2007, page A–01.

44. UNICEF, "Children's Parliament of Guinea-Bissau Presents Its 'Manifesto' to Candidates," accessed at http://www.unicef.org/adolescence/guineabissau_46308.html.

45. UNFPA, "Women and Young People in Humanitarian Crises" in *State of World Population 2005*, accessed at http://www.unfpa.org/swp/2005/english/ch8/chap8_page3.htm.

46. Sheila Meintjes, Anu Pillay, and Meredeth Turshen, "There Is No Aftermath For Women," in *The Aftermath: Women in Post-Conflict Transformation*, eds. Sheila Meintjes, Anu Pillay, and Meredeth Turshen (New York: Zed Books, 2001): 3–18.

47. Plan International, *Because I Am A Girl: The State of the World's Girls 2008, Special Focus: In The Shadow of War*, accessed at http://www.plan-international.org/pdfs/BIAAG_2008_english.pdf

48. Angela Veale, *From Child Soldier to Ex-fighter: Female Fighters, Demobilisation and Reintegration in Ethiopia*, Monograph No. 85 (Pretoria: Institute for Security Studies, 2003).

49. World Health Organization, "Post-Conflict Rehabilitation of the Health Sector", accessed at http://who.int/reproductive-health/publications/conflict_and_displacement/pdf/chapter16.en.pdf

50. UNICEF, *The State of the World's Children 2008: Child Survival* (New York: UNICEF, 2008). See http://www.unicef.org/sowc08/index.php.

51. The under-five mortality rate is the probability of dying between birth and exactly five years of age. See UNICEF, *The State of the World's Children 2008: Child Survival* (New York: UNICEF, 2008).

52. Paul Spiegel et al., "Prevalence of HIV Infection in Conflict-Affected and Displaced People in Seven Sub-Saharan African Countries: A Systematic Review," *The Lancet* 369, no. 9580 (2007): 2187–2195.

53. Susanne Schall and Thomas Elbert, "Ten Years After the Genocide: Trauma Confrontation and Posttraumatic Stress in Rwandan Adolescents," *Journal of Traumatic Stress* 19, no. 1 (2006): 95–105.

54. Nina Arnhold et al., *Education for Reconstruction: The Regeneration of Educational Capacity Following National Upheaval*, Oxford Studies in Comparative Education (Oxfordshire: Symposium Books, 1998); Alan Smith and Tony Vaux, "Education, Conflict, and International Development", (London: Department For International Development, 2003).

55. Thyne, 2006.

56. John R. Rogge, "Repatriation of Refugees: A Not So Simple 'Optimum' Solution," in Tim Allen and Hubert Morsink (eds.), *When Refugees Go Home* (London: James Currey, 1994): 14–49.

57. Philip Stabback, "Curriculum Development, Diversity, and Division in Bosnia and Herzegovina," in Sobhi Tawil and Alexandra Harley (eds.), *Education, Conflict, and Social Cohesion* (Geneva: International Bureau of Education, 2004): 41.

58. Collier et al., 2003; Paul Collier, "Doing Well Out of War: An Economic Perspective," in Mats R. Berdal and David M. Malone (eds.), *Greed and Grievance: Economic Agendas in Civil Wars* (Boulder: Lynne Rienner Publishers, 2000): 91–111.

59. L. J. Saha and I. Fägarlind, "Education and Development", in T. Husén and T. N. Postlethwaite (eds.), *The International Encyclopedia of Education*, 2nd ed. (Oxford: Elsevier Science Ltd., 1994): 1648–1655); Joop Hartog, "Human Capital as an Instrument of Analysis For the Economics of Education," *European Journal of Education,* 35, no. 1 (2000): 7–20.

60. See Ellen Carm et al, *Education and its impact on poverty: an initial exploration of the evidence.* Special study commissioned by NORAD (Oslo, Norway: Oslo University College, 2003). It should be noted, however, that countries such as India, China, and Britain all achieved significant economic growth without first achieving anywhere near universal primary education.

61. Henrik Urdal, "A Clash of Generations? Youth Bulges and Political Violence," *International Studies Quarterly* 50, no. 3 (2006): 607–629; Nicholas Sambanis, "Using Case Studies to Expand Economic Models of Civil War," *Perspectives on Politics* 2, no. 2 (2004): 259–279.

62. Mark Bils and Peter J. Klenow, "Does Schooling Cause Growth?" *The American Economic Review* 90, no. 5 (2000): 1160–1183.

63. Kenneth W. Beasley, "Job Creation in Postconflict Societies," USAID Issue Paper No. 9 (January 2006), accessed at http://digitalcommons.ilr.cornell.edu/cgi/viewcontent .cgi?article=1277&context=key_workplace.

CHAPTER 6

Summary and Conclusion

The previous chapters provided a lot of information about the situation of and challenges facing children and young people in situations of armed conflict and postwar reconstruction. They also discussed the many development programs and initiatives of local, national, and international organizations and states which are implemented to help young people to cope with their situations and to improve them. It became clear that children and young people can respond to and act completely differently when confronted with conflict: some flee and actively look for livelihood opportunities—whether in a displacement camp or just on their own—while others may decide to take part in a conflict as child soldiers or young combatants. A similarly wide range of scenarios can be distinguished in post-conflict situations where some young people are turned into passive recipients of aid (if they receive any support at all), while others are actively engaged in making peace and rebuilding their countries. However, more often than not, children and young people have no or very limited choices in wartime and in times of postwar reconstruction.

To improve the situation for young people in conflict and post-conflict situations, a wide range of means are used: there is an increasing body of conventions, principles, and treaties stipulating and protecting the rights of children in conflict situations. There are also numerous initiatives for young people during and after war to help them with (rebuilding) their lives.

This chapter will begin by presenting a short summary of each chapter and listing key points and lessons learned from it. It then presents an overview of the Machel Review study. This review, which appeared 10 years after the Machel report was written, provides an overview of the achievements made so far in relation to children in situations of armed conflict, and further stipulates some of the major challenges ahead.

Chapter 1: Children, Youth, and Armed Conflict starts with a short introduction to the phenomenon of armed conflict. It then discusses contemporary conflicts —those which took, or are still taking place, after the end of the Cold War— and explains the relevance of the changed nature of warfare with regard to consequences for children and young people. The characteristics of the so-called New Wars are discussed as well as the main explanations for why warfare has changed and why the 1990s witnessed an increase in the number of armed conflicts. The chapter then looks at young people. It observes that there are different definitions of who actually is a child and what childhood should look like. It is shown that a chronological, age-based division between "child" and "adult" has limitations and that the idea of childhood is a culturally-specific construction, rather than a universally agreed-upon concept. This is also acknowledged by researchers, policymakers, and practitioners in the field who increasingly prefer to refer to young people affected by war, rather than to children. The chapter concludes with a short overview of some of the most important international laws and conventions which address the issue of children and young people in the context of war.

Some of the key lessons and observations made in Chapter 1 are:

• War is neither a recent phenomenon, nor is it limited to certain geographical areas. After the end of the Second World War, international relations were dominated by Superpower rivalry. The end of the Cold War in the early 1990s saw at first an increase in the number of armed conflicts in the world but since 1995 a steady decrease.
• Post-Cold War armed conflicts are often referred to as "New Wars" and are predominantly intrastate conflicts with a high percentage of civilian casualties. The fighting and violence often seems to be senseless, extremely brutal, and deprived of any political aim. Increasingly, armed factions seem to have economic motives for waging or continuing their wars.
• Different explanations are given for the New War phenomenon, including deep hatreds along ethnic or religious lines ("New Barbarism"); diminishing natural resources and increasing populations (neo-Malthusianism); interests in economic gain ("Greed, not Grievance"); collapse of a specific type of political system (neo-patrimonialism); and eroding state authority as a result of globalization (Identity Politics).
• Nations in the developed world are frequently involved in war, but these seldom take place on their home soils. It is the poor and lower-income countries which experience the most conflicts on their soils.
• Some armed conflicts can go on for decades with whole generations growing up knowing nothing other than war. The majority of children and young people in regions experiencing armed conflict just try to survive in their communities, as internally displaced people in camps, or abroad as refugees. But there is a significant group of young people who either resist or participate more actively in armed conflict.
• Who are considered to be children and what childhood is supposed to be like has differed over time and from culture to culture. To overcome the problem of labeling everyone below 18 years (a widely legal accepted age for the transition from child to adult) as

a "child," terms such as child, adolescent, teenager, young adult and youth are now used to make it possible to use more subtle categories.

- There are a series of UN declarations and conventions which stipulate the rights of children, both in peacetime and in times of war. The 1989 United Nations Convention on the Rights of the Child is the most widely signed and ratified UN treaty ever.
- States which have signed and ratified these declarations and conventions have made firm commitments to uphold these rights. Nevertheless, the rights of children are violated worldwide, during times of peace and in particular during times of war. Sometimes states are not willing to live up to their obligations, but more often they are just not capable of providing for and protecting the rights of children.

Chapter 2: Growing Up in the Context of War: The Impact of Armed Conflict on Children and Young People discusses how war impacts children and young people's social and economic situation. The effects can be wide-ranging and long-lasting, and include limited access to health facilities, disrupted educational opportunities, and decreasing apprenticeship and employment possibilities. This takes place in a context of increasing poverty levels. The chapter starts with the story of Peter, one of the "lost boys" from Sudan and his search for a safe place to live. It then discusses issues of forced displacement and separation—and the impact of displacement on family and community structures—more generally. The chapter then discusses the impact of war on education. It observes that education can be a way to hold communities together and build up peace but at the same time it can be a cause for conflict—either when young people are frustrated about the poor quality of education or because the educational system is used to spread prejudices and messages of hate.

The economic impact, and the impact on family and community structures, of war on young people is considerable and is the focus of the next two sections. The chapter concludes with a discussion of the impact of war on children and young people's physical and mental health. The physical health of young people can be directly affected by war—if, for instance, they get wounded during an attack—or indirectly—because of malnutrition or limited access to health services. The impact of war on young people's mental health can be significant and may take years to heal, if it heals at all. When looking at health issues—and how they are affected by war—it is pointed out that one should always be aware of gender dimensions, or to say it differently: war has a gendered impact. The last few pages of the chapter outline an encouraging example: child clubs and the Children as Zones of Peace initiative started during times of war.

Some of the key lessons and observations made in Chapter 2 are:

- Children and young people are often highly vulnerable to the effects of war because they are to a more or lesser degree still dependent on adults and are still developing physically and psychologically. The effects of war can thus have a very long-term impact on the development of young people and their growth into adulthood.
- The targets and victims of violence during armed conflicts are predominantly civilians and civilian infrastructure. An estimated 90 percent of deaths that occur during armed

conflicts are civilians, while upwards of 50 percent of refugees are children under the age of 18.

- Young forced migrants (both refugees and internally displaced persons) can face significant security threats, such as the risk of experiencing gender-based violence (i.e. rape), becoming separated from one's parents, armed attacks on displacement camps, and the recruitment of young people living in displacement camps to serve as combatants in an armed group.
- Armed conflicts occur predominately in poor countries, where young people constitute a large section of the population. Young people in poor countries often have limited access to basic social services, such as education and health. A situation of armed conflict makes this worse, forcing young people to leave their homes and depriving them of access to the resources and social services they need to develop.
- War often deprives young people of the opportunity to go to school and worsens conditions in the education system. Nearly half of the world's out-of-school children live in conflict-affected countries. Yet, education can also play a role in the outbreak of a conflict, and in why young people become combatants. This occurs where the quality of education is poor, identity issues are not recognized in the education system, and access to schooling is limited.
- Education is now largely viewed as being a fourth pillar of humanitarian assistance. This includes the provision of education to refugees and IDPs. Some of the challenges inherent in providing education to displaced populations include whether the curriculum of the host or home country should be followed and in what language the instruction should be carried out.
- The economic consequences of armed conflict directly impact on young people. During a conflict, state resources are reallocated away from the education and health sectors to the military, and employment and income-earning opportunities become limited. As a result, parents have less money to invest in their children's schooling, adequate nutrition, and health care needs. This can force young people to take on new economic responsibilities, such as working to earn an income.
- The physical health of young people is directly threatened by a situation of armed conflict. Land mines constitute one such threat: children and young people are more likely to die or be seriously injured by a land mine because they are smaller and thus physically more vulnerable than adults to the effects of land mine explosions.
- The indirect effects of conflict, such as malnutrition and disease, heavily impact on children and young people. The highest rates of children who die before reaching their fifth birthday are found in countries that are currently experiencing war or that have recently emerged from war. As much as 95 percent of all child deaths in recent African conflicts have been the result of starvation or illness.
- War also affects the mental health of children and young people when they witness traumatic events, such as the killing or torture of family members and friends. This can result in young people developing post-traumatic stress disorders and other negative psychological responses.
- While war generally has a negative impact on the lives of children and young people, positive changes and opportunities can also result during times of war, such as when young people in refugee camps get access to education for the first time in their lives or when national and international organizations advocate for and facilitate the implementation the rights of the child.

In *Chapter 3: The Recruitment and Roles of Children and Young People in Fighting Forces*, the child soldier phenomenon is discussed. It starts with the real story of Samuel, a child soldier in the conflict in Sierra Leone. His story is illustrative of the lives of tens if not hundreds of thousands of other underage combatants. It is noted that young people are and probably always have been associated with fighting groups in various capacities throughout history. The chapter then explains why and how young people are recruited into these groups. It shows how the prewar conditions for young people—such as social exclusion and marginalization—in countries experiencing war, can have as much an impact on recruitment patterns of young people into fighting forces, as do unscrupulous warlords forcibly recruiting underage combatants to swell their ranks. A further discussion of voluntary, coerced, and forced enrollment of children into armed forces is given, as is an overview of the debate between those who argue that children indeed can voluntarily join an armed faction versus those who argue that in the case of children it is always forcible recruitment. Whether or not children voluntary join an armed faction can have legal implications. This is further explained by a discussion of the various conventions and treaties relating to children and armed conflict. But the question of voluntary or forced recruitment can also have practical implications; if young people join voluntarily for certain reasons and these reasons are not addressed, there is a real chance that at some stage they may decide to join an armed faction again. The chapter then discusses how young people are inducted into an armed group and made loyal or obedient. It concludes with a discussion of the various roles and tasks children and young people have in fighting forces, such as manning checkpoints, spying, engaging in active combat, and providing domestic and sexual services. Special attention is paid to the roles and tasks of female child soldiers.

Some of the key lessons and observations made in Chapter 3 are:

- It is estimated that during the armed conflicts of the 1980s and 90s, at any one time there were about 300,000 underage people active as child soldiers. From the start of the new millennium this number has gone down slightly, and has now been put at around 250,000. But the active involvement of those under the age of 18 in armed conflict has occurred in all times and places.
- The definition of a child soldier does not only refer to a child who is carrying, or has carried weapons. Child combatants can be part of any kind of regular or irregular armed group. Some are cooks, porters, or messengers or are used for sexual purposes and/or forced marriage.
- Child soldiers often fight in highly complex conflicts, which can take many years or even decades—and many broken cease-fires or peace-accords—before enduring peace is achieved. Often there are more armed factions involved than just the state and one opposition group.
- There are several risk factors which make young people more vulnerable to conscription or likely to join an armed faction. These include poverty, family separation, and living in a war-zone. Personal factors, such as the character of the child and his or her capacity to

overcome difficult circumstances, often referred to as "resilience," also play an important role.

- To prevent young people from joining or being forcibly recruited is difficult but community-based approaches in protecting young people have worked in the past. Schools which remain open and running during difficult times can be another incentive for not joining an armed faction.
- Female child soldiers are probably as common as male child soldiers. They are involved in the fighting but predominantly in serving commanders and soldiers in the camps or barracks. Often they are exposed to sexual harassment or even rape.
- Three different types of conscription can be distinguished for child soldiers: *voluntary conscription*, which is joining an armed faction out of one's own free choice; *coercive conscription*, which is joining an armed faction as a result of pressure to do so mainly by family, relatives, religious leaders, etc., but without explicit use of force; and *forced recruitment*, which is conscription into an armed faction against one's will or choice, with the use of threats, force, or violence.
- Forced conscription of people below the age of 18 is never allowed, neither in international treaty law nor in international customary law, but voluntarily conscription of children of 16 years and older is not always against the law.
- Children are inducted into armed factions through military training, but often also through exposure to combat without proper training or by being forced to kill people, including sometimes their own family members. Indoctrination, threats, punishments, but also rewards if they are brave, further increase loyalty or at least obedience.
- To prepare child soldiers for battle and to force them to overcome their fear, commanders can provide them with drugs. Sometimes traditional rituals are used to make the children believe that they have become invincible.
- There are about 500 million small arms in the world and many circulate in developing countries and regions experiencing armed conflict. More than 90 percent of the conflicts which took place during the 1990s involved only light weapons. These weapons make the use of children as combatants more effective.

Chapter 4: The Disarmament, Demobilization, and Reintegration of Young Ex-Combatants, discusses the transition from war to peace for young ex-combatants. The special provisions made for ex-child combatants in demobilization, disarmament, and reintegration (DDR) programs are outlined. The disarmament and demobilization of child soldiers present unique challenges. While many adult ex-combatants may return straight home after disarmament and demobilization, underage ex-combatants often stay in temporary care. In these so-called Transit Centers, the ex-combatants are reintroduced to a civilian style of life. The chapter discusses some of the most important activities taking place in these centers, which include vocational training, catch-up education, sports and recreational activities and counseling and therapy to deal with the war traumas many young people have. The chapter concludes with a discussion of the family tracing and reunification process and the more long-term reintegration process. The reintegration process—as is showed in the chapter—has many different aspects to it and can take different forms. It does not always mean that ex-child soldiers will have to live with their parents again. To measure the degree

of successful reintegration, both social and economic indicators can be used.
  Some of the key lessons and observations made in Chapter 4 are:

- The population of a state emerging from armed conflict faces enormous challenges as it must rebuild the country after years or sometimes decades of war. Destroyed infrastructure (roads, bridges, schools, hospitals, etc.) and abandoned and overgrown farmland have to be rehabilitated. Massive population movements are likely to take place when IDPs and refugees return home.
- Countries emerging from violent conflict have to find a way to make a peaceful transition from combatant to civilian life possible for the tens of thousands, or sometimes hundreds of thousands soldiers and fighters. Failing to do so will pose a direct threat to the recently achieved peace since disgruntled ex-combatants may start to cause mayhem or even take up (secretly hidden) arms again.
- Disarmament, Demobilization and Reintegration (DDR) programs stipulate when and under what conditions fighters and commanders of the armed factions will disarm; how their chains of command are broken and if temporary encampment will take place; and what kind of assistance (such as vocational training and/or financial) they will receive upon demobilization.
- DDR normally takes place at the end of the conflict. But DDR programs for child soldiers sometimes start to run while the conflict is still going on, since it is against international law to have underage combatants among the ranks. Nevertheless, the reluctance of commanders to give up their fighters, even child soldiers, remains.
- The participation of children in judicial and nonjudicial approaches to address past human rights abuses—normally referred to as "transitional justice"—is often limited. "Truth and Reconciliations Commissions" (TRCs) and "War Tribunals or Courts" are two of the most widely-used approaches by post-conflict countries, but it is widely agreed that underage combatants should for instance not be indicted by a War Tribunal.
- It is now common practice to provide institutionalized care for ex-child combatants for a certain period of time. So-called "Interim Care Centers" (ICCs) or "Transit Centers" (TCs) have been established by a number of local, national, and international NGOs and international organizations—or in some cases by the army itself—during and after the conflict. These centers aim to provide a safe environment in which the ex-child fighters are helped with their transition from a fighter's life to that of a civilian.
- The time spent in these centers can vary, but on average it is about six to nine months. During this time the ex-child soldiers receive education and skills training and enjoy recreational activities. They are provided with shelter, food, and medical care and they often take part in formal and informal counseling activities, which help them to overcome the traumatic experiences many have had. The overall aim of these activities is to bring some structure and routine back into the lives of these young people.
- Ex-child soldiers in ICCs are normally provided with a so-called "catch-up education" program. This is a compressed curriculum, designed to quickly bring them to a level more in line with their age. Although no wonders can be expected from this special form of education, the lower teacher-pupil ratio can turn out to be very effective.
- The majority of the slightly older ex-child soldiers usually prefer to be trained in a vocational skill, with the expectation that they will be able to make a living out of their newly mastered skill once they have returned to their communities or places of reintegration.

- In general, the most common skills which are made available to ex-child combatants when they are in an ICC are carpentry, tailoring, and masonry. Popular among girl ex-combatants in particular are skills like hairdressing and soap-making.

- Play and sport usually make up an important part of the day in an ICC. Keeping the young people busy is helpful in taking their minds away from the things they did and experienced while they were with the armed group, and it helps them to get rid of extra energy in a nonviolent way.

- The need for some form of counseling or therapy seems obvious: the majority of ex-child soldiers have experienced highly traumatic events, often repeatedly and over many years. Programs helping ex-child soldiers with their transition to civilian life include some form of counseling or therapy. These can vary from structured one-on-one sessions with a counselor, psychologist, or psychiatrist to group sessions wherein through means of drama or creative arts, ex-child combatants are encouraged to reflect on their past lives and subsequently focus on their strengths and the future.

- There is now an emerging understanding that counseling or therapeutic sessions have to have some resonance with practices of healing and helping that are common in the specific culture. As with so many programs that aim to help people, Western blueprint approaches are not always helpful, and can even be counterproductive.

- Ex-child soldiers, who may have spent five or even ten years with an armed faction and away from home and relatives, have to find their parents or family members after being demobilized. Child agencies helping ex-child soldiers can establish so-called Family Tracing and Reunification (FTR) teams. These teams try to gather as much information as possible from former child combatants in order to locate their families and home towns or villages.

- Various child organizations have experimented with alternative forms of care, mainly small group living in the community and foster-parent care. Successes have varied, and it seems that residential care is still needed, in particular where large groups of underage combatants disarm in a short time frame and are unlikely to be aware of the whereabouts of their families.

- Evidence gathered over a number of years shows clearly that only a part of the ex-child combatants will return and stay with their parents after they have been demobilized. Others will live with friends or relatives, for instance in urban or mining centers. There is even a group who will continue to stay with their commanders in a postwar setting. The idea that successful reintegration equals reunification and living with one's parents is too limited.

- We can distinguish between reintegration indicators that are more focused on social aspects and those more focused on economic ones. Some of the indicators which fall into the category of social reintegration include whether the young ex-combatants live with their parents and whether or not they are going to school, or are a member of a sport team or a youth association. For those ex-child combatants who are slightly older, reintegration also has economic aspects to it. Having some kind of employment is often a good indicator of reintegration.

Chapter 5: After the War: War-Affected Young People in Post-Conflict Environments discusses some of the issues already addressed in the previous chapter with regard to the reintegration of ex-combatants, but also for young war-affected people more generally. The chapter focuses on the aftermath and consequences of war on children and young people. It starts with a discussion of the conflict in Guatemala and its aftermath, which saw a rapid increase in the levels of gang-violence. It then looks at the role of UN peacekeeping missions in helping war-affected countries in their transition process. While overwhelmingly positive, peacekeeping missions can also have negative impacts on children in conflict/post-conflict settings. The issue of increased child prostitution and HIV/AIDS infection rates are used to illustrate this. The needs and rights of young people are, to some extent, but should be much more, addressed in peace-accords. The same is true for the extent young people are actively involved in the design and implementation of peace agreements and peace-building initiatives. The chapter then looks in more detail at the return and reintegration process of IDPs and refugees, and how different aid organizations help young people in this process. This is followed in the chapter by the challenge to address the economic needs of war-affected populations and the need for re-establishing social services. In many cases the reconstruction and reform of the educational sector are needed and are of great importance to young people. But at the same time, as the chapter argues, economic opportunities must be created to increase the chance of sustained peace.

Some of the key lessons and observations made in Chapter 5 are:

- The transition period from war to peace is a difficult and long-term process for conflict-affected countries. Conflict has long-ranging consequences for young people which, if not addressed after the official end of fighting, can result in the resumption of violence. Building peace entails establishing both a negative peace (that is, getting people to lay down their weapons and halting violence) and a positive peace (that is, working toward the provision of social justice).
- While the deployment of peacekeeping missions is often necessary to keep warring parties apart, such missions can also negatively impact children and young people, such as when peacekeepers sexually abuse or fail to protect young people from harm. In an effort to offset such negative consequences, the United Nations has mainstreamed Child Protection Advisors and Officers into its peacekeeping missions since 2000.
- The needs and concerns of children and young people have been taken into account during peacemaking processes and in peace agreements. Past peace agreements have addressed children and young people through, for example, attention to education issues, child soldiers, DDR processes, and the return of young forced migrants.
- The United Nations considers peacebuilding to consist of three elements: (a) the consolidation of internal and external security; (b) the strengthening of political institutions and good governance; and (c) the promotion of economic and social rehabilitation and transformation. The United Nations Peacebuilding Commission is a relatively new body that is tasked with assisting conflict-affected states in the transition from war and peace.
- Peacebuilding is a long-term process that takes place both from "above" (at the national level) and from "below" (by empowering communities that are affected by conflict to actively contribute to the consolidation of peace).
- The international community considers there to be three acceptable "durable" solutions to end existing refugee and IDP situations: integration into the country or community of

asylum; resettlement in a third country or in another part of the home country; and repatriation and return back to the country and/or community of origin.

- Repatriation is the preferred donor option for ending refugee situations. Once refugees have returned home, they must reintegrate into their communities. But for young forced migrants who repatriate, they may not be returning "home" in the same way as their parents or older family members if they have lived for a long period of time in a protracted situation of displacement.
- The effects of conflict are still experienced by women and girls long after the end of a conflict, such as continuing to lose out on the opportunity to go to school due to conflict-deepened poverty. Even in cases where gender equality may have been an important aspect of a conflict (i.e. part of the ideology of a rebel group), this does not mean that the ideals about gender equality will also automatically change gender roles and perspectives at a local level after the end of a conflict.
- Rebuilding the education and health sectors and addressing security threats such as removing land mines is important in reducing the impact of conflict on young people. Health clinics and education facilities must be rebuilt and new and existing personnel trained. Many children may have missed out on schooling during a conflict, necessitating the implementation of catch-up schooling, such as accelerated learning programs.
- Conflict can indirectly create opportunities to facilitate the participation of young people in society. For instance, children's parliaments have been created in several post-conflict countries. Improving the participation of young people, particularly in peacebuilding processes, is critical to mitigate the impact of war on young people and to help young people learn to resolve problems in nonviolent ways.

The Machel Review

This book started with a preface dedicated to the 1996 Machel report on the *Impact of armed conflict on children*. The Machel report was a seminal study which started a decade of numerous research activities into the issue of underage combatants and helped NGOs and international organizations such as the United Nations to increase the number and improve the quality of its interventions aimed at reducing the impact of war on young people. These interventions were both of a legal nature (in the form of principles and conventions or the prosecutions of perpetrators by international tribunals) and of a practical nature (such as programs to help the rehabilitation process of ex-child combatants). As is evident from this textbook, since the release of the report much has changed—fortunately for the better—in terms of conflict and its impact on young people. Not least among these changes is the fact that the number of armed conflicts has decreased, which cannot have anything other than a positive effect on the lives of young people who might have otherwise have grown up in war situations.

To better understand the impact of all the changes since 1996, the UN requested a new report or, better put, a review of the old 1996 report. On 13 August 2007 the Special Representative of the Secretary-General for Children and Armed Conflict (SRSG CAAC), together with UNICEF, released a report named the *Machel Study 10-Year Strategic Review: Children and Conflict in a*

Changing World. Explaining the rationale behind the review, the SRSG CAAC and UNICEF state that

> Since the original release of the Machel Study, the context of conflict has changed dramatically. Diverse forms of political and armed violence have presented new threats to the protection of children. The overall aim of the Strategic Review is to provide a visionary and forward looking platform to address issues of children and armed conflict for the next 10 years.[1]

The last few pages of this book will be used to give an overview of the Review report and will look at how the changing context of conflict impacts on children and young people these days.

Like the Machel study did in 1996, the Review underlines the importance of "youthhood" and "agency." The first page of the review states that "the present report focuses on children, but at times analysis is extended to youth, defined by the General Assembly to be those age 15 to 24. We should recognize the capacities and agency of children and youth, and avoid characterizing children and youth as vulnerable or as delinquents who pose a threat to security."[2] As the title of the review suggests, conflict takes place in a changing world and the nature of conflict is changing too. These changes were already hinted at in the 1996 Machel report but are further specified in the Review. One of the most important changes in situations of armed conflict today is that there is an increase in the level of one-sided violence, wherein poorly resourced armed factions prey on civilians.[3] As a result of this low-intensity (as far as the number of battle-deaths are concerned) but often prolonged situation of armed violence and insecurity, the number of direct casualties may be relatively low but the number of indirect war-related casualties can be extremely high, and women and children are often among the most affected populations. The Review refers to a study by the International Rescue Committee which found that in the conflict in the Democratic Republic of Congo, 86 percent of deaths were caused by the indirect consequences of war.[4] Limited access to health facilities, malnutrition, and no access to clean drinking water are just some of the factors responsible for this high percentage.

Another aspect of the changing nature of warfare, which was not yet fully noted by the 1996 Machel report, is the role that natural resources can have in a war. The Review identifies the significant increase in our knowledge of ' "asset wars' where economic interests commercialize and prolong conflict"[5] and how these type of conflicts can increase the vulnerability of children and undermine their positions in peace agreements and postwar reconstruction. It is not hard to imagine that if warring factions fight over access to economic resources rather than over grievances around education or employment, children can be forcibly conscripted and forced to do hazardous work (like diamond mining), and peace agreements are likely to include few details addressing the sociopolitical issues which may improve the lives of children and young people.

The Review also shows an increasing awareness of the fading borders between organized armed opposition and organized transnational crime. Likely related to the commercialization of conflict, armed factions (including the official army) can involve themselves in activities which are normally associated with organized crime, such as drug and arms trafficking, or the smuggling of natural resources or humans. The impact of this on children can be considerable, as the Report notes: "A child recruited by an armed group one day may be labeled a gang member the next as political realities evolve".[6] However, it is important to remain cautious whenever armed opposition groups are portrayed as criminal networks, since it can be used by the enemy to deny or obscure a more genuine political agenda of the opposition group.

The same is true for the next issue the Review identifies, which is "terrorism." Again, "terrorism" and "terrorists" are labels that are quickly used by states to deny any platform to the political demands some armed groups make. However, the targeting of children by armed groups (such as the Beslan school hostage-taking in the northern Caucasus in 2004 by the Riyadus-Salikhin Reconnaissance and Sabotage Battalion of Chechen Martyrs group, which killed nearly 200 children) or the use of children in violent acts (such as in suicide bombings) quickly undermine any righteous claim to a political agenda, since they directly violate basic human rights. Referring to the trend where states limit civic rights to counteract terrorism, the Review notes that "also of great concern are situations where children are subject to legal grey areas and counter-terrorism measures that violate international juvenile justice standards."[7]

Finally, the Review—in its description of the changing context of war—draws attention to the continuing proliferation of small arms and light weapons. While the report acknowledges the progress made in banning land mines, the wide availability of small arms and light weapons contributes to a sustained culture of violence and the "rule of the gun," while the millions of land mines still in the ground are likely to continue to kill and maim young people in many conflict and post-conflict countries for decades to come. Children constitute more than a third of casualties from explosive remnants globally.[8]

While the Review states that—on a normative level—significant progress in addressing the recruitment and use of child soldiers has been made since the publication of the 1996 Machel study, the use of children in armed factions is by no means something of the past; estimates vary considerably, but between 18 countries (Secretary-General) and 43 countries (Coalition to Stop the Use of Child Soldiers) were either involved in illegal recruitment or used children since 2002.[9]

To underline the massive impact war has on education and health facilities—the Review notes that attacks on schools or hospitals have actually increased in recent years—the report provides the example of Afghanistan: "in Afghanistan, over 100 bombing, arson and missile attacks were made against educational facilities in the first half of 2006, and approximately 105,000 children were denied access to education because of insecurity."[10] The impact of this is likely to be experienced for years if not decades.

Another example of what has both immediate and long-term effects is war-related rape, which is a crime against humanity. Unfortunately, the Review has to conclude that rape and other acts of grave sexual violence continue to take place in nearly all contemporary armed conflicts.[11] The "normalization" of sexual violence during times of war and a climate of impunity often results in a continuation of these practices after war, and young people make up a significant part of the victims. In addition to the direct trauma of sexual violence, long-term consequences can include early pregnancies—with children born as a result of rape often being marginalized and stigmatized—fistula, infections, HIV/AIDS, and psychological trauma.[12]

The number of child soldiers is now probably below a quarter of a million, down from an estimated 300,000 in the mid 1990s. However, the number of forcibly displaced children and youths is not counted in the hundreds of thousands but in the millions. Analysis undertaken for the report found that "an estimated 18.1 million children were among populations living with the effects of displacement; within that group, there were an estimated 5.8 million refugee children and 8.8 million internally displaced children."[13] In general, children in situations of forced displacement are extremely vulnerable to violations of their basic human rights.

Interestingly, the Review raises attention to the impact of war on children and young people in light of the 2000 Millennium Development Goals (MDGs).[14] Goal 4 of the 8 MDGs entails the reduction of child mortality. The Review finds that "of the 20 countries with the highest under-five mortality rate, 15 are currently experiencing complex emergencies in at least a part of the country."[15] Goal 2 of the MDGs is about achieving Universal Primary Education, but "at least 50 per cent of out-of-school children of primary-school age are living in conflict-affected countries."[16]

The Review then discusses political engagement and the legal normative framework. It refers to a series of UN Security Resolutions including Resolutions 1261 (from the year 1999), 1279 (2001), 1460 (2003), 1460 (2003) and 1612 (2005), which all focus on children and young people in situations of armed conflict (see Appendix II for outlines of these resolutions). In 2000 the Optional Protocol to the Convention on the Right of Child on the Involvement of Children in Armed Conflict was adopted, raising the minimum age of participation to 18 years and outlining standards against the use of underage people in armed conflict. Moreover, child soldiering was defined as among the worst forms of child labor by International Labour Organization Convention No. 182. The Review also draws attention to the 2002 special session on children when the General Assembly adopted the final document, entitled "A World Fit for Children."[17] This report lists 21 goals for children in four priority areas of action—namely a) creating a World Fit for Children; b) goals, strategies and actions; c) mobilizing resources and d) follow-up actions and assessment. These goals are considered to be a vital step toward the achievement of the Millennium Development Goals. While it is acknowledged by the Review that the goals stipulated in the "A World Fit for Children" report and the MDGs are likely not to be met by several countries—some war affected countries even see regression toward the achievement of the goals—the Review states that rather than "concluding that those goals are too ambitious, efforts towards their achievement should be accelerated."[18]

At a system-level there also have been a series of initiatives since the release of the 1996 Machel study. Most notable among these are the 2006 Integrated Disarmament, Demobilization and Reintegration Standards; the 2007 Paris Principles and Guidelines on Children Associated with Armed Forces and Armed Groups (see Appendix II); the 2004 Minimum Standards for Education in Emergencies, Chronic Crises and Early Reconstruction; and the 2004 Inter-Agency Guiding Principles on Unaccompanied and Separated Children.[19] The 1996 Machel study asked for more involvement by regional and sub-regional bodies in the protection of children in situations of armed conflict. Since then, the European Union formulated guidelines and a protection strategy and the Economic Community of West African States established a special child protection unit in 2002 (which however ceased to exist in 2006). In general, the Review observes an improvement in the extent to which children's issues and concerns are included in peace agendas as well as a higher degree of involvement of young people in all kind of peace initiatives, although their participation in decision making remains limited.[20]

Since the original Machel study, the world has witnessed the first indictments of commanders and warlords on counts of recruiting and using children in hostilities. The 1998 Rome Statute of the International Criminal Court provided strong legal tools to do so and since then, Ugandan, Congolese, and Sierra Leonean commanders have been charged and found guilty, among others.[21] Where on the legal side it seems that legislation has finally translated into some action on the ground, as evidenced by these indictments, the Review identified a number of cross-cutting issues where agreements on approaches are emerging but implementation is slow and not sufficiently resourced.[22] According to the Review, partly to blame for this is "the inertia imposed by some community customs, traditions and history."[23] These issues include:

1. *Community-based reintegration and youth opportunities*: The Review notes the need for community-based programs which facilitate the reintegration process of war-affected children, but which at the same time should not single them out as a group and by doing so increase the perpetuating stigma. It is also noted that reintegration should be understood as much more than just the final component of the formal disarmament, demobilization, and reintegration process.
2. *Gender-based violence and sexual exploitation and abuse*: The Review draws attention to the need for addressing the long-term health needs, including reproductive health issues, of young people affected by gender-based violence and abuse. In addition, to limit the risk of postwar sexual exploitation, the review urges for the development of sustainable livelihood opportunities for young girls.
3. *Justice processes and reconciliation*: There is significant evidence now that traditional—community based—approaches to reconciliation and justice can play a positive role

in the reintegration process of war-affected children. However, more research is needed on this, according to the Review.

What may be considered as one of the greatest achievements of the 1996 Machel Study is the mainstreaming of children's concerns in policies and programs concerned with armed conflict and postwar reconstruction. For example, since 1999, the UN Department of Peacekeeping Operations, UNICEF, and the Special Representative of the Secretary-General for Children and Armed Conflict have worked together "to ensure that peacekeeping operations incorporate children's issues and include child protection advisers."[24] Child-specialized staff are also deployed in the early phase of response by the Office of the United Nations High Commissioner for Refugees.

The Review concludes with a series of recommendations which reflect the current state of our understanding of children in situations of armed conflict and shows which areas still need improvements—whether through legal means or through better implementation. The details of the 15 recommendations provided by the Review can be accessed via the Review's web site[25], and the recommendations are as follows:

— Recommendation 1: Achieve universal adherence to international standards and norms;
— Recommendation 2: End impunity for violations against children;
— Recommendation 3: Prioritize children's security;
— Recommendation 4: Strengthen monitoring and reporting;
— Recommendation 5: Promote justice for children;
— Recommendation 6: Ensure access to basic services;
— Recommendation 7: Support inclusive reintegration strategies;
— Recommendation 8: End gender-based violence;
— Recommendation 9: Improve capacity and knowledge for quality care and protection of children;
— Recommendation 10: Ensure complementarity among key actors and mainstream children and armed conflict concerns;
— Recommendation 11: Operationalize the engagement of regional bodies;
— Recommendation 12: Ensure that funding matches children's needs and priorities;
— Recommendation 13: Consolidate the role of United Nations peacekeeping in child protection;
— Recommendation 14: Increase the participation of and support for children and youth;
— Recommendation 15: Integrate children's rights in peacemaking, peacebuilding, and preventive actions.

The above recommendations clearly indicate that there is still an enormous amount of work needed to be done to protect young people in situations of armed conflict and to facilitate their postwar reintegration process. The Review study, however, clearly showed how much has been achieved since the publication of the 1996 Machel study. This is also confirmed by the material presented in this

book. Still, in a quickly changing world with a rapid change in the nature of conflicts, standing still often means moving backward. Fortunately, academics,
policymakers, and practitioners have "discovered" a new ally which can and
already does make research, policies, and programs much better: these are the
world's young people themselves. With their involvement there is a good chance
that the quality of life for war-affected young people will significantly improve in
the next decade.

Notes

1. Text taken from the following webpage: http://www.un.org/children/conflict/
english/machel10.html.
2. Special Representative of the Secretary-General for Children and Armed Conflict
(SRSGCAC), 2007, "Machel Study 10-Year Strategic Review: Children and Conflict in a
Changing World", 15. Text accessed at http://www.un.org/children/conflict/_documents/
machel/MachelReviewReport.pdf.
3. Ibid, 17
4. Ibid, 17.
5. Ibid, 17.
6. Ibid, 17.
7. Ibid, 17.
8. Ibid, 18.
9. Ibid, 18.
10. Ibid, 18.
11. Ibid, 18.
12. Ibid, 18.
13. Ibid, 19.
14. Ibid, 20.
15. Ibid, 20.
16. Ibid, 20.
17. See http://www.unicef.org/specialsession/wffc/.
18. Machel, 21.
19. Ibid, 24.
20. Ibid, 27.
21. Ibid, 23.
22. Ibid, 31.
23. Ibid, 30.
24. Ibid, 26.
25. See http://www.un.org/children/conflict/_documents/machel/MachelReview
Report.pdf.

Biographies

Coalition to Stop the Use of Child Soldiers

The Coalition to Stop the Use of Child Soldiers is a consortium of nongovernmental organizations which have joined forces and aim by means of advocacy, education, research, monitoring, and capacity-building to prevent the recruitment and use of children as soldiers, to demobilize child soldiers, and to rehabilitate and reintegrate them into society. The Coalition states its goal is to "promote the adoption and adherence to national, regional and international legal standards (including the Optional Protocol to the Convention on the Rights of the Child on the involvement of children in armed conflict) prohibiting the military recruitment and use in hostilities of any person younger than eighteen years of age; and the recognition and enforcement of this standard by all armed groups, both governmental and non-governmental."[1]

The Coalition was formed in 1998 by six human rights and humanitarian organizations including the International Save the Children Alliance, Amnesty International, and Human Rights Watch. At international, regional, and national levels, the Coalition campaigns for the demobilization and reintegration of existing child soldiers, lobbies governments and armed groups known to be using child soldiers, and makes recommendations about how to best demobilize child soldiers. Public education and media campaigns are used by the Coalition to raise public awareness of the issue of child soldiers, and the Coalition further works with national and regional coalitions to develop research and campaigning expertise.

The Coalition's research activities have resulted in a number of reports and papers on the issue. One of the primary activities of the Coalition is the production of an extensive research report, the so-called *Child Soldiers Global Report*,

---

[1]From http://www.child-soldiers.org/coalition/the-coalition.

which is published every three to four years. This report provides detailed information on a country-by-country basis about the recruitment and use of children in conflict and about the demobilization and reintegration of child soldiers. Three such reports have been produced thus far, in 2001, 2004, and 2008. The 2008 report noted that there were many achievements since 2004. For example, the Optional Protocol to the Convention on the Rights of the Child regarding the involvement of children in armed conflict has been ratified by 120 states, nearly double the number from 2004. The 2008 report also observed that several individuals have been charged with war crimes relating to the conscription and use of child soldiers in the Democratic Republic of Congo, Uganda, and Sierra Leone. Lastly, the report acknowledges that the United Nations Security Council adopted Resolutions 1539 and 1612 on children and armed conflict and established a working group on children and armed conflict.

The Child Soldiers Global Report can be accessed at: http://www.childsoldiers .globalreport.org.

Further information about the Coalition to Stop the Use of Child Soldiers can be found on the organization's web site: http://www.child-soldiers.org.

Save the Children

The International Save the Children Alliance is an international network of national child-focused organizations which has worked for over 90 years to improve the lives of children all over the world. The first Save the Children organization was founded in Britain in 1919 by two sisters who were concerned about the impact of World War I and the Russian Revolution on the lives of children and young people. It was the first British organization to advocate for global children's rights, and it has since grown into the world's largest independent organization, with offices in over 120 countries. Much of the 10 years of preparation for the United Nations Convention on the Rights of the Child was done by the Save the Children Alliance.

Save the Children organizations work in nearly all conflict-affected countries, including the Democratic Republic of Congo, Somalia, Afghanistan, Sri Lanka, Colombia, and Georgia. Save the Children responds to the needs of children living in such countries, and has launched a series of programs and campaigns to address the impact of conflict on children and young people. For example, in eastern Democratic Republic of Congo, where fighting has displaced and killed thousands of people, Save the Children has supported war-affected people and communities with education, health and nutrition support, and shelter materials. Furthermore, it has registered separated children and reunified them with their families and has set up child-friendly spaces where children can play in a safe environment and work to overcome trauma. Save the Children also supported the development of child clubs during the Nepalese civil war, delivered food supplies to children and their families during the Gaza emergency of December 2008 and January 2009, and has supported schools and built health clinics and children's centers for war-affected children and communities in Darfur, Sudan.

In 2006, Save the Children launched a global campaign called *Rewrite the Future*, which focuses on improving educational provision in conflict-affected countries and aims to provide quality education for 8 million children living in such countries. The campaign has been initiated in countries such as Nepal, Guatemala, and Liberia. Thus far, as part of the campaign, thousands of teachers have received teacher training from Save the Children. War-damaged schools have been rehabilitated, new schools have been built, and school materials have been distributed. Additional efforts have been concentrated on helping to craft new national education policies, laws, and strategies in countries such as Afghanistan and southern Sudan, while in Nepal, Save the Children has focused on creating safe and protective learning environments through the "schools as zones of peace" initiative (see Chapter 2).

You can find out more about the many ways in which Save the Children assists war-affected children and young people on the following web sites:
Save the Children's United States office: http://www.savethechildren.org.
International Save the Children Alliance: http://www.savethechildren.net.

War Child International

War Child International is a nongovernmental organization that works in conflict-affected countries around the world to help children living in these countries. Founded in 1993 in response to the wars in Yugoslavia, War Child International's principal aim is to "advance the cause of peace through investing hope in the lives of children caught up in the horrors of war".[2] The organization consists of two head offices, one in Canada and one in the Netherlands. War Child Holland was founded in 1994, and War Child Canada in 1998. Both offices focus on peacebuilding within their projects, to include providing psychosocial aid and vocational training to children and young people.

War Child Canada currently works in nine conflict-affected countries: Afghanistan, Sudan, Iraq, Sierra Leone, Sri Lanka, Ethiopia, Georgia, Northern Uganda, and the Democratic Republic of Congo. In Iraq, War Child Canada has rehabilitated schools and provided educational materials, and it runs programs to build the skills of young people through training in English language, information technology, conflict resolution, and human rights. In Sri Lanka, War Child Canada supports programs that provide education and psychosocial support to children, and it has rebuilt schools and conducted art and drama classes to help children heal from the trauma of the country's long-running civil war.

War Child Holland currently works in 10 conflict-affected countries, in some cases alongside War Child Canada: Afghanistan, Chechnya, Colombia,

[2]Text accessed at http://www.warchild.org..

Democratic Republic of Congo, Sierra Leone, Sri Lanka, Sudan, Uganda, and the occupied Palestinian territory and Israel. The Holland office stresses the importance of working with children and young people in their environments to increase their resilience and strengthen their protection. War Child Holland uses three intervention strategies to make positive changes for children and young people: one, delivering services to young people when governments are not able to do so; two, building the capacity of communities, organizations, and institutions to fulfill their duties toward children; and three, advocating for political, social, and other changes that positively affect children and young people. In Chechnya, War Child Holland has conducted psychosocial workshops for young people to help them, their parents, and their teachers to better deal with children's psychosocial problems. War Child Holland has a similar psychosocial focus in its programs in Uganda, where it has conducted workshops to teach children how to address behavioral problems, how to deal with emotions and form relationships, and how to deal with conflicts. Furthermore, the office raises awareness amongst Northern Ugandan communities about child protection and recruitment of children into armed groups, and has conducted catch-up education programs for children who have missed out on school due to the conflict in the region.

You can find out more about War Child International and the Holland and Canada offices by accessing the following web site: http://www.warchild.org.

UN Special Representative of the Secretary-General for Children and Armed Conflict

The 1996 report delivered by Graça Machel on the Impact of Armed Conflict on Children (see the biographical profile of Graça Machel, as well as the authors' preface) led to the creation in 1997 of the office of the Special Representative of the United Nations Secretary-General for Children and Armed Conflict. Mandated by United Nations General Assembly resolution number 51/77, the Office of the Special Representative was initially intended to be three years in duration, but this three-year mandate has been extended several times. Two Special Representatives have been appointed since 1997: Mr. Olara A. Otunnu (1997 to 2005) and Ms. Radhika Coomaraswamy (2005 to present).

The mandate of the Office of the Special Representative, as set out in resolution number 51 / 77, is the following:

- To assess progress achieved, steps taken, and difficulties encountered in strengthening the protection of children in situations of armed conflict;
- To raise awareness and promote the collection of information about the plight of children affected by armed conflict and encourage the development of networking;
- To work closely with other United Nations entities, and non-governmental organizations;
- To foster international cooperation to ensure respect for children's rights in these situations and contribute to the coordination of efforts by Governments, relevant United Nations bodies, and other non-governmental organizations;

- To submit an annual report to the United Nations General Assembly and the Commission on Human Rights containing relevant information on the situation of children affected by armed conflict.

The Special Representative is primarily engaged in advocacy efforts on behalf of children affected by armed conflict. In the strategic plan for the Office, the following are listed as the Office's key objectives:

- Supporting global initiatives to end grave violations against children affected by armed conflict;
- Promoting rights-based protection for children affected by armed conflict;
- Making children and armed conflict concerns an integral aspect of peacekeeping and peacebuilding missions and efforts;
- Raising awareness with regard to all other issues relating to war-affected children before, during and after conflict.

To achieve these goals, the Office of the Special Representative is engaged in monitoring and reporting efforts, advocacy, coordination and mainstreaming of the Office's agenda, and research and study. Thus far, the efforts of the Special Representative have resulted in increased global awareness about issues regarding children affected by armed conflict, including prioritization of the issue within several United Nations entities, such as the Security Council. Additionally, the Office has pushed for the application of international standards regarding children and armed conflict, such as seeking accountability for violations of children's rights through the International Criminal Court. Child protection has also received increased attention in peacekeeping operations with the addition of child protection officers to peacekeeping missions.

The web site of the Office of the Special Representative has many valuable resources on various issues regarding children and armed conflict, and can be accessed at: http://www.un.org/children/conflict.

Entities of the United Nations

In addition to the Office of the Special Representative of the Secretary General for Children and Armed Conflict (see the profile for the Office in this section), the various entities of the United Nations have different roles and responsibilities regarding how to address children affected by armed conflict.

United Nations Children's Fund (UNICEF)

http://www.unicef.org

UNICEF is the UN agency which focuses on children. Since its creation in December 1946 to assist children affected by World War II, UNICEF has worked to address the needs of children and young people affected by armed conflict in countries all around the globe and to ensure and enhance their protection.

It was made a permanent part of the United Nations in 1953 and the entity was awarded the Nobel Peace Prize in 1965 for its efforts. UNICEF supported the writing of the 1996 Machel report and helped to put the issue of children and armed conflict on the agenda of the UN Security Council. In situations of armed and post-armed conflict, UNICEF works to fulfill the needs and rights of child soldiers and to prevent their re-recruitment, helps provide emergency immunizations and to improve health conditions for war-affected children and their families, rehabilitates schools, helps to reunify separated children with their families, and works to protect women and girls from gender-based violence. Each year, UNICEF produces a report, *The State of the World's Children*, which gives information about issues affecting children. Additionally, UNICEF supports research on children in part through the UNICEF Innocenti Research Center; part of the Center's research program focuses on protecting children during times of armed conflict from exploitation and abuse, and on the impact of conflict and displacement on children.

United Nations Education, Scientific and Cultural Organization (UNESCO)

http://www.unesco.org

"Since wars begin in the minds of men, it is in the minds of men that the defences of peace must be constructed."100 So begins the constitution of United Nations Education, Scientific and Cultural Organization, founded in November 1945 to contribute to peace and security in the world by promoting collaboration among nations through education, science, and culture. Regarding children and armed conflict, UNESCO has been behind the production of much research on the topic, particularly in terms of the impact of conflict on education through UNESCO's International Bureau of Education (http://www.ibe.unesco.org). Additionally, UNESCO advocates for the achievement of the six Education For All goals adopted in 2000, as well as the achievement of the second Millennium Development Goal of achieving universal primary schooling by 2015. In this vein, UNESCO supports educational provision and reform during emergency and post-emergency situations (including situations of armed conflict), especially educational programs for forcibly displaced children.

United Nations Development Program (UNDP)

http://www.undp.org

The United Nations Development Program was founded in 1965 to help coordinate and achieve solutions to global and national development challenges and priorities in areas such as democratic governance, poverty reduction, tackling the spread of epidemics, and the environment. Each year, the UNDP produces the *Human Development Report*, which focuses on global development issues. One of the UNDP's major operating departments is the Bureau of Crisis Prevention and Recovery (http://www.undp.org/cpr); part of this department's work entails a focus on young people and conflict. In Liberia, the Bureau helped the government to create the country's National Youth Policy to prevent future armed violence and crime committed by or against youth, while in Lebanon, the Bureau conducted workshops for youth that focused on art and theater as tools for conflict resolution and mediation to give young people tools to express themselves more effectively. The Bureau is engaged in other work that addresses the impact of conflict on children and young people, such as trying to control the spread of small arms and supporting humanitarian demining efforts, operating DDR programs for ex-combatants, operating programs to reintegrate displaced persons, and helping to restart basic social services in conflict-affected areas. In 2006, the Bureau published a report entitled "Youth and Violent Conflict: Society and Development in Crisis?", which provided recommendations to the UNDP on how to work with youth during and after situations of armed conflict. This report can be accessed at http://www.undp.org/cpr/whats_new/UNDP_Youth _PN.pdf.

United Nations High Commissioner for Refugees (UNHCR)

http://www.unhcr.org
The UNHCR is the United Nations agency mandated to lead and coordinate international action to protect refugees and resolve refugee situations. This includes helping to ensure that the basic needs of refugees are met in refugee camp settings, such as access to clean water, food, shelter, medical care, and education services. Such efforts are crucial for the well-being of displaced children, as upwards 80 percent of refugee populations are composed of children, women, and the elderly, and one of the major priorities of refugee populations is access to education. The UNHCR helps to provide refugees with access to basic education in all phases of its operations, and it was involved in the creation of the Inter-Agency Network on Education in Emergencies (http://www.ineesite.org) in an effort to highlight the need to provide education during emergencies, such as conflict situations. The UNHCR has also supported the publication of several research reports and papers on refugee education, such as the report "Learning for a Future: Refugee Education in Developing Countries."

Other United Nations Entities Focused on Peace and Conflict

Several bodies of the United Nations that are explicitly focused on peace-making, peacekeeping, and peacebuilding efforts have in various ways addressed children and armed and post-armed conflict. These are the Security Council, the Department of Political Affairs, and the Department of Peacekeeping Operations. As you can see from the selected sections of Security Council resolutions in the key documents portion of this book, the Security Council has addressed the issue of children and armed conflict on a number of occasions, viewing the topic as integral to long-term peacebuilding, conflict prevention, security, and development. The Security Council also oversees the United Nations Peacebuilding Commission (see Chapter 5), which has thus far had a strong focus on addressing youth in post-conflict Burundi and Sierra Leone. Furthermore, the Council established the subsidiary Working Group on Children and Armed Conflict in July 2005 to, among other things, review reports of the monitoring and reporting mechanism called for in Resolution 1612. The monitoring and reporting mechanism monitors the following abuses against children in conflict situations:

1. Killing or maiming of children;
2. Recruiting or using child soldiers;
3. Attacks against schools or hospitals;
4. Rape and other grave sexual violence against children;
5. Abduction of children;
6. Denial of humanitarian access for children.

The United Nations Department of Political Affairs works on peacemaking and peacebuilding efforts. Part of this includes participation in peace negotiations and the crafting of peace agreements, which in some cases have addressed the concerns and needs of war-affected young people. The United Nations Department of Peacekeeping Operations focuses on implementing peacekeeping operations, which now include child protection advisors and training for peacekeepers in child rights and protection.

You can find out more about each of these entities on the following web sites:

- UN Security Council: http://www.un.org/sc
- UN Department of Political Affairs: http://www.un.org/Depts/dpa
- UN Department of Peacekeeping Operations: http://www.un.org/Depts/dpko/dpko

The work of other United Nations entities are also related to and have an impact on the needs of young people during and after situations of armed conflict. For example, the World Food Programme (http://www.wfp.org/) delivers food to needy persons during emergency situations and uses food to help communities rebuild after war. In some cases, the World Food Programme supports school-feeding programs in post-conflict countries, which can help to encourage children to enroll in and attend school and to maximize their learning potential.

Romeo Dallaire

In October 1993, the United Nations sent approximately 2,200 peacekeeping troops to Rwanda to oversee the implementation of the Arusha peace agreement signed between the warring Hutu and Tutsi ethnic groups. The UNAMIR (United Nations Mission in Rwanda) peacekeeping mission was headed by Romeo Dallaire, a lieutenant-general in the Canadian army. However, the peacekeeping forces soon found themselves understaffed when the civil war resumed. The renewed tensions culminated in the Rwandan genocide of 1994, with Hutu extremists murdering 800,000 Tutsis and moderate Hutus. Tragically, the majority of the peacekeeping troops were pulled out of the country when the fighting resumed (this was a peacekeeping, not a peace-enforcing mission), but Lieutenant-General Dallaire remained in Rwanda throughout the genocide and its aftermath. As head of the mission, he tried to prevent the genocide from happening in the first place and then when it actually happened, he tried to save as many lives as possible with only a small number of peacekeeping troops. Despite numerous pleas from the lieutentant-general, the UN Security Council did not increase the number of peacekeepers before or during the genocide.

Dallaire retired from the Canadian army in 2004, and has since focused his efforts on, among other things, war-affected children. He has served as a Special Advisor to the Canadian Government on War Affected Children and the Prohibition of Small Arms Distribution, and started the Child Soldiers Initiative in Africa, an international research and intervention campaign to eradicate the use of child soldiers. The goal of the initiative is to "develop an integrated set of tools that can be used to prevent the recruitment of children into armed groups ... by developing creative approaches to prevent the use of child soldiers, addressing both the security and humanitarian dimensions of the problem; to identify the various types of approaches that are being used...; [and] to identify opportunities for new approaches and multi-party, collaborative efforts to prevent the use of children as soldiers."[3]

In an interview with the Canadian government, Dallaire states that better regulation of small arms would entail fewer children becoming soldiers: "The more you reduce the availability of small arms, the more you reduce the availability of the ammunition for the small arms, the less the child soldiers are rendered useful."[4] He also points to a need for more and better research on child soldiers to prevent their use:

> There has been no work done on specifically why [child soldiers] are used. How do you counter that weapons system [that is, child soldiers] in the field? How do you neutralize it and make it not a useful tool?...Why do they use them more for offensive than defence; why are they trained only to this level versus that level?...Because it is one of the most effective weapons systems there is... How do you eradicate the concept of the use of children in conflict?...If you don't have children to work in many of these conflicts, you might not have a conflict... I feel that we haven't pursued that as an instrument of conflict resolution – the eradication of child soldiers.[5]

Dallaire currently serves as a senator in the Canadian Parliament, where he has chaired the Committee Against the Commercial Exploitation of Children and

---

[3]From www.romeodallaire.com/child-soldiers.html.
[4]From http://www.international.gc.ca/cip-pic/discussions/non-proliferation/video/dallaire.aspx ?lang=eng.
[5]Ibid.

Youth since 2005. You can learn more about him by accessing the following web sites:

- www.romeodallaire.com
- http://sen.parl.gc.ca/rdallaire/

Graça Machel

Graça Machel, born in 1945 in Mozambique, is an international advocate for women's and children's rights. She attended the University of Lisbon in Portugal (when Mozambique was still a colony of Portugal). When she returned to Mozambique in 1973, she joined the Liberation Front of Mozambique (FRELIMO), which fought for independence, and became a school teacher. After independence in 1975, she became the first Minister of Education and Culture. In the same year she married the Mozambican president, Samora Machel. He died, however, in 1986, and in 1998 Machel married the then-South African President Nelson Mandela. In 1995, Machel was awarded the Nansen Medal by the UNHCR in recognition of her work on behalf of refugee children, and she has won several other international prizes for her humanitarian work. Since 1994, she has served as the president of the Foundation for Community Development in Mozambique, a foundation that she started and which gives financial assistance to communities and organizations working to improve living conditions and promote human development in and for poor and vulnerable communities and socially excluded groups in Mozambique. Machel recently joined the "Group of Elders" (http://www.theelders.org), a group of elder politicians and activists convened to try to tackle some of the world's most challenging issues and which, in addition to Machel, includes people such as former U.S. President Jimmy Carter, Nelson Mandela, former UN Secretary General Kofi Annan, and South African Bishop Desmond Tutu. Each of these men has received the Nobel Peace Prize.

One of Machel's most influential achievements was her work on armed conflict and children with the United Nations. On 20 December 1993, the United Nations General Assembly adopted resolution number 48/157, which called on the UN Secretary General to appoint an expert to carry out a study on the situation of children affected by armed conflict, to assess the relevance and adequacy of international standards to protect children in conflict situations, and to make recommendations as to how to prevent children from being affected by armed conflicts and how to better protect children living in situations of armed conflict and promote their well-being. In 1994, Machel was appointed by the UN Secretary General to conduct this global investigation, resulting in the release of a study in 1996 entitled "The Impact of Armed Conflict on Children." The report was a seminal contribution to the topic and created a much-needed comprehensive, global picture of the impact of war on of children and young people. The report also led to the creation in 1997 of the office of the Special Representative of the United Nations Secretary-General for Children and Armed Conflict.

The 1996 Machel report explored the different interrelated facets of the impact of armed conflict on the lives of children in many conflict-affected countries. It included issues such as child soldiering; living in exile as refugees and IDPs; the threat of sexual exploitation and gender-based violence; the impact of land mines and unexploded ordnance; the impact of sanctions; health and nutrition issues; psychological recovery and social reintegration; and finally, the impact of conflict on education. Recommendations were provided in each of these areas as to how to mitigate the impact of armed conflict on children and ensure their protection.

In 2007, a 10-year review of the Machel report was undertaken to reflect the contemporary nature of conflict and to address new threats posed to children by the changing nature of war, such as terrorism and transnational organized crime. The report provided recommendations for the next 10 years regarding how to protect and fulfill children's rights in situations of armed conflict.

The 1996 report and the 2007 review, as well as many other key documents, can be accessed via the web site of the Office of the Special Representative of the Secretary General for Children and Armed Conflict at http://www.un.org/children/conflict/english/index.html.

Key Documents

The African Charter on the Rights and Welfare of the African Child

The African Charter on the Rights and Welfare of the African Child was adopted in 1999 by member states of the Organization for African Unity. The charter outlines the rights and duties of children, and defines a child as being a person under the age of 18. The following articles of the charter specifically address children and armed conflict:

Article 22: Armed Conflicts

- States Parties to this Charter shall undertake to respect and ensure respect for rules of international humanitarian law applicable in armed conflicts which affect the child.
- States Parties to the present Charter shall take all necessary measures to ensure that no child shall take a direct part in hostilities and refrain in particular, from recruiting any child.
- States Parties to the present Charter shall, in accordance with their obligations under international humanitarian law, protect the civilian population in armed conflicts and shall take all feasible measures to ensure the protection and care of children who are affected by armed conflicts. Such rules shall also apply to children in situations of internal armed conflicts, tension and strife.

Article 23: Refugee Children

- States Parties to the present Charter shall take all appropriate measures to ensure that a child who is seeking refugee status or who is considered a refugee in accordance with applicable international or domestic law shall, whether unaccompanied or accompanied by parents, legal guardians or close relatives, receive appropriate protection and humanitarian assistance in the enjoyment of the rights set out in this Charter and other international human rights and humanitarian instruments to which the States are Parties.

- States Parties shall undertake to cooperate with existing international organizations which protect and assist refugees in their efforts to protect and assist such a child and to trace the parents or other close relatives or an unaccompanied refugee child in order to obtain information necessary for reunification with the family.
- The provisions of this Article apply . . . to internally displaced children whether through natural disaster, internal armed conflicts, civil strife, breakdown of economic and social order or howsoever caused.

Article 25: Separation from Parents

- Any child who is permanently or temporarily deprived of his family environment for any reason shall be entitled to special protection and assistance;
- States Parties to the present Charter:
  a. shall ensure that a child who is parentless, or who is temporarily or permanently deprived of his or her family environment, or who in his or her best interest cannot be brought up or allowed to remain in that environment shall be provided with alternative family care, which could include, among others, foster placement, or placement in suitable institutions for the care of children;
  b. shall take all necessary measures to trace and re-unite children with parents or relatives where separation is caused by internal and external displacement arising from armed conflicts or natural disasters.
- When considering alternative family care of the child and the best interests of the child, due regard shall be paid to the desirability of continuity in a child's upbringing and to the child's ethnic, religious or linguistic background.

Article 26: Protection Against Apartheid and Discrimination

- States Parties to the present Charter shall individually and collectively undertake to accord the highest priority to the special needs of children living under regimes practicing racial, ethnic, religious or other forms of discrimination as well as in States subject to military destabilization.

You can access the Charter at http://www.africa-union.org/child/home.htm.

Cape Town Principles

Cape Town Principles and Best Practices on the Prevention of Recruitment of Children into the Armed Forces and on Demobilization and Social Reintegration of Child Soldiers in Africa was adopted in 1997 at a symposium held in South Africa and organized by UNICEF and the NGO Working Group on the Convention on the Rights of the Child. The principles and best practices, following the suggestions of experts, recommend a series of strategies, actions, and measures that should be taken to stop the recruitment of children into armed groups and help demobilized child soldiers with their reintegration process.

The following are the key principles which together form the essence of the document.[*]

1. To prevent child recruitment, the following measures should be taken:
   — A minimum age of 18 should be established for any person participating in hostilities and for recruitment in all forms into any armed force or group.
   — A permanent International Criminal Court should be established with jurisdiction covering the illegal recruitment of children.
   — Programs to prevent the recruitment of children should be developed, and particular attention should be paid to those most at risk of recruitment: children in conflict zones; children (especially adolescents) separated from or without families; other marginalized groups (e.g., children living or working on the streets, certain minorities, refugees and the internally displaced); and economically and socially deprived children.
   — All efforts should be made to keep or reunite children with their families or to place them within a family structure.
   — Access to education, including secondary education and vocational training, should be promoted for all children, including refugee and internally displaced children.
   — Special protection measures are needed to prevent recruitment of children in camps for refugees and internally displaced persons.
   — The international community should recognize that children who leave their country of origin to avoid illegal recruitment or participation in hostilities are in need of international protection. Children who are not nationals of the country in which they are fighting are also in need of international protection.
   — Controls should be imposed on the manufacture and transfer of arms, especially small arms. No arms should be supplied to parties to an armed conflict that are recruiting children or allowing them to take part in hostilities.
2. The following principles should guide demobilization processes:
   — All persons under the age of 18 should be demobilized from any kind of regular or irregular armed force or armed group.
   — Priority should be given to children in any demobilization process.
   — The issue of the demobilization of children should be included in the peace process from the beginning.
   — The duration of the demobilization process should be as short as possible and should take into account the child's dignity and the need for confidentiality.
   — Family tracing, contacts and reunification should be established as soon as possible.
   — Monitoring and documentation of child involvement in hostilities, as well as advocacy for demobilization and release of children, should be undertaken throughout the armed conflict.
   — To the extent possible, the return of demobilized children to their communities under conditions of safety should be ensured.
3. The following principles should guide the reintegration of child soldiers:
   — Family reunification is the principal factor in effective social reintegration.

---

[*]© United Nations Children's Fund, 27–30 April 1997. Reproduced with permission.

— Programmes should be developed with the communities, build on existing resources and take account of the context and community priorities, values and traditions.
— Programmes targeted at former child soldiers should be integrated into programmes for the benefit of all war-affected children.
— Provision should be made for educational activities that reflect: the loss of educational opportunities as a consequence of participation in hostilities; the age and stage of development of the children; and the potential of these activities for promoting the development of self-esteem.
— Provision should be made for relevant vocational training and opportunities for employment, including for children with disabilities.
— Recreational activities are essential for psychosocial well-being.
— Psychosocial programmes should assist children in developing and building those capacities that will facilitate reattachment to families and communities.

You can access the text of the Cape Town Principles at http://www.unicef.org /emerg/files/Cape_Town_Principles(1).pdf.

Convention on the Rights of the Child and Optional Protocol

The 1989 *United Nations Convention on the Rights of the Child* is an international convention adopted and ratified by every UN member state, with the exception of the United States and Somalia. The convention outlines the various rights of children, including civil, social, political, economic, and cultural rights. Children are defined as being below the age of 18 in the convention and its protocols. In 2000, the *Optional Protocol on the Involvement of Children in Armed Conflict* was adopted by the United Nations General Assembly, and is specifically aimed at preventing the recruitment of children under the age of 18 into armed groups and forces. The following are key excerpts and principles from both documents:

Convention on the Rights of the Child*

Article 38

States Parties undertake to respect and to ensure respect for rules of international humanitarian law applicable to them in armed conflicts which are relevant to the child.

States Parties shall take all feasible measures to ensure that persons who have not attained the age of fifteen years do not take a direct part in hostilities.

States Parties shall refrain from recruiting any person who has not attained the age of fifteen years into their armed forces. In recruiting among those persons who have attained the age of fifteen years but who have not attained the age of eighteen years, States Parties shall endeavour to give priority to those who are oldest.

In accordance with their obligations under international humanitarian law to protect the civilian population in armed conflicts, States Parties shall take all

---

*© United Nations, 20 November 1989. Reproduced with permission.

feasible measures to ensure protection and care of children who are affected by an armed conflict.

Article 39

States Parties shall take all appropriate measures to promote physical and psychological recovery and social reintegration of a child victim of: any form of neglect ... or armed conflicts. Such recovery and reintegration shall take place in an environment which fosters the health, self-respect and dignity of the child.

Optional Protocol*

Article 1

States Parties shall take all feasible measures to ensure that members of their armed forces who have not attained the age of 18 years do not take a direct part in hostilities.

Article 2

States Parties shall ensure that persons who have not attained the age of 18 years are not compulsorily recruited into their armed forces.

Article 3

States Parties that permit voluntary recruitment into their national armed forces under the age of 18 years shall maintain safeguards to ensure, as a minimum, that:

a. Such recruitment is genuinely voluntary;
b. Such recruitment is carried out with the informed consent of the person's parents or legal guardians;
c. Such persons are fully informed of the duties involved in such military service;
d. Such persons provide reliable proof of age prior to acceptance into national military service.

Article 4

1. Armed groups that are distinct from the armed forces of a State should not, under any circumstances, recruit or use in hostilities persons under the age of 18 years.
2. States Parties shall take all feasible measures to prevent such recruitment and use, including the adoption of legal measures necessary to prohibit and criminalize such practices.

Article 6

States Parties shall take all feasible measures to ensure that persons within their jurisdiction recruited or used in hostilities contrary to the present Protocol are demobilized or otherwise released from service. States Parties shall, when necessary, accord to such persons all appropriate assistance for their physical and psychological recovery and their social reintegration.

---

*© United Nations, 25 May 2000. Reproduced with permission.

Article 8

Each State Party shall, within two years following the entry into force of the present Protocol for that State Party, submit a report to the Committee on the Rights of the Child providing comprehensive information on the measures it has taken to implement the provisions of the Protocol, including the measures taken to implement the provisions on participation and recruitment.
You can find the full UNCRC at http://untreaty.un.org/English/TreatyEvent2001/pdf/03e.pdf.
You can find the full Additional Protocol at http://www2.ohchr.org/english/law/crc-conflict.htm.

Geneva Conventions

The four Geneva Conventions were signed in 1949, with three additional protocols signed in 1977 and 2005. These conventions lay down the principles of international humanitarian law regarding war, such as the treatment and protection of noncombatants and prisoners of war. The fourth Geneva Convention and two of the protocols specifically address the issue of children during times of war.* The contents of these documents are outlined below.

Convention (IV) Relative to the Protection of Civilian Persons in Time of War (1949)

- Article 14: In time of peace or after the outbreak of hostilities, hospitals and safety zones may be organized to protect from the effects of war ... children under fifteen.
- Article 17: The parties to a conflict shall make agreements to remove children from besieged areas.
- Article 23: The parties to a conflict shall allow the free passage of clothing, medicines, and food for children under fifteen.
- Article 24: "The Parties to the conflict shall take the necessary measures to ensure that children under fifteen, who are orphaned or are separated from their families as a result of the war, are not left to their own resources, and that their maintenance, the exercise of their religion and their education are facilitated in all circumstances. Their education shall, as far as possible, be entrusted to persons of a similar cultural tradition. The Parties to the conflict shall facilitate the reception of such children in a neutral country for the duration of the conflict with the consent of the Protecting Power, if any, and under due safeguards for the observance of the principles stated in the first paragraph. They shall, furthermore, endeavour to arrange for all children under twelve to be identified by the wearing of identity discs, or by some other means."
- Article 50: In occupied territories, "the Occupying Power shall, with the cooperation of the national and local authorities, facilitate the proper working of all institutions devoted to the care and education of children. The Occupying Power shall take all necessary steps to facilitate the identification of children and the registration of their parentage. It may not, in any

*See http://www.worldlii.org/int/journals/ISILYBIHRL/2001/2.html.

case, change their personal status, nor enlist them in formations or organizations subordinate to it. Should the local institutions be inadequate for the purpose, the Occupying Power shall make arrangements for the maintenance and education, if possible by persons of their own nationality, language and religion, of children who are orphaned or separated from their parents as a result of the war and who cannot be adequately cared for by a near relative or friend. A special section of the Bureau set up in accordance with Article 136 shall be responsible for taking all necessary steps to identify children whose identity is in doubt. Particulars of their parents or other near relatives should always be recorded if available."

- Article 82: In case of internment, "members of the same family, and in particular parents and children, shall be lodged together in the same place of internment ... Internees may request that their children who are left at liberty without parental care shall be interned with them. Wherever possible, interned members of the same family shall be housed in the same premises and given separate accommodation from other internees, together with facilities for leading a proper family life."
- Article 89: In case of internment, "expectant and nursing mothers and children under fifteen years of age, shall be given additional food, in proportion to their physiological needs."
- Article 94: In case of internment, "the Detaining Power shall .... [ensure] the education of children and young people; they shall be allowed to attend schools either within the place of internment or outside. Special playgrounds shall be reserved for children and young people."
- Article 132. In case of the release of internees, the parties to a conflict shall endeavour "to conclude agreements for the release, repatriation, and return to places of residence or the accommodation in a neutral country of certain classes of internees, in particular children."

Protocol Additional to the Geneva Conventions of 12 August 1949, and Relating to the Protection of Victims of International Armed Conflicts (Protocol I), 8 June 1977.

- Article 70: Priority shall be given to people such as children in the distribution of humanitarian relief.
- Article 77: "Protection of children:

  1. Children shall be the object of special respect and shall be protected against any form of indecent assault. The Parties to the conflict shall provide them with the care and aid they require, whether because of their age or for any other reason.

  2. The Parties to the conflict shall take all feasible measures in order that children who have not attained the age of fifteen years do not take a direct part in hostilities and, in particular, they shall refrain from recruiting them into their armed forces. In recruiting among those persons who have attained the age of fifteen years but who have not attained the age of eighteen years the Parties to the conflict shall endeavour to give priority to those who are oldest.

  3. If, in exceptional cases, despite the provisions of paragraph 2, children who have not attained the age of fifteen years take a direct part in hostilities and fall into the power of an adverse Party, they shall continue to benefit from the special protection accorded by this Article, whether or not they are prisoners of war.

  4. If arrested, detained or interned for reasons related to the armed conflict, children shall be held in quarters separate from the quarters of adults, except where families are accommodated as family units.

5. The death penalty for an offence related to the armed conflict shall not be executed on persons who had not attained the age of eighteen years at the time the offence was committed."

- Article 78: "Evacuation of children:

1. No Party to the conflict shall arrange for the evacuation of children, other than its own nationals, to a foreign country except for a temporary evacuation where compelling reasons of the health or medical treatment of the children or, except in occupied territory, their safety, so require. Where the parents or legal guardians can be found, their written consent to such evacuation is required. If these persons cannot be found, the written consent to such evacuation of the persons who by law or custom are primarily responsible for the care of the children is required. Any such evacuation shall be supervised by the Protecting Power in agreement with the Parties concerned, namely, the Party arranging for the evacuation, the Party receiving the children and any Parties whose nationals are being evacuated. In each case, all Parties to the conflict shall take all feasible precautions to avoid endangering the evacuation.

2. Whenever an evacuation occurs pursuant to paragraph 1, each child's education, including his religious and moral education as his parents desire, shall be provided while he is away with the greatest possible continuity.

3. With a view to facilitating the return to their families and country of children evacuated pursuant to this Article, the authorities of the Party arranging for the evacuation and, as appropriate, the authorities of the receiving country shall establish for each child a card with photographs, which they shall send to the Central Tracing Agency of the International Committee of the Red Cross" that shall bear information about the child, such as the child's name and date of birth.

Protocol Additional to the Geneva Conventions of 12 August 1949, and Relating to the Protection of Victims of Non-International Armed Conflicts (Protocol II), 8 June 1977

- Article 4.3: "Children shall be provided with the care and aid they require, and in particular:
  a. they shall receive an education, including religious and moral education, in keeping with the wishes of their parents, or in the absence of parents, of those responsible for their care;
  b. all appropriate steps shall be taken to facilitate the reunion of families temporarily separated;
  c. children who have not attained the age of fifteen years shall neither be recruited in the armed forces or groups nor allowed to take part in hostilities;
  d. the special protection provided by this Article to children who have not attained the age of fifteen years shall remain applicable to them if they take a direct part in hostilities despite the provisions of subparagraph (c) and are captured;
  e. measures shall be taken, if necessary, and whenever possible with the consent of their parents or persons who by law or custom are primarily responsible for their care, to remove children temporarily from the area in which hostilities are taking place to a safer area within the country and ensure that they are accompanied by persons responsible for their safety and well-being."

- Article 6.4: "The death penalty shall not be pronounced on persons who were under the age of eighteen years at the time of the offence and shall not be carried out on pregnant women or mothers of young children."

The text of the Geneva Conventions and additional protocols can be accessed at http://www.icrc.org.

Paris Commitments and Principles

The *Paris Commitments and Principles* are the result of an extensive review process of the Cape Town principles (1997) and aim to protect children from recruitment into armed groups and lay down guidelines for the protection, release, and reintegration of children associated with armed groups. Two documents were the outcome of talks conducted during 2007: *The Paris Commitments to Protect Children Unlawfully Recruited or Used by Armed Forces or Armed Groups* and *The Principles and Guidelines on Children Associated with Armed Forces or Armed Groups*. These documents define a child as "any person less than 18 years of age."

The Paris Principles detail guidelines as to how the Commitments should be implemented. The signatory states to the Paris Commitments commit themselves to upholding 20 principles to end the use of children during armed conflict. Below is a summary of some of the key obligations for the signatory states*:

- To spare no effort to end the unlawful use or recruitment of children by armed forces or groups in all regions of the world;
- To ensure that conscription and enlistment procedures for recruitment into armed forces are established, including establishing mechanisms to ensure that age of entry requirements are respected;
- To take measures to prevent armed groups operating within the jurisdiction of a State that are distinct from armed forces from recruiting children under the age of 18;
- To seek and secure the release of children recruited or used unlawfully by armed forces or groups at all times, to include during conflict situations, and that such release does not depend on a cease-fire or peace agreements or any release or demobilization process for adults;
- To investigate and prosecute those persons who have unlawfully recruited children into armed forces or groups, or used them to participate actively in hostilities, and to refrain from giving amnesty to such persons in peace agreements;
- To support monitoring and reporting efforts at national, regional, and international levels on violations of child rights;
- To fully cooperate with the implementation of targeted measures taken by the United Nations Security Council against parties to an armed conflict which unlawfully recruit and use children;
- To ensure that children who have been unlawfully recruited or used by armed forces or groups and who are accused of crimes against international law are considered primarily as victims of violations against international law and not only as perpetrators;

---

* © United Nations, February, 2007. Reproduced with permission.

- To ensure that, where truth-seeking and reconciliation mechanisms are established, the involvement of children is supported and promoted, that measures are taken to protect the rights of children throughout the process, and that children's participation is voluntary;
- To ensure that children who have exited armed groups are not used for political purposes;
- To ensure that children who flee to another country to escape unlawful recruitment can seek asylum;
- To ensure that children who are granted asylum or are recognized as refugees are fully entitled to the enjoyment of their human rights on an equal basis with other children;
- To advocate for the inclusion in peace agreements and ceasefires minimum standards regarding the cessation of all recruitments and for the registration, release and treatment of children in armed forces or groups, including provisions for the special needs of girls and their children for protection and assistance;
- To ensure that armed forces or groups having unlawfully recruited or used children are not allowed to secure advantages during peace negotiations or security sector reforms, such as using the number of children in their ranks to increase their troop size in a power sharing arrangement;
- To ensure that sufficient funding is made available as early as possible to achieve full and effective (re)integration of war-affected children.

You can access the full text of the Paris Principles at http://www.un.org/children/conflict/_documents/parisprinciples/ParisPrinciples_EN.pdf.
You can access the full text of the Paris Commitments at http://www.un.org/children/conflict/_documents/pariscommitments/ParisCommitments_EN.pdf

Recent Peace Agreements Which Address Issues of Relevance to Children and Young People

While in general children and young people are not addressed specifically or feature prominently in peace agreements, issues relevant to young people are raised in many peace agreements. For instance, provisions are made in various peace agreements for the resumption of formal schooling and vocational training; for the demobilization, disarmament, and reintegration of young ex-combatants; for the provision of assistance to young returning refugees and IDPs; for the creation of opportunities for young people to participate in the political system of their country; and for general attention to be given to war-affected children, including the delivery of humanitarian assistance. Some agreements make calls for stopping the use of children as combatants in conflict.

Table A.1 contains five examples of peace agreements that address children and young people, and the specific points of each agreement that address issues relevant to children and young people.

All agreements can be accessed on the web site of UN Peacemaker, at http://peacemaker.unlb.org.

Table A.1

Country or parties to the agreement	Year of the agreement	Title of Agreement	Specific contents that address children and young people
Israel-Palestine	1995	Israeli-Palestinian Interim Agreement on the West Bank and the Gaza Strip	This agreement addresses educational matters. Chapter 4, Article XXII states that "Israel and the [Palestinian] Council will ensure that their respective educational systems contribute to the peace between the Israeli and Palestinian peoples and to peace in the entire region, and will refrain from the introduction of any motifs that could adversely affect the process of reconciliation."
Mexico	1996	The San Andrés Accords	These accords primarily address educational matters, requiring the federal government to: • Ensure education and training for indigenous peoples that respects and takes advantage of their knowledge, traditions, and forms of organization, and promotes their development. • Respect the educational activities of indigenous peoples within their own cultural space, and commit resources to allow indigenous peoples to implement educational activities that they have decided upon. • Education provided by the State should be intercultural and multicultural and should recognize and disseminate the culture, history, customs, and traditions of indigenous peoples. • Education should be conducted in indigenous languages in order to promote, develop, preserve, and practice these languages so that people can acquire reading and writing skills in these languages. Indigenous peoples shall also be given opportunities to learn and master Spanish. • The state shall fulfill the rights of indigenous peoples to free, quality education and to a bilingual and intercultural education, and shall promote the involvement of indigenous communities in selecting and removing teachers. The content of teaching shall be regional in nature, and the regions will have the authority to design and develop academic programs. • The content of national textbooks should be reviewed to reflect on the multicultural nature of the country. • Establishment of a scholarship system for indigenous youth to access higher levels of education.

Table A.1. *continued*

Country or parties to the agree-ment	Year of the agree-ment	Title of Agreement	Specific contents that address children and young people
Kosovo	1999	Kosovo peace agreement 1 (Interim Agreement for Peace and Self-Government in Kosovo)	This agreement addresses educational issues in the following ways: Chapter 1, Article VII In order to preserve, protect, and express their national, cultural, religious, and linguistic identities, national communities are granted the right to "provide for education and establishing educational institutions, in particular for schooling in their own language and alphabet and in national culture and history, for which relevant authorities will provide financial assistance; curricula shall reflect a spirit of tolerance between national communities and respect for the rights of members of all national communities in accordance with international standards." The communes shall be given the responsibility for "providing education, consistent with the rights and duties of national communities, and in a spirit of tolerance between national communities and respect for the rights of the members of all national communities in accordance with international standards." Further educational provisions are made throughout the text.

Country or parties to the agreement	Year of the agreement	Title of Agreement	Specific contents that address children and young people
Nepal	2006	Comprehensive Peace Accord	Section 7.5.4 states the following: "Acknowledging that the right to education should be ensured and respected, both parties are committed to maintaining appropriate academic environment in educational institutions. Both sides agree to guarantee that the right to education will not be impeded. They agree to put to an end, on an immediate basis, to activities like taking the educational institutions under control and using them, abducting teachers and students, taking them under control and disappearing them, and to not to establish barracks in a way that it would impede them." Section 7.6 on the rights of women and children states the following: "Both parties fully agree to provide special protection to the rights of women and children, to immediately stop all types of violence against women and children, including child labor, as well as sexual exploitation and abuse, and not to include or use children who are 18 years old and below in the armed force. Children thus affected would be immediately rescued and necessary and appropriate assistance will be provided for their rehabilitation."

(continued)

Table A.1. *continued*

Country or parties to the agreement	Year of the agreement	Title of Agreement	Specific contents that address children and young people
Uganda	2008	Agreement on Disarmament, Demobilization, and Reintegration	The needs of children and young people are covered in several sections of this agreement. The agreement requires the Government of Uganda to: • Implement a return and reintegration program for children associated with the Lord's Resistance Army (LRA) that is in line with international standards and policies, and to provide reintegration support for children returning from the LRA with inclusive community-based programs for conflict-affected children and youth. This support should focus on providing educational and livelihood opportunities, and give priority to girls and young mothers and to vulnerable children. • Provide reintegration programs that are relevant to youth combatants of the LRA. During disarmament, child-specific measures are to be adopted, such as making available child-appropriate facilities and specialized staff. During repatriation and reception processes, special consideration will be given to the needs of children, and separate transitional accommodation provided for men, women, and children.

United Nations Security Council Resolutions Regarding Children and Armed Conflict

The United Nations Security Council (http://www.un.org/sc/) is one of the most powerful and important organs of the United Nations. According to the charter of the United Nations, the primary function of the Security Council is to maintain international peace and security. Security Council Resolution 1361 (August 2001) also explicitly identifies conflict prevention and the maintenance of global peace and security as the key purposes of the Council. Conflict prevention by the Security Council can take many shapes and forms, from investigating disputes and regulating and policing arms trade, calling on member states of the Council to apply economic sanctions in order to stop aggression, to taking direct military action by sending peacekeeping missions to conflict-affected states. Subsidiary bodies of the Security Council include the United Nations Peacebuilding Commission (see Chapter 5) and a Working Group on Children and Armed Conflict.

The Security Council has addressed the impact of armed conflict on children in several resolutions, of which the most relevant parts are summarized and outlined below.*

Resolution 1261 (August 1999) on Children and Armed Conflict

- Calls on all parties to end the targeting of children in situations of armed conflict, and for the intensification of efforts to end the recruitment and use of children in armed conflict;
- Urges all parties to armed conflicts to ensure that the protection, welfare, and rights of children are taken into account during peace negotiations and throughout the process of consolidating peace in the aftermath of conflict;
- Calls upon parties to armed conflicts to undertake feasible measures during armed conflicts to minimize harm suffered by children, such as "days of tranquility" to allow the delivery of basic necessary services, and for all parties to armed conflicts to allow the access of humanitarian personnel and delivery of humanitarian supplies to all children affected by armed conflict;
- Urges all parties to armed conflicts to take special measures to protect children, in particular girls, from rape and other forms of sexual abuse and gender-based violence in situations of armed conflict and to take into account the special needs of the girl child throughout armed conflicts and their aftermath;
- Urges the facilitation of the disarmament, demobilization, rehabilitation, and reintegration of children used as soldiers.

Resolution 1265 (September 1999) and 1296 (April 2000) on the Protection of Civilians in Armed Conflict

- Underlines the special rights and needs of children in situations of armed conflict, including those of the girl-child (1265);
- Expresses support for the inclusion in peace agreements and mandates of UN peacekeeping missions of specific and adequate measures for the disarmament,

---

*© United Nations, 1999–2006. Reproduced with permission.

demobilization, and reintegration of ex-combatants, with special attention given to the demobilization and reintegration of child soldiers (1265);

- Notes the importance of including in the mandates of peacemaking, peacekeeping and peace-building operations special protection and assistance provisions for groups requiring particular attention, including women and children (1265);
- Calls upon the parties to a conflict to make special arrangements to meet the protection and assistance requirements of women, children, and other vulnerable groups, including through the promotion of "days of immunization" and other opportunities for the safe and unhindered delivery of basic necessary services (1296);
- Affirms that United Nations peacekeeping missions should include a mass-media component that can disseminate information about international humanitarian law and human rights law, including peace education and children's protection (1296).

Resolution 1314 (August 2000) on Children and Armed Conflict

- Urges member states and parties to armed conflict to provide protection and assistance to refugees and internally displaced persons, as appropriate, the vast majority of whom are women and children;
- Calls upon all parties to armed conflict to ensure the full, safe and unhindered access of humanitarian personnel and the delivery of humanitarian assistance to all children affected by armed conflict;
- Requests parties to armed conflict to include, where appropriate, provisions for the protection of children, including the disarmament, demobilization and reintegration of child combatants, in peace negotiations and in peace agreements and the involvement of children in these processes;
- Reaffirms the UN's readiness to include child protection advisers in future peacekeeping operations;
- Underlines the importance of giving consideration to the special needs and particular vulnerabilities of girls affected by armed conflict, including those heading households, orphaned, sexually exploited and used as combatants, and urges that their human rights, protection and welfare be incorporated in the development of policies and programs, including those for prevention, disarmament, demobilization and reintegration;
- Reiterates the importance of ensuring that children continue to have access to basic services during the conflict and post-conflict periods, including education and health care;
- Indicates its willingness to consider assessing the potential unintended consequences of sanctions on children and to take appropriate steps to minimize such consequences;
- Welcomes recent initiatives by regional and sub-regional organizations and arrangements for the protection of children affected by armed conflict, and urges them to:
  - (a) Consider establishing, within their secretariats, child protection units for the development and implementation of policies, activities and advocacy for the benefit of children affected by armed conflict, including children in the design and implementation of such policies and programs where possible;
  - (b) Consider including child protection staff in their peace and field operations and providing training to members of their peace and field operations on the rights and protection of women and children;

(c) Undertake initiatives to curb the cross-border activities deleterious to children in times of armed conflict, such as the cross-border recruitment and abduction of children, the illicit movement of small arms and the illicit trade in natural resources;

- Encourages Member States, relevant parts of the United Nations system and regional organizations and arrangements to undertake efforts to obtain the release of children abducted during armed conflict and their family reunification;
- Calls on Member States, relevant parts of the United Nations system, and civil society to encourage the involvement of young persons in programs for peace consolidation and peace-building.

Resolution 1379 (November 2001) on Children and Armed Conflict

- Expresses its intention to address the linkages between armed conflict and terrorism, the illicit trade in precious minerals, the illicit trafficking in small arms and light weapons, and other criminal activities, which can prolong armed conflict or intensify its impact on civilian populations, including children;
- Calls upon parties to armed conflict to:
  — provide protection and assistance to refugees and internally displaced persons, the majority of whom are women and children;
  — take special measures to promote and protect the rights and meet the special needs of girls affected by armed conflict, and to put an end to all forms of violence and exploitation, including sexual violence, particularly rape;
  — ensure the protection of children in situations of armed conflict;
  — provide protection of children in peace agreements, including provisions relating to the disarmament, demobilization, reintegration and rehabilitation of child soldiers and the reunification of families, and to consider the views of children in those processes;
- Urges member states to ensure that parties to armed conflict respect international norms for the protection of children, and to consider measures against corporate actors, individuals and entities under their jurisdiction that engage in illicit trade in natural resources and small arms;
- Requests the Secretary General to take the protection of children into account in peace-keeping plans submitted to the Security Council by including child protection staff in peacekeeping and peace-building operations; and to ensure that all peacekeeping personnel receive and follow training in international human rights, humanitarian, and refugee law relevant to children;
- Requests all entities of the United Nations to:
  — devote particular attention and adequate resources to the rehabilitation of children affected by armed conflict, particularly their counseling, education and appropriate vocational opportunities, as a preventive measure and as a means of reintegrating them into society;
  — ensure that the special needs and particular vulnerabilities of girls affected by armed conflict, including those heading households, orphaned, sexually exploited and used as combatants, are duly taken into account in the design of development assistance programs, and that adequate resources are allocated to such programs;
  — promote a culture of peace, including through support for peace education programs and other non-violent approaches to conflict prevention and resolution, in peace-building activities

- Encourages the international financial institutions and regional financial and development institutions to:
  — devote part of their assistance to rehabilitation and reintegration programs that have taken effective measures to comply with their obligations to protect children in situations of armed conflict, including the demobilization and reintegration of child soldiers, in particular those who have been used in armed conflicts contrary to international law;
  — support the efforts of the regional organizations engaged in activities for the benefit of children affected by armed conflict, by providing them with financial and technical assistance, as appropriate.

Resolution 1460 (January 2003) on Children and Armed Conflict

- Expresses its intention to enter into dialogue, as appropriate, or to support the Secretary-General in entering into dialogue with parties to an armed conflict in violation of the international obligations applicable to them on the recruitment or use of children in armed conflict, in order to develop clear and time bound action plans to end this practice;
- Calls upon all concerned parties to ensure that the protection, rights and well-being of children are integrated into the peace processes, peace agreements and the post-conflict recovery and reconstruction phases;
- Calls upon Member States and international organizations to ensure that children affected by armed conflict are involved in all disarmament, demobilization and reintegration processes, taking into account the specific needs and capacities of girls, and that the duration of these processes is sufficient for a successful transition to normal life, with a particular emphasis on education, including the monitoring, through schools, of children demobilized in order to prevent re-recruitment.

Resolution 1539 (April 2004) on Children and Armed Conflict

- Notes the advances made for the protection of children affected by armed conflict but remains concerned over the lack of overall progress on the ground;
- Strongly condemns the recruitment and use of child soldiers by parties to armed conflict;
- Requests the Secretary General to devise an action plan for a systematic and comprehensive monitoring and reporting mechanism to provide reliable information on the recruitment and use of child soldiers;
- Calls upon groups using child soldiers to develop time-bound action plans to halt recruitment and use of children, and to consider imposing sanctions on assistance and arms exports if such parties refuse to enter into dialogue or fail to develop an action plan;
- Calls upon states and the United Nations to recognize the important role of education in conflict areas in halting and preventing recruitment and re-recruitment of children;
- Notes with concern all the cases of sexual exploitation and abuse of women and children, especially girls, in humanitarian crisis, including those cases involving humanitarian workers and peacekeepers, and requests contributing countries to develop appropriate disciplinary and accountability mechanisms.

Resolution 1612 (July 2005) on Children and Armed Conflict

- Stresses the primary role of national Governments in providing effective protection and relief to all children affected by armed conflicts, and recalls the responsibilities of States to end impunity and to prosecute those responsible for genocide, crimes against humanity, war crimes and other egregious crimes perpetrated against children;
- Convinced that the protection of children in armed conflict should be regarded as an important aspect of any comprehensive strategy to resolve conflict;
- Gravely concerned by the documented links between the use of child soldiers in violation of applicable international law and the illicit trafficking of small arms and light weapons and stressing the need for all States to take measures to prevent and to put an end to such trafficking;
- Requests the Secretary-General to implement the monitoring and reporting mechanism, and to provide an assessment of the overall effectiveness of the mechanism, as well as the timeliness, accuracy, objectivity and reliability of the information compiled through the mechanism;
- Decides to establish a working group of the Security Council consisting of all members of the Council to review the reports of the monitoring and reporting mechanism, and to review progress in the development and implementation of the action plans.

Resolution 1674 (April 2006) on the Protection of Civilians During Armed Conflict

- Recognizes the important role that education can play in supporting efforts to halt and prevent abuses committed against civilians affected by armed conflict, in particular efforts to prevent sexual exploitation, trafficking in humans, and violations of applicable international law regarding the recruitment and re-recruitment of child soldiers;
- Recalls the particular impact which armed conflict has on women and children, including as refugees and internally displaced persons, as well as on other civilians who may have specific vulnerabilities, and stressing the protection and assistance needs of all affected civilian populations;
- Calls upon all parties concerned to ensure that all peace processes, peace agreements and post-conflict recovery and reconstruction planning have regard for the special needs of women and children and include specific measures for the protection of civilians including (i) the cessation of attacks on civilians, (ii) the facilitation of the provision of humanitarian assistance, (iii) the creation of conditions conducive to the voluntary, safe, dignified and sustainable return of refugees and internally displaced persons, (iv) the facilitation of early access to education and training, (v) the re-establishment of the rule of law, and (vi) the ending of impunity;
- Condemns in the strongest terms all sexual and other forms of violence committed against civilians in armed conflict, in particular women and children, and *undertakes* to ensure that all peace support operations employ all feasible measures to prevent such violence and to address its impact where it takes place;
- Condemns in equally strong terms all acts of sexual exploitation, abuse and trafficking of women and children by military, police and civilian personnel involved in United Nations operations, and welcomes the efforts undertaken by United Nations agencies and peacekeeping operations to implement a zero-tolerance policy in this regard.

Chronology

1100–146 BCE

Young people are recruited into the armed forces of the city states of ancient Greece.

1212

Children's Crusade

1429

Teenager Joan of Arc leads several victorious military battles during the Hundred Years' War in France.

1600 and 1700s

Young men participate in European armies and navies, primarily in support roles.

1775–1783

A limited number of young people participate in the American Revolution, primarily in support roles.

1861–1865

A limited number of young people participate in the American Civil War, primarily in support roles.

1914–1918

World War I

1922

Hitler Youth Organization (Hitler Jugend) is founded; the group becomes militarily active in 1943, taking on combat roles. As the war proceeds, the age of new recruits becomes even younger, and some recruits are as young as 12 years old.

1936–1939

Young people participate on both government and opposition sides in combat and support roles during the Spanish Civil War.

1939–1945

World War II

1949

Geneva Conventions are signed.

1947–1979

Young people are used as combatants by both government and opposition forces during the Indochina Wars (involving Vietnam, Cambodia, Laos, France, and the United States).

1955–1972 and 1983–2005

Thousands of young people participate in both combat and support roles during the first and second North-South civil wars in Sudan.

1962

Military junta comes to power in Myanmar (Burma), the country with the highest number of child soldiers. Young people participate in both government and rebel group forces in both combat and support roles; the junta currently remains in power.

1964–present

Young people participate in rebel, government, and paramilitary forces during the Colombian civil war.

1975–1979

Young people participate in carrying out the genocide by the Khmer Rouge in Cambodia.

1975–2002

Young people participate in both combat and support roles in both government and opposition forces during the Angolan civil war.

1977

Additional Protocols I and II (addressing children and armed conflict) of the Geneva Conventions are signed.

1980–1988

Young people serve in combat roles during the Iran-Iraq war.

1983–present

Young people participate in both combat and support roles in the Sri Lankan civil war, primarily in the ranks of the rebel Liberation Tigers of Tamil Eelam (LTTE).

1987–present

Years during which the Lord's Resistance Army has operated in Uganda and neighboring countries, forcefully recruiting thousands of children to serve in support and combat roles.

1989

The United Nations Convention on the Rights of the Child signed.

1989–2003

Thousands of young people serve as combatants during the Liberian civil war.

1990

Cold War ends. The African Charter on the Rights and Welfare of the African Child is adopted.

1991–2002

Thousands of young people serve as combatants during the Sierra Leonean civil war.

1994

Young people participate in carrying out the Rwandan genocide and are victims of the genocide.

1996–1997 and 1998 to present

Dates of the first and second Congo Wars, and of the subconflicts in the eastern region of the country.

1996

Machel report on the Impact of Armed Conflict on Children is published.

1997

Cape Town Principles are adopted. The office of the Special Representative of the Secretary General for Children and Armed Conflict is established.

1999

First UN Security Council Resolution on children and armed conflict is passed.

2000

Optional Protocol to the Convention on the Rights of the Children on the Involvement of Children in Armed Conflict is adopted. The first child protection advisor is deployed to the UNAMSIL peacekeeping mission in Sierra Leone.

2003

 Former Liberian president Charles Taylor is charged by the International Criminal Court with war crimes and crimes against humanity committed during the Sierra Leonean civil war, to include the use of child soldiers. Taylor's trial is currently ongoing.

2005

Congolese militia leader Thomas Lubanga is arrested and flown to the International Criminal court in the Hague to face charges that he recruited child soldiers. Lubanga's trial is currently ongoing.

2007

Paris Principles are adopted.

Glossary

Adolescent	According to the United Nations, adolescents are boys and girls who are between the ages of 10 and 19 years old
Armed conflict	Armed conflict is political violence between two or more organized parties involving the use of armed force. Armed conflicts usually revolve around one or more incompatibilities between groups of people, such as disputes over government or territory. There are different types of armed conflict, depending on the duration, levels, and intensities of a conflict and on the nature of the parties participating in the conflict.
Armed group	A group that uses armed force to achieve its objective. Such groups are often not associated with the government or state (and are, as such, labeled "non-state actors" or "armed opposition group").
Cantonment	Cantonment refers to a process ranging from the processing of individual combatants in temporary centers to the massing of troops in camps designated for this purpose. Cantonment sites can be encampments, assembly areas, or barracks.
Cease-fire	A cease-fire is a temporary stoppage of hostilities during an armed conflict, wherein the warring parties agree to stop aggressive, violent activities for a period of time to, for instance, start peace

	negotiations or allow the delivery of humanitarian supplies.
Child	According to the United Nations, a child is a person who is between 0 and 17 years old. However, other factors beside chronological age determine who is considered to be a "child" versus a "youth" or "adult," such as cultural and social norms and beliefs, economic status, gender, religion, and national and international law.
Childhood	The period of time and state of life during which an individual is considered to be a "child." Perspectives on what exactly entails childhood differ from culture to culture and over time.
Child-headed household	A household where the occupants are younger than 18 years old. This often occurs because the children living in the household have been orphaned or abandoned by or separated from one or both parents. In such a household, one or more children take on adult responsibilities for providing food, caring for younger siblings, and maintaining and running the household.
Child soldier	As defined by UNICEF in the 1997 Cape Town principles, a child soldier is any person under 18 years of age who is part of any kind of regular or irregular armed force or armed group in any capacity, including but not limited to cooks, porters, messengers, and anyone accompanying such groups, other than family members. The definition includes girls recruited for sexual purposes and for forced marriage. It does not, therefore, only refer to a child who is carrying or has carried arms.
Civilian	An individual who is not part of the military or an armed group; a noncombatant.
Combatant	An individual who, as part of an army or armed group, directly participates in an armed conflict, usually bearing weapons.
Complex humanitarian emergency	Usually a man-made disaster characterized by high levels of violence, such as an armed conflict or genocide, and which affects a large

civilian population and leads to large-scale forced displacement, poor living conditions (such as restricted access to food, water, shelter, clothing, and medical care), and high mortality rates among civilians. Such situations may last for a limited period of time (days or weeks), but in many cases last for much longer (months or years).

Conscription | The act of joining the military or an armed group. Voluntary conscription entails joining by choice, without coercion; coercive conscription is the result of pressure to join an armed group, but without the explicit use of force; and forced recruitment is conscription into an armed group against one's will and with the use of force or threats.

Counterinsurgency | A military campaign undertaken in an effort to stop a rebellion.

DDR | The process of disarmament, demobilization, and reintegration (including reinsertion) that ex-combatants often go through in disengaging from an armed group and returning to civilian life after the end of a conflict.

Demobilization | As part of the DDR process, demobilization is the formal and controlled discharge of active combatants from armed forces or other armed groups.

Disarmament | As part of the DDR process, disarmament is the collection, documentation, control, and disposal of the small arms, ammunition, explosives, and light and heavy weapons in the possession of combatants and of the civilian population.

Emergency education | The rapid provision of education for people affected by disasters.

Gender | The social construction of role differences between men and women in society.

Gender-based violence (GBV) | Defined in 1993 in the United Nations Declaration on Violence Against Women as violent acts that are likely to or do result in physical, sexual, or psychological harm to women. While women

	are often the primary victims of GBV, men can also be victims.
Genocide	One-sided violence against unarmed civilians, characterized by acts committed with the intent to destroy, in whole or in part, a national, ethnical, racial or religious group.
Humanitarian demining	The process of removing land mines in order to return the use of the land back to normal, civilian purposes. Mine action includes demining activities to remove land mines; mine-risk education; victim assistance; stockpile destruction; and advocacy to campaign against the use of land mines.
Induction	A process whereby new recruits in the army or armed group receive military training and undergo certain experiences such as ideological indoctrination or forced participation in violent acts to secure their loyalty and prevent defection from the group.
Interim Care Center	Also labeled a "transit center," such centers are designed to provide a safe environment in which ex-child combatants can be helped with their transition from a combatant to a civilian life.
Internally displaced person (IDP)	A person who has fled from his or her home, but remains in his or her country of origin. IDPs are forced migrants.
International community	Refers to actors including the United Nations, non-government organizations, donors and agencies that provide humanitarian aid, international financial institutions such as the World Bank, and governments who provide humanitarian and development aid and assistance to people affected by humanitarian emergencies.
Land mine	An explosive device laid in the ground, intended to detonate when a person, animal, or vehicle comes into contact with it, or when an operator detonates it.
Militia	A militia is an armed group that may or may not be aligned with the state. A militia may be formed by citizens to defend a territory or group

	or people, or it may be a privately operating group of combatants that operate on behalf of the government or other group but which is not part of the government.
Non-government organization (NGO)	A private organization that operates independently of the government, such that government representatives are not participating in or being represented in its operations. NGOs are also often called civil society organizations, and those NGOs that function to assist people during times of war are also labeled as humanitarian aid organizations.
Peace	Negative peace entails the absence of conflict and direct violence; positive peace entails the presence and promotion of social justice.
Peace agreement, peace-accord	A formal arrangement designed to stop the violence of an armed conflict through a cease-fire, and intended to permanently end a conflict through the establishment of new political, social, economic, and legal structures. Peace agreements are often the end result of peace processes, which are the diplomatic and political efforts that aim to reach a negotiated end to a conflict.
Peacebuilding	A process that attempts to address the root, structural causes of conflict in order to change behaviors and relationships between the warring parties, as well as to transform identities and institutions at national and local levels so that conflict does not re-erupt. The United Nations considers peacebuilding to consist of three elements: the consolidation of internal and external security, the strengthening of political institutions and good governance, and the promotion of economic and social rehabilitation and transformation.
Peacekeeping	The insertion of foreign, international armed forces into a conflict-affected country with the consent of the warring parties. The mandate of a peacekeeping operation is often to keep the warring parties apart and to enforce peace by preventing violence.

Peacemaking	The process whereby warring parties move toward reaching a voluntary negotiated settlement of a conflict in order to end an armed conflict.
Rebel	A member of a rebel group; such a group participates in hostilities against the state during an armed conflict and as such is an armed group. Rebel groups are also non-state groups, in that they are political actors which are not states.
Recruitment	The act and methods used to enroll individuals in the military or an armed group. Recruitment methods may be voluntary, coercive, or involuntary (forced). See the definition for *conscription*.
Refugee	An individual who has been forcibly displaced from his or her home country and is living in another country, and who is unable or unwilling to return to their home countries due to insecurity and poor living conditions. Refugees are forced migrants.
Reinsertion	Reinsertion is the short-term material and/or financial assistance offered to ex-combatants during demobilization but prior to the longer-term process of reintegration.
Reintegration	Reintegration is the longer-term process by which ex-combatants acquire civilian status and gain sustainable employment and income.
Repatriation	One of three acceptable durable solutions to end existing refugee and IDP situations (the other two are resettlement abroad and local integration in the host country). Repatriation entails the return of a forced migration (refugee or IDP) back to the home country and/or community from which that person originates.
Separated children	Separated children are separated from both parents, but not necessarily from other relatives. This is in contrast to **unaccompanied children**, who are separated from both parents and are not being cared for by an adult who, by law or custom, is responsible to do so. A child is an **orphan** only if both parents are dead.
Small arms and light weapons	Weapons that can be transported by an individual person or animal, and which can be fired by

	individuals (small arms) or by individuals working together (light weapons). They include guns, pistols, submachine guns, grenade launchers, and anti-tank missiles.
Teenager	According to the United Nations, teenagers are boys and girls who are between the ages of 13 and 19 years old.
Transitional justice	The range of judicial and nonjudicial approaches that can be undertaken during the transition from a violent conflict or authoritarian regime to address past human rights abuses. These approaches include truth and reconciliation commissions and war tribunals or courts.
Unexploded remnants of war, unexploded ordnance	Explosive weapons such as grenades, bombs, and rockets that remain after the end of a conflict. These weapons were either abandoned, or did not explode when they were originally deployed, but are at risk of exploding.
Vocational training	Vocational training is intended to provide students with practical skills for employment within a profession and can be provided within the formal education system, though civil society organizations may provide such training outside of the formal education system. Apprenticeship is a type of vocational training carried out by craft-based organizations which train new practitioners, for instance to become an electrician, doctor's assistant, carpenter, baker, or tailor.
War	An armed conflict in which there are 1,000 or more battle deaths per year (that is, in which 1,000 or more individuals die as a direct result of fighting).
Young adult	According to the United Nations, a young adult is a person who is between the ages of 20 and 24 years.
Young person	This category includes individuals who might be considered a child, teenager, adolescent, or youth, but who are not considered to be adults.
Youth	According to the United Nations, a youth is a person who is between the ages of 15 and 24 years old.

Annotated Bibliography

Recommended Print Readings

On Conflict Causes, Dynamics, and Resolution and Peace

Collier, Paul, et al. *Breaking the Conflict Trap: Civil War and Development Policy*. Washington, D. C. : The World Bank, 2003.

Crocker, Chester, Fen Osler Hampson, and Pamela R. Aall, eds. *Leashing the Dogs of War: Conflict Management in a Divided World*. Washington, D. C. : United States Institute of Peace Press, 2007.

Crocker, Chester, Fen Osler Hampson, and Pamela R. Aall, eds. *Turbulent Peace: The Challenges of Managing International Conflict*. Washington, D. C. : United States Institute of Peace Press, 2001.

Elias, Robert, and Jennifer Turpin, eds. *Rethinking Peace*. Boulder: Lynne Rienner Publishers, 1998.

Human Security Centre. *Human Security Report 2005*. Oxford: Oxford University Press, 2005.

Kaldor, Mary. *New Wars and Old Wars: Organized Violence in a Global Era*, 2nd ed. Palo Alto: Stanford University Press, 2007.

Ramsbotham, Oliver, Tom Woodhouse, and Hugh Miall. *Contemporary Conflict Resolution: The Prevention, Management, and Transformation of Deadly Conflicts*, 2nd ed. Cambridge: Polity Press, 2005.

Rupesinghe, K. (with S. N. Anderlini). *Civil Wars, Civil Peace*. London: Pluto Press, 1998.

Wallensteen, Peter. *Understanding Conflict Resolution: War, Peace, and the Global System*. London: Sage, 2007.

On Youth, Conflict, and the Impact of Conflict on Children and Young People

Barber, Brian K. *Adolescents and War: How Youth Deal With Political Violence*. Oxford: Oxford University Press, 2008.

Cairns, Ed. *Children and Political Violence*. Cambridge, MA: Blackwell, 1996.

Machel, Graça. *The Impact of War on Children: A Review of Progress Since the 1996 United Nations Report on the Impact of Armed Conflict on Children*. London: Hurst & Company, 2001.

McIntyre, Angela. *Invisible Stakeholders: Children and War in Africa*. Pretoria: Institute for Security Studies, 2004.

Peters, Krijn, Paul Richards, and Koen Vlassenroot. "What Happens to Youth During and After Wars? A Preliminary Review of Literature on Africa and Assessment on the Debate." RAWOO Working Paper (October 2003). Accessed at http://www.rawoo.nl/pdf/youthreport.pdf.

Richards, Paul. *Fighting for the Rainforest: War, Youth, and Resources in Sierra Leone.* Oxford: Currey, 1996.

Sommers, Marc. "Youth and Conflict: A Brief Review of Available Literature", 2006. Accessed at http://www.crin.org/docs/edu_youth_conflict.pdf.

United Nations Development Programme. "Youth and Violent Conflict: Society and Development in Crisis?" New York: UNDP, 2006.

On Child Soldiers and Ex-Child Soldiers

Brett, Rachel and Irma Specht. *Young Soldiers: Why They Choose to Fight.* Boulder: Lynne Rienner Publishers, 2004.

Eichstaedt, Peter. *First Kill Your Family: Child Soldiers of Uganda and the Lord's Resistance Army.* Chicago: Lawrence Hill Books, 2008.

Gates, Scott, and Simon Reich, eds. *Child Soldiers in the Age of Fractured States.* Pittsburgh: University of Pittsburgh Press, 2009.

Goodwin-Gill, Guy, and Ilene Cohn. *Child Soldiers: The Role of Children in Armed Conflict.* Oxford: Oxford University Press,1993.

Honwana, Alcinda. *Child Soldiers in Africa.* Philadelphia: University of Pennsylvania Press, 2006.

Singer, Peter. *Children at War.* Berkeley: University of California Press, 2006.

Vigh, Henrik. *Navigating Terrains of War: Youth and Soldiering in Guinea-Bissau.* New York: Berghahn Books, 2006.

Wessells, Michael. *Child Soldiers: From Violence to Protection.* Cambridge, MA: Harvard University Press, 2006.

On Education, Conflict, and Peace

Buckland, Peter. *Reshaping the Future: Education and Postconflict Reconstruction.* Washington, D. C. : The World Bank, 2005.

Crisp, Jeff, Christopher Talbot, and Diane B. Cipollone, eds. *Learning for a Future: Refugee Education in Developing Countries.* Geneva: UNHCR, 2001.

Davies, Lynn. *Education and Conflict: Complexity and Chaos.* London: Routledge Falmer, 2004.

Retamal, Gonzalo, and Ruth Aedo-Richmond, eds. *Education as a Humanitarian Response.* London: Cassell, 1998.

Tawil, Sobhi, and Alexandra Harley, eds. *Education, Conflict, and Social Cohesion.* Geneva: International Bureau of Education, 2004.

On Forced Displacement and Young People

Boyden, Jo, and Joanna de Berry, eds. *Children and Youth on the Front Line: Ethnography, Armed Conflict and Displacement.* New York: Berghahn Books, 2004.

Chatty, Dawn, and Gillian Lewando Hundt, eds. *Children of Palestine: Experiencing Forced Migration in the Middle East.* New York: Berghahn Books, 2005.

Hart, Jason, ed. *Years of Conflict: Adolescence, Political Violence, and Displacement.* New York: Berghahn Books, 2008.

On Health, Weapons, and Young People

Simon, Bennett, and Roberta J. Apfel, eds. *Minefields In Their Hearts: The Mental Health of Children in War and Communal Violence.* New Haven: Yale University Press, 1996.

Small Arms Survey. *Yearbook* (annual publication). Geneva: Graduate Institute for International Studies. Accessed at http://www.smallarmssurvey.org.

Krug, Etienne G., et al, eds. *World Report on Violence and Health.* Geneva: World Health Organization, 2002.

On Gender, Conflict, and Young People

Mazurana, Dyan, Angela Raven-Roberts, and Jane Parpart. *Gender, Conflict, and Peacekeeping.* Lanham, Maryland: Rowman & Littlefield, 2005.

Nordstrom, Carolyn. "Girls and War Zones: Troubling Questions." In *Engendering Forced Migration: Theory and Practice*, Doreen Indra, ed., New York: Berghahn Books, 1999.

Plan International. *Because I Am a Girl: The State of the World's Girls 2008, Special Focus: In the Shadow of War.* Working, U.K.: Plan International, 2008.

On the Human Rights of and Protection of Children and Young People During Conflict

Ensalaco, Mark, and Linda C. Majka, eds. *Children's Human Rights: Progress and Challenges for Children Worldwide.* Lanham, Maryland: Rowman & Littlefield, 2005.

Greenbaum, Charles W. , Philip Veerman, and Naomi Bacon-Shnoor, eds. *Protection of Children During Armed Political Conflict: A Multidisciplinary Perspective.* Antwerpen: Intersentia, 2006.

On Young People and Post-Conflict

Kemper, Yvonne. *Youth in War-to-Peace Transitions: Approaches of International Organizations.* Berlin: Berghof Research Center for Constructive Conflict Management, 2005.

McEvoy-Levy, Siobhan, ed. *Troublemakers or Peacemakers? Youth and Post-Accord Peace Building.* Notre Dame: University of Notre Dame Press, 2006.

Internet Sites

Special Representative of the Secretary General for Children and Armed Conflict: www.un.org/children/conflict.

Web site with full text of the 1996 Machel report: http://www.unicef.org/graca/.

The Children and Armed Conflict Unit at the University of Essex: http://www.essex.ac.uk/armecon/.

Watchlist on Children and Armed Conflict: http://www.watchlist.org/.

Child Rights Information Network (CRIN): http://www.crin.org.

UNICEF Innocenti Research Center: http://www.unicef-irc.org/.

Human Security Report Project: Human Security Gateway (on conflict): http://www.humansecuritygateway.info.

Human Rights Watch (many reports about children and war): http://www.hrw.org.

International Crisis Group (information about conflicts in the world): http://www.crisisgroup.org.

Eldis (on children and war): http://www.eldis.org/go/topics/resource-guides/children-and-young-people/children-and-conflict.

International Committee of the Red Cross (on children and war): http://www.icrc.org/eng/children.

Center for Defense Information (on children and armed conflict): http://www.cdi.org/program/index.cfm?programid=21.

BBC: Children of Conflict: http://www.bbc.co.uk/worldservice/people/features/childrensrights/childrenofconflict/.

Beyond Intractability (resources about conflict): http://www.beyondintractability.org.

IRIN, on children: http://www.irinnews.org/Theme.aspx?theme=CHI.

Non-Print Sources: Films

Child Soldiers (2002): A documentary film about child soldiers.

Children in War (2000): An examination of the effects of war and terrorism on children.

Ezra (2007): A film about the experiences of Sierra Leonean child soldiers (fictional).

Johnny Mad Dog (2008): A film about the experiences of child soldiers in Africa.

Lost Boys of Sudan (2004): A film about the Lost Boys of Sudan.

War Child (2006): Film about the life of a former child soldier from Sudan who is an emerging hip-hop artist.

Index

About the Authors

KENDRA E. DUPUY is a researcher at the International Peace Research Institute, Oslo. She researches education, peace, and armed conflict; children and youth in developing countries; the socioeconomic impact of land mines; and post-conflict power-sharing and wealth-sharing. From 2006 to 2008, she worked a large research project in conjunction with Save the Children Norway on transforming armed conflict and building peace through education systems. She is the author of several publications on education, peace, and conflict.

KRIJN PETERS is a rural development sociologist specialized in armed conflict and postwar reconstruction. He has over 10 years of research experience on the issue of child soldiers and young combatants and their disarmament, demobilization, and reintegration process. He has considerable experience in consultancy and advisory work with a range of organizations including the World Bank, European Union, Royal Institute of the Tropics, Special Court for Sierra Leone, and nongovernmental organizations, such as Save the Children and Plan International. His consultancy work has focused on child and youthful soldiers and postwar reintegration trajectories, evaluations of Interim Care Centers for underage ex-combatants, and war crimes and crimes against humanity.